I0421311

SOCIAL SCIENCES STUDIES *IN TURKEY*

EYUP SARITAS
Editor

Order this book online at www.trafford.com
or email orders@trafford.com

Most Trafford titles are also available at major online book retailers.

Print information available on the last page.

ISBN: 978-1-4907-8850-0 (sc)
ISBN: 978-1-4907-8851-7 (hc)
ISBN: 978-1-4907-8853-1 (e)

Library of Congress Control Number: 2018942105

Trafford rev. 04/23/2018

North America & international
toll-free: 1 888 232 4444 (USA & Canada)
fax: 812 355 4082

Contents

PART TWO

LITERARY STUDIES

PART THREE

PHILOSOPHICAL STUDIES

PART FOUR

ECONOMICS STUDIES

Foreword

This book is a compilation of research articles covering topics in the areas of history, literature, philosophy and economy from international perspective. The book contains 4 parts and 13 chapters in total. The first part of the book contains historical studies and made up of six chapters. The second part of the book consists of literary studies and three chapters. The third part of the book is about philosophical studies and the fourth part of the book is about studies of economy.

Chapter 1 analyses the use of ideology and the creation of a warrior ideal in the Japanese army following the Meiji restoration. While it has been a common misconception in popular culture and public imagination that the Japanese warrior culture and ethics continued into the modern era without alteration in many aspects of Japanese life, especially the army, this paper tries to look into the roots of the "modern" warrior culture and ideology that was actually created during the Meiji restoration. Chapter 2 focuses on the Mongol court politics during the Ögedeid rule during which the four different Jinggisid houses became irreconcilably separate political entities. Following the death of Jinggis Khan, the Mongol Empire continued its unity for a period of four rulers, Ögedei and his son Güyük, Möngke and his younger brother Khublai. Khublai was the last Mongol Khan to be recognized universally as the Great Khan within the Mongol realm, but by his death, the Mongol Empire had already dissolved into smaller Khanates and the Mongol civil war that not only devastated the pax Mongolica but also ended the Mongol supremacy in Eurasia had already started. Chapter 3 provides an overview of the research on the role and importance of the mixed courts in the Ottoman Provinces. From the beginning of the 19th century it appeared that the European the legal, social, economic and political effects of these courts on Egypt were tried to be revealed by Ottoman and especially English archival documents during the period beginning from the Mixed Courts were established in 1875 until they were officially abolished in 1949. Chapter 4 explains the biography of the 27th Regimental 3rd Army Commander Gazi Major Halis Ataksor and his participation in battle front because of Anzac landing on 25 April 1915 is explained. While this work was being done, it was benefited from documents and various sources from the archives of Serdar Hâlis Ataksor, the grandchild of Gazi Hâlis. In addition, it has benefited from the related part of Halis Ataksor's autobiography which he wrote his life from his birth to his death, from the diary he held during the war, from his own draw war sketch and himself photo album. In the direction of the information given by Battalion Commander Major Halis himself, the initial phase of the Çanakkale Land Wars will be tried to be elucidated and an attempt will be made to show how effective the first day's defense and strategies at the result of the war. The findings are expected to contribute to the biographies that academics study about them, and to the new work about the April 25 Anzac Landing. Chapter 5 examines Bulgarian politics of Russia during the First World War in Russian diplomatic documents. Chapter 6 mentions about history of modern medicine education in China. Chapter 7 is about Wang Zengqi's short stories which are unique in terms of literary language, characters' temperament and story's organization. Chapter 8 is about the activities of homeland literature of Palestine which has characterized and edited in the migration environment and representatives of homeland literature in Turkey. Despite the abundance of literary works in this area, it has been seen that there are few scientific knowledge studies on the area during the study. Witnessing and researching living Arabic literature is very important in terms of releasing a document about today's world to the next generation. Perhaps the literary activities carried out by the Arabic literati in our country, which has been heavily immigrated from the Arab countries, are the footsteps of a new kind of sectarian literature in the future. From this point, our study gains a different point of view. Chapter 9 gives information about the life, literary personality and style of Şehrnûs-i Pârsîpûr (b. 1946) which has started to give work since 1970's years, the attitudes and the impressions of the writer has tried to been examined against the social transformations and the traumas by handling the story called "Temperature in the Zero Year" and it was tried to reflect the effects of these people on culture and civilization of Iran at that time. In the context of the story of Şehrnûs-i Pârsîpûr's "Temperature in the Zero Year", Iran's culture, lifestyle and social fluctuations in the modern era has been looked by perspective of women and at the same time, the effects of pre-revolutionary and post-revolutionary censorship on literary works and culture have been observed. Chapter 10 examines Balkan migrations of the novel and of our realm. Our realm in the novel, are subject to the political upheaval in the Balkans that took place during migration events. I. after the Declaration of constitutional monarchy against the Ottoman Empire Greek, Bulgarian, and with the instigation of Armenians of Russia are rebelling. The Ottoman state left to live in this mess of a hard time. Chapter 11 provides an overview of the pioneer of Modern Chinese Literature Ba Jin and his masterpiece "The Torrents Trilogy: The Family". This study provides information about effects of "May Fourth" movement upon modern Chinese literature, as well as the role and literary identity of Ba Jin, a pioneering figure in modern Chinese literature, within the context of "May Fourth" movement. Also, "The Torrents Trilogy", a masterwork by Ba Jin, is discussed, and particularly "The family", the first serial of the trilogy, which is loaded with anti-feudalism findings and traces, is quoted. Chapter 12 is about call of conscience and risk of accusation and Chapter 13 is about OPEC' s dwindling influence on oil prices.

Edited by Prof. Dr. Eyup Saritas and Res. Asst. Lale Aydin, this book contains result of most recent scientific studies by thirteen academicians from Turkey and China. All those academicians have profound professional experience on their field of interest. Except perspective of Turkey, every part of the book has global academic perspective such as from China, Japan, Russia, Bulgaria, Palestine and Iran.

PART ONE
HISTORICAL STUDIES

CHAPTER 1

THE ROOTS OF WARRIOR IDEALS AND IDEOLOGY IN MEIJI ARMY

Murat Kadıoğlu[1*]

Abstract

This paper analyses the use of ideology and the creation of a warrior ideal in the Japanese army following the Meiji Restoration. While it has been a common misconception in popular culture and public imagination that the Japanese warrior culture and ethics continued into the modern era without alteration in many aspects of Japanese life, especially the army, this paper tries to look into the roots of the "modern" warrior culture and ideology that was actually created during the Meiji restoration.

Keywords: Japan, warrior, Samurai, Meiji Restoration, military ideology

Japanese modernization has been the focus of historians as well as sociologists and other academics from the social sciences field since the early 20th century. Many aspects of Japanese modernization in the areas including but not limited to its economy, culture, military and industrial technology, judicial system, social structure, art, architecture, literature etc. have been the subject of meticulous research for over a century by now. however, there is a common conception that the Japanese ideology and intellectual culture did not change much since the transition from

1 * PhD Candidate in Selçuk University, Department of History

the Tokugawa to Meiji Restoration, and that Japan despite receiving Western technology, still remained as a "closed country"[2] to the western ideologies and thought. However, the fact is that, Japanese ideology druing the modern era was largely influenced by the ideas stemming from Europe, and the military warrior cuts and the connected warrior ideals that were imposed on the soldiers were no exception as this paper will try to demonstrate.

The most commonly used word in Japanese for warrior code today is bushido.[3] The meaning of the word is "the way of the warrior". However, the word itself became popular in Japan after the publication of a book in English language in the United states by a Japanese author with the aim of introducing Japanese culture to the American readers. The book was written by Inazo Nitobe and was published in 1900 under the title of *Bushido: The Soul of Japan*.[4] This book was later on translated into Japanese and became very popular in Japan becoming one of the classics to be read for understanding the samurai[5] culture and virtues of the past.[6]

---

2 Closed country or sakoku as it was named in Japanese by the mid-Edo period intellectual Hayashi Razan was a term coined by him and is used to describe the era in Japan in which it was forbidden fort he western Powers except the Dutch to enter Japan while relations with China and Korea actually continued an deven florished despite the limitations. For a detailed analysis of sakoku see: Robert Hellyer, "Historical and Contemporary Perspectives on the 'Sakoku' Theme in Japanese Foreign Relations: 1600-2000," *Social Science Japan Journal* 5, no. 2 (October 1, 2002): 255–59; Tashiro Kazui and Susan Downing Videen, "Foreign Relations during the Edo Period: Sakoku Reexamined," *Journal of Japanese Studies* 8, no. 2 (July 1, 1982): 283–306, https://doi.org/10.2307/132341; Ronald P. Toby, "Reopening the Question of Sakoku: Diplomacy in the Legitimation of the Tokugawa Bakufu," *Journal of Japanese Studies* 3, no. 2 (July 1, 1977): 323–63, https://doi.org/10.2307/132115.

3 Bushido in Japanese.

4 Inazo Nitobe, *Bushido, The Soul of Japan* (New York: Dover Publications, 2012).

5 The term samurai derives from the verb saburau in classical Japanese which means to serve, thus originally it means retainer. The samurai in the Heian period were seen as the henchmen of the aristocracy. Peter Duus, *Feudalism in Japan* (New York: McGraw-Hill, 1993), 13.

6 The other classics are: Miyamoto Musashi, *The Book of Five Rings: Miyamoto Musashi*, trans. D. E. Tarver, The Warrior Series 2 (New York: Writers Club Press, 2004); Yamamoto Tsunetomo, *The Hagakure: Yamamoto Tsunetomo*, trans. D. E. Tarver, The Warrior Series 3 (New York: Writers Club Press, 2002); Yagyu Munenori, *The Life-Giving Sword: Secret Teachings from the House of the Shogun*, trans. William Scott Wilson (Boston: Shambhala Publications, 2012).

However, most of the ideals and the concepts in the book were actually Meiji Era inventions and adaptations. The concept of an unchanging warrior etiquette and culture was in this respect, a pure imagination. First of all, the feudal armies of the Edo Period and previous periods were mostly made up of the professional warriors called under different names such as bushi[7] and samurai.[8] These warriors were more like the landed aristocracy of the European medieval armies than the modern armies. While the Japanese armies has for the first time become a national army after the Meiji restoration, it consisted of two types of soldiers at the beginning. At the top were the new officers the majority of whom used to be feudal samurai belonging to the local daimyo[9] armies of various han[10], below them were the newly recruited soldier the great majority of whom were paesants and merchants who were previously denied any right to even carry weapons, not to mention becoming soldiers, following the unification of Japan and the strict observation of the laws brought by Toyotomi Hideyoshi prohibiting people from changing their class, joining the army, leaving the army if one was already a soldier, and carrying weapons if one was not a soldier. In fact, even the ranks of the soldiers passed from father to son for centuries.[11] In this respect, the social, economic and political background of the premodern and modern Japanese armies were very different from each other. As a result, most of the premodern Japanese warrior ideals did not necessarily appeal to the new soldiers coming from agrarian or merchant family and social backgrounds. In fact, there were differences between the warrior ideals of the different periods in Japanese history, and the unchanging idea of a bushido, or a warrior code is again nothing but an illusion. In order to understand the Meiji Era ideology that stipulated the large peasant

---

7 Bushi

8 Toru Sagara, *Bushi No Shisō* (Tokyo: Perikansha, 2004), 74.

9 Daimyo were feudal lords who ruled over at least one or more provinces. Mark Ravina, "State-Building and Political Economy in Early-Modern Japan," *The Journal of Asian Studies* 54, no. 4 (November 1, 1995): 79, https://doi.org/10.2307/2059957.

10 Han were originally the provinces in Japan, but in time they were used for denoting the daimyo lands, and their borders were shifting until the Edo period in which wars between the daimyo were prohibited by the shogunate. John Whitney Hall, "Feudalism in Japan-A Reassessment," *Comparative Studies in Society and History* 5, no. 1 (October 1, 1962): 87.

11 Matsuda Hirataro, *Edo jidai seido no kenkyū* (Tokyo: Buke Seido Kenkyukai, 1919), 23.

and merchant population to behave and think in accordance with the imagined or invented warrior codes of the Edo and more previous periods, we must first briefly have a look at the warrior codes of conduct in the previous eras.

As in most other cultures of the world, Japan was governed by elites coming from military backgrounds from the very early times onwards. Although we do have archeological findings suggesting the dominance of a military class from prehistoric times onwards.[12] However, with the introduction of Confucianism and Confucian ethics from Korea.[13] in fact, the eight samurai virtues[14] are actually the Confucian virtues that are deemed to exist in gentleman. Especially beginning with the Heian[15] Period (794-1185), thanks to the advanced shipping technology brought to China by the Muslim merchants that allowed safer journey on the ocean[16] the interactions between Japan and China accelerated as a result of direct exchanges rather than through Korea. thus, the Japanese nobility who came from a military aristocracy best represented by the imperial Yamato clan as seen in Kojiki[17] and Nihonshoki[18] began

---

12 For the Pre-Yamato Prehistoric culture of Japan see: Jonathan Edward Kidder, *Himiko and Japan's Elusive Chiefdom of Yamatai: Archaeology, History, and Mythology* (Honolulu: University of Hawaii Press, 2007).

13 Contrary to the general view, Japan did not receive Buddhism, Confucianism and Daoism as well as Chinese writing and other technical and intellectual know-how directly from China for the first time, but from the kingdoms in the Korean peninsula. For more details on the early cultural interactions between Japan and the Korean kingdoms see: Wontack Hong, *Relationship Between Korea and Japan in Early Period: Paekche and Yamato Wa* (Seoul: Ilsimsa, 1988).

14 These are: justice, courage, mercy, politeness, honesty, honor, loyalty, self-control (Kiri Paramore, *Japanese Confucianism*, vol. 14 (Cambridge University Press, 2016), 89.

15 Heian is the old name of Kyoto.

16 For the shipping technology brought to China by the Muslim merchants see: Pierre-Yves Manguin, "Trading Ships of the South China Sea. Shipbuilding Techniques and Their Role in the History of the Development of Asian Trade Networks," *Journal of the Economic and Social History of the Orient/Journal de L'histoire Economique et Sociale de l'Orient*, 1993, 253–280.

17 Anonymous, *Kojiki: Records of Ancient Matters* (Tuttle Publishing, 2012), 27.The Kojiki: Records of Ancient Matters is Japan's classic of classics, the oldest connected literary work and the fundamental scripture of Shinto. A more factual history called the Nihongi or Nihon Shoki (Chronicles of Japan

18 Shisei Tanigawa, *Nihonshokitsūshō* (Tokyo: Kokumin Seishin Bunka Kenkyūjo, 1939), 19.

adopting Buddhism and more importantly Confucianism. However, the dissemination of the Chinese culture was initially limited to this military nobility in Heian, and until the inclusion of the local warriors outside of Heian into politics and the usurpation of power by these new military men called "samurai", the concepts deriving from China were limited to the educated nobility of Heian city. Thus, when the samurai warrior class began to emerge in the provinces, their ideological and social backgrounds for legitimacy were profoundly different from the previous Heian nobility despite both groups being from warrior origins. It was the first shogun Minamoto no Yoritomo who established not only the Kamakura Shogunate (1185-1333), but also a warrior code.[19] While the Heian aristocracy had turned into a Chinese style educated elite bureaucrats, these new warriors acted under the leadership of local chieftains and despite adopting many of the Confucian ideas and concepts at their face value, these ideas and concepts were changed in order to accommodate them with the needs of the Samurai class who lived in the provinces. While China had long been a monetary economy and a centralized government, Japan was more like medieval Europe with its fractured government and the lack of a strong monetary economy. Thus, although in theory Japan was governed by the emperor and the central government from Heian, by the time the Kamakura shogunate was established, appointing Minamoto no Yoritomo as the Shogun and giving him authority over the taxation and jurisdiction issues of the provinces was actually merely recognizing the facts. While the emperor and the Heian aristocracy derived their legitimacy from the Shinto myths which claimed that the emperors and the aristocrat families were descendants of gods, the samurai did not have such claims and they derived their authority from their military power and the recognition of their authority in the provinces by the emperor which came as a result of their military power and actual control over the provinces vis-à-vis the nominal control of the central government in the provinces. This equilibrium in which both sides recognized each other's rights and legitimacy was broken after the Kamakura Shogunate fell as a result

19 Nagai Michiko, *Kamakura: Chūsei-shi no fūkei*, (Tokyo: Iwanami Shoten, 1984), 67.

of the Mongol invasions[20] and a process called gokekijo[21] changed the structure of the warrior class as well. Thus, during the era called Sengoku Jidai or the Warring States it was sheer military power that decided the authority of the provincial rulersand the warrior class code of conduct underwent major changes.one of the major works written by Miyamoto Musashi one of the most renowned warriors of the Sengoku Jidai is *The Book of Five Rings.* This book is today mainly popular among the practitioners of martial arts both in Japan and abroad. However, the ideas that Musashi mentions in his book reflect the warrior class ideology and code of conduct in this era and is therefore very important for the intellectual history of Japan as well. In his book Musashi states that it is not reasonable to die in vain for the glory of one's name and surviving is more important, he also recommends that one should rely on his own power rather than the divine powers of the Shinto gods, Buddha or other spiritual beings. For him it was not a shame to leave the battlefield in order to survive and he survived three battles on the losing side and did not commit seppuku.[22]

However, these ideas changed profoundly with the unification of Japan by Tokugawa Ieyasu following the battle of Sekigahara in 1600. The Tokugawa shogunate managed to establish a centralized feudal state that lasted for over two and a half centuries until the Meiji restoration of the imperial power and the period called as the Edo Period after the Edo city which was the old name for Tokyo and the capital of the Tokugawa shogunate was essential for the later modernization of Japan in many aspects. Although the battle of Sekigahara was the final decisive battle that determined the establishment of Tokugawa hegemony over the other daimyo, the process of Japanese unification began earlier by the last half of the 16th century. Although a few number of clans had been fighting over land and annexing their neighbors' lands for a long time following the fall of the Ashikaga shogunate, it was Oda Nobunaga who began the unification of Japan in earnest. What Oda Nobunaga used for overcoming his enemies was to use the western firearms that did not need a long period of training to use as well as the peasant soldiers in huge numbers. He also did not allocate the new lands that he conquered among

---

20 For a detailed study of the Mongol invasions of Japan see: Aida Niro, *Môko Shûrai no Kenkyû: Research on the Mongol Invasions* (Tokyo: Yoshikawa Kobunkan, 1982).

21 Gekokujō in Japanese.

22 Musashi, *The Book of Five Rings: Miyamoto Musashi*, v.

his generals. Thus he did not only conquer lands but began to rule these lands with a centralized governmental system. However, he was killed by one of his generals.[23] But his reforms and conquests were continued by one of his generals, Toyotomi Hideyoshi who, despite coming from a humble peasant background, rose rapidly in the serveice of Oda Nobunaga thanks to his talent. After having united Japan to a large extent, Toyotomi Hideyoshi banned the use of weapons by people other than the samurai, he also prohibited merchants and peasants from entering the samurai class although he himself came from a peasant origin.[24] Thus, after a long period of time following the fall of the Kamakura shogunate, for the first time the authority to use force and carry weapons was collected in the hands of the central authority and was taken from non-military people such as peasants and Buddhist monks who used to setup gangs and even armies and not only fought among each other[25] but also challenged the authority of the daimyos and shoguns and Oda Nobunaga had to fight long battles against the Buddhist monasteries, especially the one in Hieizan which he not only captured and burnt down, but also raised to the ground and used its stones for building a castle.[26] After the right to use force and carry weapons was concentrated in the hands of samurai by these two figures, it was time for the central government to put the samurai under control. One of the first decrees that Tokugawa Ieyasu issued after the battle of Sekigahara was the publication of a code of conduct for the samurai and stipulate the laws on a country-wide level that limited the samurai and the daimyo from acting independently on their own.[27] The daimyo were

23 Gyūichi Ōta, *The Chronicle of Lord Nobunaga* (BRILL, 2011), 17.the work translated here into English under the title "The Chronicle of Lord Nobunaga," is the most important source on the career of one of the best known figures in all of Japanese history—Oda Nobunaga (1534-1582

24 For the life of Hideyoshi and detailed political events of his era see: Mary Elizabeth Berry, *Hideyoshi* (Boston: Harvard University Asia Center, 1989).

25 The Buddhist monks went so far as to burn each other's temples. For a detailed account see: Susan L. Burns, *Before the Nation: Kokugaku and the Imagining of Community in Early Modern Japan* (Londra: Duke University Press, 2003), 77–92.

26 Ōta, *The Chronicle of Lord Nobunaga*, 58.the work translated here into English under the title "The Chronicle of Lord Nobunaga," is the most important source on the career of one of the best known figures in all of Japanese history—Oda Nobunaga (1534-1582

27 Lee A. Butler, "Tokugawa Ieyasu's Regulations for the Court: A Reappraisal," *Harvard Journal of Asiatic Studies* 54, no. 2 (December 1, 1994): 62.

restricted by the shogunate in their actions in their own hans and they were obliged to take residence in Edo and their own han for periods of three years and they had to leave their families in their Edo residences as hostages during their absence.[28] This system not only put the daimyo under firm control, it also created a more centralized and monetary economy since the daimyo proceeded between their own han and Edo city with a large group of retainers as well as merchants who carried local goods with them and sold them on the markets on the way. Thus, the Edo period became one of the most centralized and united periods of premodern Japan. A national consciousness began to apper as a result of the samurai class living together and interacting with samurai from other regions of the country resulting in the creation of a common culture and ideology among the samurai from all over the country. another famous book about the warrior code wa written by a samurai during the Edo period was *Hagakure.*[29] The author of the book Tsunetomo had actually never been to a war and he was influence by the neo-confucian movement and its ideas. In this respect his ideas about the duties of a samurai and warrior code were in stark contrast with those of Miyamoto Musashi. For him it was the duty of a samurai to serve his lord even if it meant death, and a samurai should be ready to die rather than to leave the battlefield. The center of a samurai's code of conduct was serving his lord and clan. In this respect Miyamoto Musashi's time was more individualistic and the samurai could switch sides, act more as individuals and rebel against their overlords whereas by the mid-Edo period it was almost impossible for a samurai to switch his allegiance from one daimyo to another, and the only rebellion until the end of the Edo period was the Christian Shimabara revolt which had nothing to the with the lord vassal relations or the Tokugawa hegemony.[30] By the late Edo period however, another change was taking place in terms pf the samurai ideology. The wagaku school which focused on the study of Japanese myths and history reexamined and influenced the thinking of the samurai class deeply. According to this school of thought, the allegiance of the samurai should only belong to the emperor who was the real ruler of Japan y decree of the gods and who was also a descendent of the supreme goddess of

---

28 This system was called sankin kotai and continued until the end of the Edo period. For detailed information on the sankin kotai system see: Toshio George Tsukahira, *Feudal Control in Tokugawa Japan: The Sankin Kotai System* (New York: Publication for the East Asian Research Center, 1966).

29 Tsunetomo, *The Hagakure: Yamamoto Tsunetomo*, 7.

30 Yamaoka Sōhachi,*Tokugawa Iemitsu* (Tokyo: Kōdansha, 1981), 98.

the Japanese pantheon, the sun goddess Amaterasu. They claimed tht the shoguns including the Tokugawas usurped the power from the emperors and it was the duty of the samurai to serve the emperor.[31] This school of thought was essentially very different from the previous ones.while it contained some of the core ideas of the previous schools such as putting the samurai in a special place as in the Kamakura period, or referencing the divine right of the emperor as in the Heian period before it and creating a mutual recognition and benefit for both groups as Yoritomo designed. But the old Heian aristocracy was not included and the original property rights or right of taxation for the old aristocracy and the imperial family were ignored. The allegiance of a vassal to his lord was seen as divine but this allegiance was not only to the daimyo, but also to the emperor. And in fact, the allegiance to the emperor was deemed as more important than the allegiance to the daimyo or the shogunate. As a result, the young samurai from different clans began to support the idea that the shogun should be overthrown and the emperor should be the sole ruler.

As a result of a combination of some developments such as the sonno joi movement that emerged as a result of the reactions against the western incursions into Japan and the coup d'etats in the richest and strongest hans by the young samurai who were influenced by the wagaku movement a coordinated revolt overthrew the Tokugawa shogunate and emperor Meiji became the head of state.

During the Meiji period, a new state ideology needed to be created in order to accommodate with the nation-state system that became prevalent first in Europe and later in the rest of the world. Thus, the Japanese created a new set of ideas during their nation-building process in the Meiji era. One of the most influential schools that continued until the end of the second world war as a dominant state ideology was the state "Shinto". The idea of an emperor as a descendant of Amaterasu and a living god to be worshipped not only became a cult but also a state orthodoxy. This cult was different from the wagaku shool of thought in that the emperor worship cult was never prevalent in Shinto thought, and even the number of temples and shrines dedicated to Amaterasu the chief goddess of the imperial family were limited compared to the local cults and shrines dedicated to them. But perhaps the biggest difference was the diffusion of warrior ideals and codes to the general public. The

[31] Kubilay Atik, "Japonya, Kapalı Ülke, İdeoloji ve Din," *Doğu-Batı*, no. 60 (May 2012): 72.

main difference was that the Japanese army adopted the conscription system after the Meiji restoration which resulted in the inclusion of the peasants and merchants not only in the army but also in the politics. Thus, the peasant majority as well as the merchants and the industrial workers were also doctrinized through compulsory education. Thus, the innovated version of the wagaku school of thought was imposed on the general population as the "traditional" samurai ideas. The peasants and the merchants in medieval Japan were in fact excluded and did not even have the right to carry arms or join the army or politics as mentioned above. But in the process of nation-building, these groups had to be persuaded in complying with the state ideology. Through education the whole population was indoctrinized and the soldiers regardless of their rank or social background were honored in the state Shinto as servants of the emperor who was a living god. While the originally Confucian virtues which were adopted by the samurai class as the ruling elite were changed to a certain extent and adopted to the whole population, the class distinctions and hereditary nature of the samurai class disappeared altogether as a result of nation-building process. Thus, the new ideaology carried the ideals of the feudal warrior class such as valor on the baatlefield, giving one's life for his lord or clan, fidelity to the general public, and made certain changes such as switching from the necessary allegiance to a lord to allegiance to the nation and the emperor, thus replacing the clan and the lord with nation and the emperor, giving the peasants the duty of fighting for the nation instead of only toiling the soil and paying taxes, placing the merchants at a higher position who were seen as the lowest class in the traditional Confucian system.[32]

In conclusion, the warrior ideology of premodern Japan was actually a constantly changing group of ideas that changed from period to period following the necessities and the socio-economic conditions of the times and the political developments. While the Heian period warriors focused on the Chinese Confucian ideals, the Kamakura period warriors were more feudal in their way of thinking and the idea of a supreme emperor to whom all the people owed allegiance was rather an alien thought for them despite their having derived their legitimacy from the emperor. By the Muromachi period and the Warring States era, the samurai were no more willing to recognize the rights of the emperor and the Heian

---

32 James T. C. Liu, "How Did a Neo-Confucian School Become the State Orthodoxy?," *Philosophy East and West* 23, no. 4 (October 1, 1973): 83, https://doi.org/10.2307/1397719.

aristocracy, and they felt they did not need to derive their authority from the legitimacy given to them by the emperor. When reunification of Japan happened under the Tokugawa shogunate however, there was a fundamental change following the political unification and the need to restrict the rights and the power of the local clans and the samurai in order to maintain the unified state structure. Neo-confucianism and Zen Buddhism were used for creating a new warrior code which would make no sense to the samurai of the earlier epochs, and did not become the dominant ideology until the mid-Edo period. This ideology also became the root of the Meiji militarism, despite undergoing some changes and despite the Meiji intellectuals' claims that the ideology was derived from the ancient Shinto myths and the unchanging Samurai ideals.

Bibliography

Aida Niro. *Môko Shûrai no Kenkyû: Research on the Mongol Invasions.* Tokyo: Yoshikawa Kobunkan, 1982.

Anonymous. *Kojiki: Records of Ancient Matters.* Tuttle Publishing, 2012.

Atik, Kubilay. "Japonya, Kapalı Ülke, İdeoloji ve Din." *Doğu-Batı*, no. 60 (May 2012).

Berry, Mary Elizabeth. *Hideyoshi.* Boston: Harvard University Asia Center, 1989.

Burns, Susan L. *Before the Nation: Kokugaku and the Imagining of Community in Early Modern Japan.* Londra: Duke University Press, 2003.

Butler, Lee A. "Tokugawa Ieyasu's Regulations for the Court: A Reappraisal." *Harvard Journal of Asiatic Studies* 54, no. 2 (December 1, 1994): 509–51.

Duus, Peter. *Feudalism in Japan.* New York: McGraw-Hill, 1993.

Hall, John Whitney. "Feudalism in Japan-A Reassessment." *Comparative Studies in Society and History* 5, no. 1 (October 1, 1962): 15–51.

Hellyer, Robert. "Historical and Contemporary Perspectives on the 'Sakoku' Theme in Japanese Foreign Relations: 1600-2000." *Social Science Japan Journal* 5, no. 2 (October 1, 2002): 255–59.

Hong, Wontack. *Relationship Between Korea and Japan in Early Period: Paekche and Yamato Wa.* Seoul: Ilsimsa, 1988.

Kazui, Tashiro, and Susan Downing Videen. "Foreign Relations during the Edo Period: Sakoku Reexamined." *Journal of Japanese Studies* 8, no. 2 (July 1, 1982): 283–306. https://doi.org/10.2307/132341.

Kidder, Jonathan Edward. *Himiko and Japan's Elusive Chiefdom of Yamatai: Archaeology, History, and Mythology*. Honolulu: University of Hawaii Press, 2007.

Liu, James T. C. "How Did a Neo-Confucian School Become the State Orthodoxy?" *Philosophy East and West* 23, no. 4 (October 1, 1973): 483–505.

Manguin, Pierre-Yves. "Trading Ships of the South China Sea. Shipbuilding Techniques and Their Role in the History of the Development of Asian Trade Networks." *Journal of the Economic and Social History of the Orient/Journal de L'histoire Economique et Sociale de l'Orient*, 1993, 253–280.

Matsuda Hirataro. *Edo jidai seido no kenkyū*. Tokyo: Buke Seido Kenkyukai, 1919.

Munenori, Yagyu. *The Life-Giving Sword: Secret Teachings from the House of the Shogun*. Translated by William Scott Wilson. Boston: Shambhala Publications, 2012.

Musashi, Miyamoto. *The Book of Five Rings: Miyamoto Musashi*. Translated by D. E. Tarver. The Warrior Series 2. New York: Writers Club Press, 2004.

Nagai Michiko. *Kamakura: Chūsei-shi no fūkei*. Tokyo: Iwanami Shoten, 1984.

Nitobe, Inazo. *Bushido, The Soul of Japan*. New York: Dover Pubşications, 2012.

Ōta, Gyūichi. *The Chronicle of Lord Nobunaga*. BRILL, 2011.

Paramore, Kiri. *Japanese Confucianism*. Vol. 14. Cambridge University Press, 2016.

Ravina, Mark. "State-Building and Political Economy in Early-Modern Japan." *The Journal of Asian Studies* 54, no. 4 (November 1, 1995): 997–1022. https://doi.org/10.2307/2059957.

Sagara, Toru. *Bushi No Shisō*. Tokyo: Perikansha, 2004.

Tanigawa, Shisei. *Nihonshokitsūshō*. Tokyo: Kokumin Seishin Bunka Kenkyūjo, 1939.

Toby, Ronald P. "Reopening the Question of Sakoku: Diplomacy in the Legitimation of the Tokugawa Bakufu." *Journal of Japanese Studies* 3, no. 2 (July 1, 1977): 323–63. https://doi.org/10.2307/132115.

Tsukahira, Toshio George. *Feudal Control in Tokugawa Japan: The Sankin Kotai System*. New York: Publication for the East Asian Research Center, 1966.

Tsunetomo, Yamamoto. *The Hagakure: Yamamoto Tsunetomo*. Translated by D. E. Tarver. The Warrior Series 3. New York: Writers Club Press, 2002.

Yamaoka Sōhachi. *Tokugawa Iemitsu]*. Tokyo: Kōdansha, 1981.

CHAPTER 2

COURT POLITICS IN THE MONGOL EMPIRE FROM ÖGEDEI UNTIL MÖNGKE

Kubilay Atik[33*]

Abstract

Following the Death of Jinggis Khan, the Mongol Empire continued its unity for a period of four rulers, Ögedei and his son Güyük, Möngke and his younger brother Khublai. Khublai was the last Mongol Khan to be recognized universally as the Great Khan within the Mongol realm, but by his death, the Mongol Empire had already dissolved into smaller Khanates and the Mongol civil war that not only devastated the pax Mongolica but also ended the Mongol supremacy in Eurasia had already started. This paper focuses on the Mongol court politics during the Ögedeid rule during which the four different Jinggisid houses became irreconcilably separate political entities.

Keyword: Mongols, Ögedei, Güyük, Möngke, court politics

Although there have been many studies about the Mongol Empire, court struggles and court politics of the early Mongol empire has so far mostly been neglected. The focus has mostly been either Jinggis or

33 * Dr. Kubilay Atik teaches in Medieval History in Nevşehir Hacı Bektaş Veli University, Faculty of Sciences and Letters, Department of History.

his more successful grandsons such as Khubilai or Batu. Ögedei has probably been one of the most neglected Mongol Khans since his reign has mostly been seen as a transition period. But it was during the reign of Ögedei that the later military and political struggles of the Mongolian royal houses began fermenting. Therefore, the court politics of the reign of Ögedei needs further attention in order to better grasp the background of the later struggles. The choice of Ögedei as a Khan was an exception in many ways. He was nominated as the heir by Jinggis while he was alive and therefore he was one of the very few Mongol Khans to be elected without much struggle and bloodshed. The nature of his selection by Jinggis Khan has mostly been given in an anecdote by the Persian historian Rashid al Din as a result of a fight between his two elder brothers Jochi and Chaghadai during a banquet. Sensing that there might arise a civil war for supremacy between the followers of the two eldest brothers, Jinggis as a result nominated Ögedei who was on good terms with both brothers according to traditional accounts. Although such an inheritance was against the Mongol custom of primogeniture, both brothers agreed this decision. Actually, this event probably simply gave Jinggis Khan the excuse he needed for selecting an heir apparent. As the founder of a new state, Jinggis Khan had already been considering appointing an heir apparent in his later years. According to Juvaini Jinggis assigned certain roles to four of his sons from his primary consort Börte. Jochi was responsible for hunting, Chaghadai for law, Ögedei for political administration and Tolui for the army. From this arrangement, it is evident that Jinggis actually planed his inheritance scheme from an earlier date and the fight between the two brother simply set the stage for him to announce his decision.

After the death of Jinggis Khan in 1227 during the punitive campaign against the Tangut Xi Xia state, Ögedei was selected as the great Khan of the Mongols almost unanimously, at least there was no other candidate or open opposition to his being selected as the Khan. This was, as stated above, an abnormal situation according to the Persian historian Rashid-al Din Fazlallah as he records in his Compendium of History.[34] Normally in a traditional Mongol family, the youngest son would inherit his father's house and was called "the hearth protector"

---

34 Rashiduddin Fazlullah, *Jami'u't-Tawarikh: Compendium of Chronicles*, trans. Wheeler M. Thackston, vol. 3, Classical Writings of the Medieval Islamic World: Persian Histories of the Mongol Dynasties (London: I. B. Tauris & Co, 2012).

and his elder brothers were expected to leave the paternal household and establish their own houses as they come of age. Jinggis Khan broke with this tradition. He did not select his fourth son as his heir and he gave the control of the whole realm to Ögedei. Before the rise of Jinggis Khan to power, the Mongol tribes were disunited and were in a constant war with each other. Jinggis ended this situation and he established the road for a Mongolian style feudal system. Under the influence of more developed Khitan, Jürchen and Chinese civilizations, he adopted a series of new measures towards changing Mongolian inheritance patterns. The abolition of the ultimogeniture inheritance system in favor of an sovereign selected by the father was one of these steps towards feudalization. But Jinggis Khan was careful in considering these changes and he continued to comply with the old traditions to a certain extent. As Rashid-al Din narrates vividly:

> "When Jinggis examined the duties to be given to his men, he hesitated on arranging the inheritance to the throne, sometimes he thought of giving the throne to Ögedei Khan, and sometimes to his youngest son Tolui Khan. Although according to ancient Mongol customs, the youngest son would inherit his father's yurt, later on Jinggis Khan said: Affairs of the throne and state are difficult, let Ögedei rule. However, as for my yurt, family, army, treasure and like, let them be given to Tolui."[35]

Tolui was Jinggis Khans favorite son since he came along with Jinggis Khan in all his campaigns and became in a way his companion during his long campaigns. With the aforementioned step, he probably compensated and gave security to his beloved companion. As a result of this arrangement however, the Tolui line possessed more military power and wealth which had an important effect on the outcome of the later court struggles. At the same time the ultimogeniture inheritance custom continued to survive and was kept as a basis for selecting the next khan by some of the Mongol rulers and ministers. The reason lying behind the struggle of Arigh Böke and Khubilai Khan was the continuity of this custom alongside other practices of selecting a khan.

---

35 Ibid., 3:17–18.

Juvaini and Rashid al Din states that when Jİnggis Khan expressed his wish for the inheritance of his sons, they all agreed. But according to more reliable *The Secret History of the Mongols* Jinggis Khan's announcement of his will was just before the beginning of his western campaign, and a struggle between his sons had already surfaced. Regarding the delicate question of inheritance, there two camps emerged: one camp was that of Chaghatai and Ögedei, the other was that of Juchi and Tolui. Actually, Rashid al Din points out to the struggles between Juchi and his younger brothers Chagahatai and Ögedei, and also he mentions the good relations between the family members of Juchi and Tolui and Tolui dous not resent stories regarding Juchi's birth.[36] These personal struggles between the two parties later on constituted the struggles and the ensuing civil war within the Mongol Court. Members of the both parties did not hesitate to conspire, kill, or perform coup d'états in order to seize the imperial power for their own lineage.

The stance of Juchi and Tolui was not so strong, they could not defy the orders of Jinggis Khan and thus they could not openly oppose the election of Ögedei. But Juchi's opposition to Ögedei soon surfaced. When Jİnggis Khan set for the expedition against the Kharazmians in the west, he took Tolui alongside him and he left his other three sons to capture the Kharazmian capital Ürgenj. According to *The Secret History of the Mongols* and Rashid al Din, Juchi and Chaghadai had an argument and they could not attack the city. They sent a message to Jinggis Khan asking for determining who should bear the command of the army.[37] Such a question by Juchi was a hint of opposition at the selection of Ögedei as the heir apparent rather than a simple argument between brothers who should lead the army since Ögedei was elected as the heir apparent at the eve of the Kharizmian campaign, it was apparent that Ögedei should lead the army, and Juchi also probably guessed what the answer to his question would be. But this seems to be a subtle show of opposition rather than an actual question. Rashid-al Din continues to narrate that the three sons were temporarily united under the command of Ögedei and managed to conquer Ürgenj. Afterwards, Chaghatai and Ögedei met with Jinggis Khan while Juchi remained behind in his own camp. Originally Jinggis Khan ordered Juchi to move towards the Qipchaq steppe for further conquests there and his disobedience angered the great Khan. But later

36 Ibid., 3:98.

37 Ibid., 3:118.

on he was ill and he died after which Ögedei and Chaghata, continued the campaign. Jinggis was so raged that at one point he ordered Ögedei and Chaghatai to attack the forces of Juchi as the front and he himself prepared to attack with the main force. But just as they preapared for this campaign, the news of Juchi's death arrived and Jinggis regretted his decision to attack his own son whom he regarded as a great soldier.[38] Although there is no mention of reasons for Juchi's opposition to his father, the most probable reason seems to be his dissatisfaction with his father's choice of a heir.

Jinggis Khan passed away in the August of 1227 during a punitive campaign against the Tangut Xi Xia state. According to Juvaini, he gathered his sons around him at his death bed and bid them to unite under the command of Ögedei. In a story reported by Juvaini from Jinggis Khan's mouth, in a cold night a group of snakes were trying to enter a hole, but they were all hindering each other from entering the hole and in the end all the snakes died, if they let at least one of them to enter the hole, their whole generation would have been saved.[39] In the feudal system that Jinggis probably tried to build, the heir apparent would ascend the throne upon the ruler's death, but in the Mongol system a Khurultai had to be convened and Ögedei had to be elected as the Khan although this Khurultai was a mere procedure after Jinggis's will was in favor of Ögedei. But until this Khurultai could be convened and Ögedei could ascend the throne as the great Khan, Tolui ruled as the regent for a period of two years as the protector of the hearth of Jinnggisid house as Jinggis Khan's youngest son. A Khurultai was not merely convened for electing a Khan. It was also a gathering where all the heads and important members of each tribe could come together and decide on affairs such as war and peace. For instance, in the Khurultai of 1201 waging war was decided by the tribal leaders of eleven Mongolian tribes. Therefore, the Khurultais were not mere instruments of electing a Khan from among the ruling elite, but they were rather gatherings of decision-making where all the tribes had to be persuaded for acting in unison. Therefore, the Jinggisids had to persuade and influence the members of the tribes who attended the Khurultai, and even more so, to persuade the parties to attend the Khurultais since a Khurultai convened in the

---

38 Ibid.

39 Ala' al-Din 'Ata Malek Juvaini, *The Tar̓ ikh-I-Jahan-Gusha of Alaud̓-Din Ata Malik-I-Juwayni: Containing the History of Chingiz Khan and His Successors*, trans. Muhammad Qazvini (London: Luzac, 1912), 181.

absence of one or more important figures could be put into question in terms of the legitimacy of the decisions made. According to the Persian historians, the Khurultai that elected Ögedei as the great Khan went smoothly and Ögedei was unanimously elected as the great Khan and he has respectfully rejected the position three times until the others insisted that he must just as the Mongol tradition demands. On the other hand, the Chinese sources seem to contradict this smooth transition of power in harmony. *Yuanshi* relates the events under a different light than in the Persian histories of Rashid al Din and Juvaini. According to the passage in the biography of Yelü Chucai who was an old Jin official of Khitan origin and who began serving Jinggis Khan after the Mongol conquest of the Jin Dynasty, the decision making process dragged on for a while and Tolui and Ögedei alongside Yelü Chucai argued about the prolonging of the final decision.[40] Also according to *Yuanchao Mingchen Shilue*[41] the passage in the biography of Yelü Chucai again relates a similar situation. According to this passage, the decision to elect the Khan was declared on the 24th of August 1229, but until the 22nd of August, there was still discussions going on. According to Juvaini, the Khurultai continued for forty days. The first three days were the welcoming banquets, and compared with the Chinese sources at hand, it seems that the decision-making process took thirty-five days and it was probably no smooth operation given the length of the decision-making process. If Ögedei was accepted as the undisputed heir of Jinggis Khan, then the time for selecting a Khan would not have been so long. The other possible candidate for the throne was Tolui. He, as the youngest son, was the protector of the hearth, and according to old Mongol tradition, had the right to inherit his father's belongings. This fight was not a mere fight for inheritance between the two brothers. This kind of a fight had been going on for centuries in different dynasties established by an elite of a nomadic background but conquered sedentary areas and created a hybrid administration. While one party always insisted on preserving the steppe traditions, the other party wanted innovation in order to adapt better to the new environment. The Wei dynasty of the Tabgach[42], Khitan Lia, and

40 Song Lian, *Yuanshi: History of Yuan]*, Ershı Wushı Shı: The Twenty-Four Histories (Beijing: Zhonghua Publishing House, 2000).

41 Tianjing Su, *Yuanchao Mingchen Shilue*, vol. 1 (Beijing: Zhonghua Publishing House, 1962).

42 Tuoba was the Chinese name, but the Orkhon inscriptions name them as Tabgach which was most probably the original pronounciation of this group.

more recently the Jürchen Jin dynasty had all faced this problem until the time of Jinggis. In fact, we can see the traces of the same struggle between the traditionalists and the innovationists even in the Türk Qaghanate as seen in the argument between Bilga Qaghan who wanted to build Chinese style cities and temples, and Tonyuquq who opposed this idea rather convincingly since his ideas were accepted in the end. Thus, the supporters of Ögedei were mostly the supporters of the innovations that Jnggis Khan tried to bring in to the Mongol political entity. In fact most of the innovations attributed to him such as the decimal army system, protocol, and other political novelties were in fact Turkic, Khitan, or Jürchen innovations. The fight between Ögedei and Tolui however was the first of tis kind in the Mongolian Empire and it would later be repeated between Khubilai and his brother Arigh Böke as well as in other Khanates that emerged in the aftermath of the Mongol civil wars. According to Juvaini, when Ögedei refused the throne for three times as the custom demanded, one of the reasons he cited for refusing the throne was the fact that according to the old Mongol tradition it was Tolui who should inherit the throne.[43] But Tolui is not reported to utter a word, and seems to have accepted the fact that Ögedei was the Khan. Tolui had already been the de facto ruler for two years and he had the largest army since he inherited Jinggis Khan's main army.given these facts it seems odd that Ögedei should mention such dangerous remarks for his legitimacy and Tolui should not oppose Ögedei. But by the time the Khurultai had been held, Juchi, the main ally of Tolui was dead and Ögedei and Chaghatai were a strong coalition. Also they occupied lands that divided the Toluid house in Mongolia and parts of China from the Juchids in the Qipchaq steppe. In fact, the Juchids seem to be silent during these affairs and Toluid party most probably reckoned that they would not be able to win a war if they attempted to seize the throne by force, and by the time Ögedei was refusing the throne he was only paying lip service to the Toluids and everything had already been decided in the Khurultai. Tolui was praised by both Persian and Chinese sources for his silence in this affair as being honest and good, and not causing any trouble as a dutiful brother.[44] But it should also be remembered that these histories were written in the courts of his sons, Khubilai and Hülegü, and it was quite natural that the Toluids did not want to represent their father as a

43 Juvaini, *The Tar̓ikh-I-Jahan-Gusha of Alaud̓-Din Ata Malik-I-Juwayni: Containing the History of Chingiz Khan and His Successors*, 186.

44 Ibid., 549; Song, *Yuanshi: History of Yuan]*, chap. 115.

rebellious son who ignored his father great Khan Jinggis's wishes. To the opposite, the Toluids always tried to portray themselves as the protectors of the Jinggisid tradition and Yassaq. Thus, rather than portraying Toluid as a loser in the competition, the Persian and Chinese historians most probably under the direction of the court, saw it fit to portray him as a good son and harmonious brother.

After the enthronement of Ögedei, the struggles at court eased for a while. Tolui, the main opponent of Ögedei died for years later under suspicious conditions. Juvaini relates the death of Tolui to heavy drinking and illness. According to him, after the conquest of the Khitans, he was proud of himself and he began drinking heavily in the banquet and he died a fewdays later.[45] In *Heida Shilue* the Song diplomat Peng Daya states that the death of Tolui took place after his return from Henan.[46] But *The Secret History of the Mongols* relates the death of Tolui to self-sacrifice for his brother. According to the story in *The Secret History of the Mongols* the deities of the Jin realm were angry after the devastation that the Mongols brought to the Jin dynasty and Ögedei got ill after their return. A shaman said that in order to save Ögedei it was necessary that one of his relatives sacrifice his life for him. Tolui volunteered to sacrifice himself for his brother and after Tolui got ill and died after which Ögedei recovered. *Yuanshi* on the other hand, narrates this event in a different light. Again Ögedei gets ill and Tolui volunteers to give his soul to the deities in return for the recovery of Ögedei, but Tolui returns north after Ögedei recovers and he dies in the northern steppe. Rashid al Din mentions a wooden cup wherein the illness of Ögedei was put into so that he recovers but Tolui in order to show his respect knowingly drinks from the cup and dies. This motive of sacrificing oneself in place of a beloved relative which can be seen all the versions of the story is not unique to this story. A similar case can be seen in the case of Deli Dumrul of the Dede Korkut stories of the Oghuz tribes. But in any case, there seems to be a suspicion in the circumstances surrounding his death. whether he was poisoned as suspected or not, the supporters of Tolui did not seem to trust the Ögedeid house at all. In any case it was politically more convenient for the Toluid descendants to demonstrate their father

45 Juvaini, *The Tar̉ikh-I-Jahan-Gusha of Alaud̉-Din Ata Malik-I-Juwayni: Containing the History of Chingiz Khan and His Successors*, 549.

46 Daya Peng, *Heida Shilue Jiaozhu*, (Lanzhou: lanzhou Daxue Chubanshe, 2014).

as a loyal younger brother who could sacrifice his life for the good of the Khanate.

Ögedei after the death of Tolui made a bold ove to concile the Tolui house, and he proposed that Tolui's wife Sorghaghtani Beki be married to his son and heir Güyüg. Sorghaghtani Beki declined the offer.[47] And later on, she would manage to make her sons Khans. After this there was a long but tense peace. In the meanwhile, the heirs of the four Jinggisid houses were busy building their own powers. Güyüg participated in the campaigns in Russia and Europe. During the campaigns, he had arguments and trouble with Batu, the eldest son of Juchi as well as his own brother Kadan. The Chaghataids were mostly interested in their own business. However, after Ögedei died at the age of 55 in 1241, the peace was broken again. Batu, the eldest son of the eldest son of Jinggis Khan delayed the Khurultai proceedings by refusing to participate in the Khurultai for a number of reasons, and since for a Khurultai to be legitimate, his presence was necessary, the Empire was ruled by Töregene Khatun for an interim of three years.[48] Like his father Jinggis, Ögedei also presented a heir apparent, and his choice was again a seemingly more neutral person who could be more easily accepted by the other houses. Instead of his son Güyüg, he presented Shiremün, his grandson as his successor, but his wife Töregene after a lengthy diplomatic battle with the other houses had her son Güyüg elected as the Khan.[49] Batu did not attend the Khurultai but he did not openly oppose it either. Sübüdei, the experienced Mongol general tried to reconcile the cousins, but he did not succeed. After Güyüg ascended the throne, he was not only angry at Batu, but also suspicious of him. In order to secure his place, Güyüg decreed that from then on, the Khan title would remain in his lineage.[50] Afterwards, Güyüg began moving his forces westwards in a suspicious manner as if planning to attack Batu who was situated on the Qipchaq steppe at the moment. *Yuanshi* does not mention the reason for his move with a huge force. But Rashid al Din narrates that Güyüg had the ntention of attacking Batu with a surprise attack. He disguised his moving westwards as a hunting party. But Sorghaghtani Beki, the

47 John Man, *Kublai Khan* (London: Bantam, 2007), 19.

48 Song, *Yuanshi: History of Yuan*, chap. 121.

49 Fazlullah, *Jami'u't-Tawarikh: Compendium of Chronicles.* (20yi bul)

50 Juvaini, *The Tar'ikh-I-Jahan-Gusha of Alaud-Din Ata Malik-I-Juwayni: Containing the History of Chingiz Khan and His Successors*, 181–182.

wife of late Tolui informed Batu about Güyüg's move.[51] This was a point where for the first time two Jinggisid houses came to the brink of open warfare. It is interesting that Güyüg would attack Batu and risk civil war even if he was elected as the Khan and took what he wanted. We do not know the exact motives for his hasty move. It might either be that he considered the Toluids to be neutralized about which he seems to be wrong, but judging from the fact that he trusted them enough to confide his move to Sorghaghtani Beki or to keep them in the inner circle, so that Sorghaghtani Beki would be able to acquire such an information, this option seems to be possible. Thus, he might have thought eliminating the Juchids before they got strong would be a logical move. Also Yuan Jue, a Yuan era writer in his work *Qingrong Jushiji* states that Güyüg had the intention of eliminating the house of Batu and conquering his domain.[52] For a short while the Ögedeids seemed to be destined to rule the whole Mongol realm if they managed to beat the Juchids at war. Since the Chaghataids were on their side and the Toluids were seemingly neutral, Batu seemed to be cornered. But Güyüg died all of a sudden in 1248.

It is evident from the clues that we have both in Chinese and Persian sources that Güyüg's intention was not hunting when he moved his army westwards. And this was the first time that the Jingisid rulers waged open warfare to each other in their inner political struggles. Güyüg's mother Töregene was influential in Güyüg's election as the Khan and as he died. In Mongol court politics, the womenhad always been influential and active. Both in the election of Güyüg and his successor, it was the mothers of the Khans who played the decisive role. Sorghaghtani Beki, the wife of Tolui who warned Batu in time about Güyüg's imminent attack urged her son Möngke to visit Batu in his Orda and ask for his help. Either out of his gratitude or because he was not interrestedin becoming the great Khan from the very beginning, Batu held a Khurultai in his own domain and nominated Möngke as the Khan. Some minor Ögedeid and Chaghataid members also attended this Khurultai, but even still, a Khurultai held outside Mongolia could be deemed invalid, so accompanied by Berke and Tuqa Temür, two brothers of Batu, Möngke attended another Khurultai in Mongolia for which his mother had been making diplomatic preparations for a while. Shiremün, the heir apparent

---

51 Ibid., 120.

52 Jue Yuan, *Qingrong Jushiji*, Sibu bei yao: Ji bu bai bu congshu jicheng. Wushiliu. Yi jiatang congshu 49 (Taipei: Taiwan Zhonghua Publishing House, 1969), chap. 34.

appointed by Ögedei bu replaced by Güyüg as a result of Törenege's maneuvers wanted to attend this Khurultai along with Güyüg's eldest son Khoja from his wife Oghul Qaimish, a Turkic princess from the Merkit tribe, but they were secretly bringing the Ögedeid army and planning an ambush. However, their plan was discovered and they were rounded up which not only ruined their chance of a surprise attack but also ruined the Ögedeid house as well as the Chaghataids who sided with them. Not all the Chaghataids sided with Oghul Qaimish and her faction who was behind all the conspiracy. But the man purpotrators and their supporters were all executed, attacking a Khurulai held in the sacred area of the Mongols and the Turkic tribes was an unpardonable crime. A Khurultai was a semi-sacred affair where all the parties had to persuade at least in appearance, all the parties, ideally without the threat of war or violence. But in any case, using violence and shedding blood were completely out of the way. Thus, what the Ögedeids did was not seen as amove against the Toluids and the Juchids but against the whole Mongol customs and traditions as well as the heritage of Jinggis Khan. If the claims of poisoning of Toluid are true, and since this story was mentioned by many historians in China, Persia, and other parts of the Empire, it seems this was widely suspected and was not a secret, both Ögedei and his son, the only two Ögedeid Khans did not hesitate to shed Jinggissid blood. Wha could have been the reasons that prompted the Ögedeid rulers to shed theirbrothers' or cousins' blood? They had already become great Khans, and did not need to shed blood. In the case of Toluid, he had already stated that he willingly gives up his claim to the thone in the Khurultai in front of everyone, and even after his death, Toluids did not resort to arms until Ögedei's sons tried to eliminate them by force. Güyüg in the same way was on the way to attack Batu who neither openly, nor as far as the sources reveal secretly had no purpose of becoming the great Khan, he was content with the western part of the Empire in Russia, Qipchaq steppes, Caucasia and parts of the Balkan peninsula which gave him great wealth and power as well as autonomy. They most probably understood the consequences of such actions, it would not only bring bad reputaition to the ruler to poison or attack his own brothers who were at the same time his vassals, but it also carried the risk of uniting the rest of the houses against the leader which was what happened after Güyüg. Later on Güyüg's son and the other Ögedeid contender Shiremün also resorted to arms. But these moves might not have been completely irrational on the Mongol political scene as well. For

Ögedei, the traditionalist party wo united behind Tolui was still strong, and they opposed a new form of government that would jeopardize their interests. Tolui was raised by Jinggis Khan and he attended nearly all the wars with him. Thus, he had very close relations with the elder generation who built the Mongol Empire alongside Jinggis Khan. The Juchid house also backed him and Tolui as an inheritance took the large force of Jinggis Khans elite Khesig army. Therefore, Ögedei might have feared that a civil war would be imminent if he did not eliminate him at that moment. Later on Ögedei invested heavily on the Ortogh companies of the Central Asian merchants, and his son Güyüg was also elected like him. There was no open opposition to Güyüg's election. The sons of Tolui were still too young and Batu had no interest in becoming the Khan so he simply did not attend the Khurultai. He neither wanted to be a Khan, nor wanted Güyüg with whom he had personal troubles to be the Khan. So, he simply delayd the Khurultai by not attending. In the meanwhile, the Chaghataids in central Asia and parts of Mongolia were busy with their own internal troubles and were not of great help to their Ögedeid allies. In fact, Güyüg felt the need to intervene their inner politics, lest their leaders shift their allegiance, and had Qara Hülegü dethroned, who would join Möngke upon the death of Güyüg and represent the Chaghataid house. Therefore, it might have seemed appropriate for Güyüg to attack Batu at a moment when he did not have Toluid allies and Chaghataids were still on his side. The third instance that the Ögedeids attempted to attack another house was the Khurultai where Möngke was elected by the Mongol tribes among whom there were Chaghataids such as Qara Hülegü and dissatisfied Ögedeids such as Kadan. What Güyüg and Ögedei before him feared seemed to have come to reality when tnot only the Juchids allied with the Toluids but the Chaghataids also sided with them. Thereforethey had two options, either to accept their fate like the Toluids did and wait, or to attack and win the throne by sheer force.

At this moment, Töregene saw that the only way was a surprise attack. In this respect, she differed from another Turkic princess, Sorghaghtani Beki, who bid her time and made preparations for the oportunate moment when she could strike. Both women were of Christian Turkic origin, but they did not put forward their Turkic or Christian orgins to the fore, and acted like real Mongols. In the Mongol politics beginning from Jinggis Khan whose grand grandmother, mother and wife also came from the Onggirad tribe. The Merkits, Qaraits, and especially the Onggirads acted as consort tribes in the Mongolian Empire and played significant roles in the Mongol politics. This was not unique to the Mongols. The Khitans had the Uighur Xiao clan as their consort clan. The Jürchens following the Khitans adopted this strategy and had women from tribes who had a better grasp of politics and cultural interaction. This strategy not only helped to build stron alliances, but also brought political knowledge and cultural exchange to the new dynasty. Just as the Uighur tribes had a more developed culture and political knowledge than the Khitans and the Xiao clan not only gave daughters but also gave ministers to the Khitans, the other Turkic tribes who continued the Turkic traditions and political culture brought their own culture and knowledge to the Mongol court and played significant roles. In the nomadic Empires of the Asian steppe, wives were also political actors unlike China where women were seldom on the front scene of the politics and needed intermediaries such as the eunuchs to intervene in the court politics whereas Khitan and Mongol women could even attend the military campaigns. their ethnicity and religion or cultural background also did not matter in most cases. Sorghaghtani Beki, though a devout Christian herself if we are to believe the sources[53], did not raise her sons as Christians.[54] Töregene, Sorghaghtani Beki and Oghul Qaimish were all influential in the shaping of the Mongol politics, but what is less known is that the Onggirad consort tribe also played an important role in forging and maintaining the Juchid-Toluid alliance against the Ögedeids. Batu's mother was also an Onggirad. Thus, the not only the consorts, but also their tribes played instrumental roles in shaping the Mongol court politics at its early stages through their networks in the different courts of all the four Jinggisid houses. This did not change when the power passed to the Toluids as well. The Onggirads continued to play a decisive role, and they even brokered peace between the Juchids and the Toluids when later the Ilkhans and the Golden Horde were at war.

---

53 Johannes de Plano Carpini, *Relation des Mongols ou Tartares* (Paris: Arthus-Bertrand, 1838); William Rubruck, *Mengü Han'ın Sarayına Yolculuk 1253-1255*, ed. David Morgan and Peter Jackson, trans. Zülal Kılıç, Kitap Yayınevi ; Sahaftan Seçmeler Dizisi 229. 21 (Istanbul: Kitap Yayınevi, 2010).

54 Morris Rossabi, *Khubilai Khan: His Life and Times* (Univ of California Press, 2009), 28.

Conclusion

Although the reigns of Ögedei and his son Güyük were relatively short, they have been decisive in shaping the later political events and the alliances between the different families. These two reigns have mostly been examined in terms of the military conquests that have been made, but one of the important aspects of these reigns have been the shaping of the Ögedeid, Toluid, Chaghataid and the Juchid houses. Descended from the four sons of Jinggis Khan from his wife, these four families. Jinggis Khan originally bid his sons to unite against outsiders, but even while he was alive, his sons were struggling with each other. The struggle between his sons however, was not a mere family struggle over the inheritance of their father, but it was more a struggle of a political and ideological nature. Each party represented a certain ideology and political view and the struggle was more around whether to adopt a new political model based on the more developed Chinese, as well as Khitan and Jürchen hybrid models, or to continue the traditional steppe models that the Mongols shared with the Turkic peoples around them.

References

Carpini, Johannes de Plano. *Relation des Mongols ou Tartares*. Paris: Arthus-Bertrand, 1838.

Fazlullah, Rashiduddin. *Jami'u't-Tawarikh: Compendium of Chronicles*. Translated by Wheeler M.

Thackston. Vol. 3. Classical Writings of the Medieval Islamic World: Persian Histories of the Mongol

Dynasties. London: I. B. Tauris & Co, 2012.

Juvaini, Ala' al-Din 'Ata Malek. *The Tar'ikh-I-Jahan-Gusha of Alaud-Din Ata Malik-I-Juwayni: Containing the History of Chingiz Khan and His Successors*. Translated by Muhammad Qazvini. London: Luzac, 1912.

Man, John. *Kublai Khan*. London: Bantam, 2007.

Peng, Daya. *Heida Shilue Jiaozhu*. Lanzhou: lanzhou Daxue Chubanshe, 2014.

Rossabi, Morris. *Khubilai Khan: His Life and Times*. Univ of California Press, 2009.

Rubruck, William. *Mengü Han'ın Sarayına Yolculuk 1253- 1255*. Edited by David Morgan and Peter Jackson. Translated by Zülal Kılıç. Kitap

Yayınevi ; Sahaftan Seçmeler Dizisi 229. 21. Istanbul: Kitap Yayınevi, 2010.

Song Lian. *Yuanshi: History of Yuan*. Ershı Wushı Shı: The Twenty-Four Histories. Beijing: Zhonghua Publishing House, 2000.

Su, Tianjing. *Yuanchao Mingchen Shilue*. Vol. 1. Beijing: Zhonghua Publishing House, 1962.

Yuan, Jue. *Qingrong Jushiji*. Sibu bei yao: Ji bu bai bu congshu jicheng. Wushiliu. Yi jiatang congshu 49. Taipei: Taiwan Zhonghua Publishing House, 1969.

CHAPTER 3

THE ROLE AND IMPORTANCE OF THE MIXED COURTS IN THE OTTOMAN PROVINCES: THE CASE OF THE PROVINCE OF EGYPT (1875-1949)

Recep Kürekli[55*]

Abstract

From the beginning of the 19th century it appeared that the European legal system had begun to enter the Ottoman legal system. In this period, it is estimated that the Egyptian province was ahead of Turkey in the codification of the law. The establishment of the Mixed Courts was one of the most important developments in the history of Egyptian civilization with the expression of Khedive Ismail and was welcomed in the first place; But in the process, Egyptian nationalist administrators and the Egyptian bourgeoisie, which emerged as an efficient class, began to evaluate these courts as an influential means of intervention by the European powers on the country. As a result of international diplomatic initiatives and legal regulations, the Mixed Courts would be completely removed from the Egyptian legal system at the end of the first half of

55 * Asst. Prof. Dr. Recep KUREKLİ, Nevsehir Hacı Bektas Veli University, Education Faculty, The Department of Turkish and Social Sciences Education. Contact: recepkurekli@gmail.com

the 20th century. In this study, the legal, social, economic and political effects of these courts on Egypt were tried to be revealed by Ottoman and especially English archival documents during the period beginning from the Mixed Courts were established in 1875 until they were officially abolished in 1949.

Key Words: Mixed Courts, The Province of Egypt, Judicial System in the Late Ottoman Egypt.

Law in the Ottoman Empire

The Ottoman Empire adopted Islam as a religion, as in Muslim and the Turkic States, for which reason Islamic law was taken as the basis. Islam is a religion that regulates not only the principles of faith and worship but also the growing aspects of life. For this reason Islamic law has been adopted along with the acceptance of Islam. However, since the Ottoman State has a multinational structure, it is expressed that the law and customs together with the law of Sharia regulate the social life. Sharia law is made up of direct norms based on the Qur'an, Sunnah, Ijma and Qiyas. On the other hand, rather than being contrary to Sharia law, the common law is executed in accordance with administrative and military law, fiscal law and land law, which are shaped by the fiefs and laws of the Sultan.[56]

The capitulations given to the western powers have been used as judicial privileges and are subject to their own laws and their own judges when there are conflicts and disputes among themselves in the countries where foreigners are present, and this task was usually carried out by their consuls. The aliens' cases were seen at the consulate courts established by the consulates. There were all kinds of lawsuits involving civil law within the jurisdiction of the consuls and disputes between their compatriots. It has been reported that in the cases of disputes between different nationalities and in disputed cases, the "convicts and requests of the parties" The Ottoman authorities did not preside over this kind of case without the parties' consent. On the basis of European law, the

56 Murat Şen, "*Osmanlı Hukukunun Yapısı*", Osmanlı, C.6. Yeni Türkiye Yayınları, Ankara 1999, pp. 327-329.

lawsuits opened the plaintiffs' case to the consular courts to which the defendant belonged.[57]

The struggle between the aliens and the Ottoman subjects began to be overseen by the Ottoman courts until the beginning of the 19th century rather than the the consulate courts. In the course of time, the authorities of the consular courts have progressively expanded and have begun to look at the struggle between aliens and the Ottoman subjects.[58]

In the Ottoman Empire from the beginning of the 19th century, the need to make new arrangements in law emerged. Beginning with the 1839 Tanzimat Decree, foreign legal argument started to be made. In other words, the Europeanization of Ottoman and Turkish Constitutional legal code started in 1839.[59]

Law in the Province of Egypt

At the beginning of the 19th century Egypt, especially in the codification of the penal code was ahead of Turkey. Although Egypt was a part of the Ottoman State, Mehmet Ali Pasha had arranged the new codes according to the Egyptian conditions.[60] From the time of Mehmet

---

57 Yasemin Saner Gönen, "*Hukuki Kapitülasyonlar ve Sonuçları*", Osmanlı, C.6. Yeni Türkiye Yayınları, Ankara 1999, pp. 340.341.

58 Yasemin Saner Gönen, "*Hukuki Kapitülasyonlar ve Sonuçları*", Osmanlı, C.6. Yeni Türkiye Yayınları, Ankara 1999, pp. 348.

59 Christian Rumpf, "*Osmanlı ve Türk Hukukunda Avrupalılaştırma Hareketleri*", Osmanlı, C.6. Yeni Türkiye Yayınları, Ankara 1999, pp. 482-483. (TanzimatÇeviri hatası in a broad sense is a concept that expresses the arrangements made in the structure of the Ottoman State and in the state-society relations. See. Bülent Tanör, "*Anayasal Gelişmelere Toplu Bir Bakış*", Tanzimat'tan Cumhuriyet'e Türkiye Ansiklopedisi, C.1, İletişim Yayınları, İstanbul 1985, pp.10-26; Ali Akyıldız, "*Tanzimat*", Türkiye Diyanet Vakfı İslam Ansiklopedisi, C.40, TDV, Ankara 2011, pp. 1-10; Gabriel Baer, "Tanzimat in Egypt--The Penal Code", *Bulletin of the School of Oriental and African Studies*, University of London, Vol. 26, No. 1 (1963), pp. 29-49.)

60 Gabriel Baer, "Tanzimat in Egypt--The Penal Code", *Bulletin of the School of Oriental and African Studies*, University of London, Vol. 26, No. 1 (1963), pp. 29. (Born in Kavala in 1769 or 1770, Mehmet Ali Pasha joined the army in 1787 and was among the 300 soldiers who had taken the road from Kavala against the French occupying Egypt in 1798. After the end of French occupation, the Ottoman and Mamluks struggle started in the absence of authority emerged in Egypt. Mehmet Ali Pasha, who won this struggle in favor of the Ottomans, was appointed as the governor of Egypt on 3 July 1805. See

Ali Pasha, significant arrangements were made in the field of law. For example, during the years 1829-1830 two important penal codes had been put into force. One of them was related to crime in general, and the other was specifically related to crimes in rural areas.[61] The basic punishments given were lashing, exile and rowing (penal servitude).[62] By 1834, Mehmet Ali Pasha increased his authority. Having sent a decree to local administrators, Pasha asked that the cases be investigated locally and the criminal cases connected with the trial, especially for the death penalty sent to him to be approved by him. The aim of Pasha is to establish a centralized, rational administration, and to have the ultimate authority within the legal system.[63] Until the French legal codes were enacted in 1883, Egyptian Penal code was enforced by written law and Islamic law throughout the 19th century. Penal codes were executed by parliaments, administrative and judicial institutions, while Islamic law was applied by the Qadi.[64] The Islamic religion, whether native or foreign persons allowed to use their own law in matters related to the civil status of their internal affairs.[65]

The Egyptian rulers needed to penetrate the country to control and organize the country. The management system put into practice by Mehmet Ali Pasha developed rapidly and the effect of the administration began to be felt on the whole Egyptian people. This effect first appeared

---

about Mehmet Ali Pasha, Muhammet Hanefi Kutluoğlu, "Kavalalı Mehmet Ali Paşa", *Türkiye Diyanet Vakfı İslam Ansiklopedisi*, C.25, Ankara 2002, s. 62-65.)

61 Rudolph Peters, "For His Correction and as a Deterrent Example for Others": Meḥmed ʿAlī's First Criminal Legislation (1829-1830)", *Islamic Law and Society*, Vol. 6, No. 2, The Legal History of Ottoman Egypt (1999), pp. 164.

62 Gabriel Baer, "Tanzimat in Egypt--The Penal Code", *Bulletin of the School of Oriental and African Studies*, University of London, Vol. 26, No. 1 (1963), pp. 29.

63 Rudolph Peters, "For His Correction and as a Deterrent Example for Others": Meḥmed ʿAlī's First Criminal Legislation (1829-1830)", *Islamic Law and Society*, Vol. 6, No. 2, The Legal History of Ottoman Egypt (1999), pp. 173.

64 Rudolph Peters, "Islamic and Secular Criminal Law in Nineteenth Century Egypt: The Role and Function of the Qadi", *Islamic Law and Society*, Vol. 4, No. 1 (1997), pp. 70. (The Ottoman Qadi is the judicial and civilian authority which has a unique place in the Islamic states. See: İlber Ortaylı, "Osmanlı Devleti'nde Kadı", Türkiye Diyanet Vakfı İslam Ansiklopedisi, TDV, C. 24, Ankara 2001, pp. 69-73.

65 Mark S. W. Hoyle, "The Origins of the Mixed Courts of Egypt", *Arab Law Quarterly*, Vol. 1, No. 2 (Feb., 1986), pp. 220.

on the law. Administrative arrangements were made on legal codes and regulations, including criminal proceedings that would apply to state officials. Nevertheless, the relationship between the executives and the officials, and the relations of the citizens to each other were clearly defined. The use and ownership rights of land have been regulated by other laws and regulations, as well as other commercial issues.[66]

In the 19th and early 20th centuries Egypt had two major legal institutions. One of them was the mixed courts (al-mehakim al-muhtelitah) and the other was the domestic courts (al-mehakim al-ahliyyah).[67] Egypt was part of both of the British and Ottoman Empires internationally and was subject to the control of the Caisse de la Dette Publique in the judicial sense of the international mixed courts in the economic field.[68] Although Egypt was part of the Ottoman Empire, the Egyptian rulers had a wide range of freedom to legislate.[69] In Egyptian law, "majlis-i ahqam-i al-Misriyyah" instead of "majlis-i ahqam-i adliyah"; "Egyptian Governor's Council" instead of "Mushur"; Only "sheikh" or "faqih" or court instead of "court"; "Umera" instead of "Wukela"; have been used instead of Ottoman institutions and concepts.[70]

The mixed commercial courts, which were established during the reign of Mehmet Ali Pasha, continued with the appointment of local merchants regularly to the council during the Abbas, Said and Ismail Pasha periods, and the election of European representatives was decided by the Ministry of Foreign Affairs of Egypt, possibly by consultation

---

66 F. Robert Hunter, "State-Society Relations in Nineteenth-Century Egypt: The Years of Transition, 1848-79", *Middle Eastern Studies*, Vol. 36, No. 3 (Jul., 2000), pp. 147.

67 Will Hanley, *Foreignness and Localness in Alexandria (1880-1914)*, A Dissertation Presented to The Faculty of Princeton University in Candidacy for the Degree of Doctor of Philosophy-Recommended for Acceptance by The Department of History, April 2007, pp. 4.

68 Will Hanley, *Foreignness and Localness in Alexandria (1880-1914)*, A Dissertation Presented to The Faculty of Princeton University in Candidacy for the Degree of Doctor of Philosophy-Recommended for Acceptance by The Department of History, April 2007, pp. 77-79.

69 Rudolph Peters, "Islamic and Secular Criminal Law in Nineteenth Century Egypt: The Role and Function of the Qadi", *Islamic Law and Society*, Vol. 4, No. 1 (1997), pp. 72.

70 Gabriel Baer, "Tanzimat in Egypt--The Penal Code", *Bulletin of the School of Oriental and African Studies*, University of London, Vol. 26, No. 1 (1963), pp. 40.

with the relevant consulates. The vast majority of cases that came to the Mixed Commercial Court were complaints of Europeans against their inhabitants.[71] The first Mixed Commercial Court in Alexandria was founded in 1826 under the name of "majlis al-tijarah" or "majlis al-tujjar" and was to be rebuilt with a law promulgated in 1842. This court was established to judge disputes between domestic (Egyptian or Ottoman) merchants or disputes between domestic and foreign merchants. Two such courts were established, one in Alexandria and the other in Cairo. Each court had an evaluation committee of merchants.[72] The aliens who committed the crime were handed over to their own consulates, and the consulates sent their offenders to their own countries for trial in their country.[73]

The mixed courts, reorganized in 1861, consisted of one Egyptian president appointed by the government, two Muslim merchant-evaluators and two Europeans. Judgments were made in accordance with the 1860 Ottoman commercial code. Consuls, however, continued to make complaints about the proceedings. The Levantine officers were concentrating on issues such as clearly distorting the testimonies during the translation process and generally not having any coercion on trial. Despite all these flaws, the Mixed Courts were perhaps the most autonomous organizations established by the government. The decision of the Alexandrian court could be appealed by the Cairo court or vice versa.[74] In 1876, reformed judicial courts were opened with the power to take civil action between aliens and the state or indigenous or other aliens. In Alexandria, six local and one Belgian, one Swedish, two Greek, one Austrian, French, Norwegian, Italian, American, Russian and German judges were assigned to the court in Alexandria.[75]

---

71 Michael J. Reimer, *Social Change in Alexandria Egypt 1807-1882*, An Unpublished Dissertation, Georgetown University, Washington, D.C, March 16, 1989, pp. 278.

72 Michael J. Reimer, *Social Change in Alexandria Egypt 1807-1882*, An Unpublished Dissertation, Georgetown University, Washington, D.C, March 16, 1989, pp. 162.

73 J.V.C. Smith, *Pilgrimage to Egypt*,Gould and Lincoln, Boston 1852, p. 27.

74 Michael J. Reimer, *Social Change in Alexandria Egypt 1807-1882*, An Unpublished Dissertation, Georgetown University, Washington, D.C, March 16, 1989, pp. 278-279.

75 *PRO,FO, 881/4509*, p. 18-19 (Summary by Lord Tenterden on the History of the Administration of Egyp 1840-81, Foreign Office, October 10, 1881)

The Emergence Process of the Mixed Courts

As a great judicial mechanism, the Egyptian Mixed Courts have emerged as the most successful international organizations. Fifteen nationals contributed to the development of these courts in fifty years so that the courts were able to carry out their activities in harmony. Relevant to these courts, diplomatic battles were initiated in 1867 by Nubar Pasha (Armenian-origin foreign minister of Khedive Ismail).[76] One of the most important steps in judicial reform was the establishment of international courts. Nubar Pasha, who made a great effort in judicial reform, sent a memorandum to powerful states in 1867. A commission was established on this subject. In October 1869, representatives of the Austrian, German, United States and Cairo members of France, England, Italy and Russia in Cairo were gathered with the participation of Nubar Pasha. The Commission convened until January 5, 1870 and issued a report strongly recommending that the old judicial system be renewed and international courts established. In January 1876 new courts were formally established and courts established on 1 February 1876 were opened. Three first-instance courts, one in Alexandria, one in Cairo and one in Mansoura, and one in Alexandria, opened an appeals court. The first-instance court in Alexandria consisted of 7 local and 12 foreign judges. 4 locals and 7 foreigners in Cairo were composed of 3 local and 5 foreign judges in Mansoura. The appeals court in Alexandria consisted of 7 foreigners and 5 local judges. In addition to foreign judges, there were judges who were called to assist judges in some commercial cases. These courts were overseeing all civil proceedings between the Government and the natives, and between the aliens of the same origin, and between the different foreign nations.[77] Nubar Pasha had to compromise on the majority of foreigners in these courts. Pasha, however, adapted some special mixed legal codes from French law to the legal system. But these legal codes were alien to judges appointed by the 14 states with both

---

76 Jasper Yeates Brinton, "*The Mixed Courts of Egypt*", Advocate of Peace through Justice, Vol. 93, No. 4 (December, 1931), pp. 254-255.
http://www.jstor.org/stable/20681637 (Accessed: 23-06-2017 07:40 UTC). See about Nubar Pasha: F. Robert Hunter, "Self-Image and Historical Truth: Nubar Pasha and the Making of Modern Egypt", *Middle Eastern Studies*, Vol. 23, No. 3 (Jul., 1987), pp. 363-375.

77 PRO, *FO, 881/4509*, p. 3 (Summary by Lord Tenterden on the History of the Administration of Egyp 1840-81, Foreign Office, October 10, 1881)

domestic judges and capitulations. In Egypt's chaotic financial situation, it was inevitable to give priority to private foreign enterprises.[78] European laws have also been implemented while new courts are being established. For this reason, the Ottoman legal system also began to change. Ottoman statesmen desired to go to a legal system where the privileges are canceled and the principle of reciprocity is observed. These desires can only be reached in the period between 1917 and 1818.[79]

According to the 1877 treaty, crimes related to slave trade were being discussed by military courts. This application could be seen as an imperative when the agreement was made, because there were no civil courts in the country in 1877. The intellectual part of the indigenous people had a feeling that the military courts were no longer needed because of the dramatic improvements in civil courts over time. Later, a special court to be composed of five judges elected from the Egyptian Appeals Court will be authorized and the decisions of this court will be final.[80]

Establishment of the Mixed Courts

Many states in the Middle East have tried to develop their judicial systems, largely by modeling the European states, during the 19th century. In Egypt, one of the first steps in this direction was to set up the Mixed Courts.[81]

The idea of the Mixed Courts, which Nubar Pasha had envisaged in 1867, could not be put into practice until 1876. Khedive Ismail and Nubar Pasha were worried about struggling with the restrictions imposed by the capitulations. Disagreements between Egyptians and foreigners could not be sentenced in native Egyptian courts or consulate courts. However, the growing debts of Egypt were of a worrisome dimension.

---

78 Byron D. Cannon, "A Reassesment of Judicial Reform in Egypt, 1876-1891", *The International Journal of African Historical Studies*, Boston University African Studies Center, Vol. 5, No. 1 (1972), p. 53.

79 Yasemin Saner Gönen, "Hukuki Kapitülasyonlar ve Sonuçları, Osmanlı, C.6. Yeni Türkiye Yayınları, Ankara 1999, pp. 348

80 *PRO, FO, 881/6808*, No: 7, p. 25 (Lord Cromer to the Marquess of Salisbury, Cairo, February 3, 1896)

81 Nathan J. Brown, "The Precarious Life and Slow Death of the Mixed Courts of Egypt", International Journal of Middle East Studies, Vol. 25, No. 1 (Feb., 1993), pp. 33.

This has led to the increasing insecurities of foreigners against the Egyptian government and the judicial system. For this reason, Egyptian managers needed to protect the financial interests of their countries. In this context, Nubar Pasha suggested the establishment of a unified legal system that includes aliens and natives. The Egyptian rulers had to accept the majority of foreigners in the Mixed Courts. Nevertheless, the courts have been forced to narrow down in their work areas. As foreigners continue to oversee the consular courts for criminal cases, the Mixed Courts would oversee civil and commercial cases. In Mixed Court law, a foreigner is entitled to file a lawsuit against the Government. Thus, if the case were won, the Government had to implement the court order. It was again appointed to investigate cases in the French legal system, and to appoint civil servants who were able to sue a criminal and who could find legal advice on the jurisdictions.[82]

In Egypt, the Mixed Courts were first established in 1875.[83] These courts have begun to work amongst a great publicity and hope. These courts, operating according to completely new legal codes for the country, were also overseeing political and economic cases.[84] The established Mixed Courts were divided into two levels: first degree courts and appeal courts. First-degree courts were deployed in Alexandria, Cairo and Mansoura. The appeals court was in Alexandria. All the courts had a certain number of judges, and the majority of them were European. The Egyptian government, while having the right to choose a judge, chose judges from those recommended by European states.[85] Thus, the Mixed Courts were also used as a weapon in European intervention in Egypt. Because the judges were elected by the European governments from the Egyptian government, this situation was in favor of the Europeans in the stance.[86]

---

82 Nathan J. Brown, "The Precarious Life and Slow Death of the Mixed Courts of Egypt", International Journal of Middle East Studies, Vol. 25, No. 1 (Feb., 1993), pp. 33-35.

83 F. Robert Hunter, "Self-Image and Historical Truth: Nubar Pasha and the Making of Modern Egypt", *Middle Eastern Studies*, Vol. 23, No. 3 (Jul., 1987), pp. 367.

84 Mark S. W. Hoyle, "The Mixed Courts of Egypt 1875-1885", *Arab Law Quarterly*, Vol. 1, No. 4 (Aug., 1986), pp. 436.

85 Robert L. Tignor, *Modernization and British Colonial Rule in Egypt, 1882-1914*, Princeton University Press, New Jersey, 1966, pp. 125.

86 F. Robert Hunter, "Self-Image and Historical Truth: Nubar Pasha and the Making of Modern Egypt", *Middle Eastern Studies*, Vol. 23, No. 3 (Jul., 1987), pp. 367.

When the Mixed Courts began to work in 1876, Egypt became economically bankrupt and Khedive Ismail had to accept European control over the economy. In the meantime, the Mixed courts have begun to discuss numerous cases against the Khedive and the Egyptian government. Khedive Ismail would be demoted when he tried to get rid of the financial control of foreigners and the control of the Mixed Courts.[87]

The Mixed Courts were modeled on French law as Nubar Pasha had expected.[88] So the law was based on French law and was applied by mixed courts.[89] The Mixed Courts have accustomed the country to European law and procedures. But very few Egyptian lawyers had studied law in France. This meant that the new legal system would be placed according to the French model. The legal codes published in Arabic were drawn up in a clear and concise manner and forced the courts to follow certain precise procedures. The salaries were fixed at a sufficient level so that judges would not feel the need to corrupt themselves. But the judges were not always chosen according to merit. The difficulties arising from the lack of sufficient Egyptian judges to adhere to the new system which imposed the presence of judges in the first degree and appeal courts. The newly established courts, despite many inconveniences, made a great progress compared to the previous courts. From 1885 onwards, the work was folded four times, and few cases were not completed. Some errors were probably caused by ignorance and inexperience. A serious bribery bill was not heard.[90]

The court records continued to work without any legal delay, even after the British navy bombarded Alexandria in July 1882, in the confusion surrounding the city, and even until the defeat of Arabi Pasha forces in Tel-el-Kebir in September 1882.[91] The general principle

87 Nathan J. Brown, "The Precarious Life and Slow Death of the Mixed Courts of Egypt", International Journal of Middle East Studies, Vol. 25, No. 1 (Feb., 1993), pp. 36.

88 Robert L. Tignor, *Modernization and British Colonial Rule in Egypt, 1882-1914*, Princeton University Press, New Jersey, 1966, pp. 125.

89 *PRO, FO, 881/5322*, No: 174, p. 127 (Sir E. Baring to the Early of Rosebery, Cairo, May 13,1886)

90 *PRO, FO, 407/106*, No: 64, p. 69 (Sir E. Baring to the Marquis of Salisbury,Cairo, March 29,1891)

91 Mark S. W. Hoyle, "The Mixed Courts of Egypt 1875-1885", *Arab Law Quarterly*, Vol. 1, No. 4 (Aug., 1986), pp. 441. (It is seen that the revival of national consciousness in Egypt was in reality and as a historical event

of the Mixed Courts was to decide on the civil disputes that emerged among different nations. The courts were now regarded as sufficient to oversee the cases of people from the same nation if they were concerned with European interests. In this respect, Circassians, the Railways, the Dominions and the Alexandria Municipality undertook to take care of domestic cases in addition to foreign cases against various state institutions, even if they were registered companies (even if they were registered in Egypt).[92] The Mixed Courts continued to look at a wide range of commercial litigation regarding every segment of Egyptian society. As a specific example, employers have made decisions about the safety of the workers they work with, making sure that workers are as safe as possible, and they have made compensation decisions for occupation accidents.[93]

The Mixed Courts have had a well-deserved reputation for impartiality and legal knowledge in the field of judges, as well as complaints about the cumbersome and expensive procedures. There is no doubt that these judges offer great services to the country. They maintain the equilibrium required by their legal qualifications and at the same time protect the plaintiffs against the arbitrary implementation of the Egyptian Government. On the other hand, it protected the Egyptian Government against the extreme demands of the Europeans. However, judges of the Mixed Court were not under any surveillance or control. The Egyptian government did not have any control over the courts. Only international control was alternative to other controls; but it was not in practice either.[94]

The fact that the local Justice system has gradually ceased to be effective since the 1880s had by then become one of the topics discussed

---

firstly manifested in 1881 with the Arabî Pasha rebellion. As a result of this movement identified with the slogan "Egypt for Egyptians", the country was under a new invasion and ended with the death of many Egyptians. Arabi movement could be considered as the beginning of resistance against foreign invasion and foreign domination for many years under the consciousness of Egyptians. See. Yakup Kadri Karaosmanoğlu, "Mısır'da Milli Şuurun Uyanışı", *Orta Doğu*, Year 1, Number 2, Ankara 1961, pp. 3-4.)

92 *PRO, FO, 881/6965*, No: Inclosure in No 81, p. 57 (Further Memorandum on the Judgement of the Mixed Courts, December 2,1896)

93 Mark S. W. Hoyle, "The Mixed Courts of Egypt 1906-1915", *Arab Law Quarterly*, Vol. 2, No. 2 (May, 1987), pp. 177.

94 *PRO, FO, 407/106*, No: 64, p. 66-67 (Sir E. Baring to the Marquis of Salisbury,Cairo, March 29,1891)

at the local press as a matter of complaint. On the contrary, "Al-Hukuk", the magazine of Egyptian lawyers, admitted that the Mixed courts benefited Egypt.[95] In 1883, after the British occupation, a new penal code based on French law was put into force. In the following years a series of modern penal codes would be enacted.[96]

In 1883, the Egyptians and the Ottomans were regarded as the same and were being tried as native citizens. Foreigners who did not benefit from the capitulations and beneficiaries were mostly tried in mixed courts in civil and commercial matters. However, the new penal code did not introduce any exemption, so foreigners who did not benefit from the capitulations were tried in domestic courts.[97]

Serious progress has been made against crime in the justice system. Punishment of crime was more clear. There were not crowded rogue bandits anymore. The murder cases decreased from 347 in 1891 to 270 in 1892, and one-third of these murders were for robbery purposes. Other crimes were revenge, jealousy and land dispute related. But there was still highway robbery, cattle abduction, and such minor crimes were at high levels, and these cases before the judge were showing an increase. People did not help to prevent crime and identify it, they did not say what they know.[98] The police could not reveal the crime because often people, especially village guards, did not report crimes quickly, and did not give evidence to make criminals come out. With the expression of "Sir E. Baring," people did not understand that it was a public duty to do the best of each person's ability to provide order and suppress crime.[99]

In 1896, the total number of crimes committed was 1,850. In 1897, this number was 1,437 with a 22% decrease. The types of crime, which were usually related to the security situation of the country, showed the effectiveness of the police and the crime rate was rather low. Among the

---

95 Byron D. Cannon, "A Reassesment of Judicial Reform in Egypt, 1876-1891", *The International Journal of African Historical Studies,* Boston University African Studies Center, Vol. 5, No. 1 (1972), p. 61-65.

96 Gabriel Baer, "Tanzimat in Egypt--The Penal Code", Bulletin of the School of Oriental and African Studies, University of London, Vol. 26, No. 1 (1963), pp.. 47.

97 Mark S. W. Hoyle, "The Mixed Courts of Egypt 1875-1885", *Arab Law Quarterly*, Vol. 1, No. 4 (Aug., 1986), pp. 443.

98 *PRO, FO, 407/119,* No: 152, p. 110 (Lord Cromer to the Earl of Rosebery, Cairo, March 9,1893)

99 *PRO, FO, 407/106,* No: 64, p. 71-72 (Sir E. Baring to the Marquis of Salisbury,Cairo, March 29,1891)

people, the robbery, known as banditry decreased from 51 to 17, violently and with pressure, fell from 440 to 280, from the constitutional raids of 98 to 75. The feedbacks indicating the decrease in crime show that not only in a specific place, but also in the country as a whole. This decrease showed itself to the full moon throughout the year.[100] From 1896 to 1899, it was observed that serious crimes had been steadily declining. However, the proportion of each case that resulted in the sentence increase from 73% in 1896 to 80% in 1899.[101] By 1899, there were 242 Europeans in the Joint Courts, including judges, and only 17 of them were British citizens. 101 of these courts were working in Egypt.[102]

The British Chamber of Commerce in Alexandria had long insisted on the regulation of fraudulent bankruptcy in the Mixed Law and the need to deal with this problem for a long time.[103] Indeed, the criminal proceedings of the mixed courts had been extended to include simple and fraudulent bankruptcy crimes. Fraudulent bankrupts could be sentenced to two to five years in prison. Simple bankruptcy involving crimes such as negligence and unjustified expenditure, fraudulent receivers and bookkeeping was considered as a mild crime, and simple bankruptcy criminals could be sentenced from one to two years in prison. If a foreigner was charged with this crime, "Parquet"'s investigation in this context would be carried out by a European magistrate.[104] The Alexandria Court of Jurisdiction (Mahkeme-i Muhtelitah), who committed fraudulent bankruptcy; But those living within the borders of the Ottoman State who did not reside in Alexandria were sent to Alexandria to withdraw their punishment from the court.[105]

---

100 *PRO, FO, 881/7158*, No: 116, p. 88-89 (Lord Cromer to the Marquess of Salisbury, Cairo, February 27, 1898)

101 *PRO, FO, 881/7510*, No: 29, p. 40 (Viscount Cromer to the Marques of Salisbury, Cairo, February 20,1900)

102 *PRO, FO, 407/150*, No: 142, p. 133 (Viscount Cromer to the Marquess of Salisbury, Cairo, February 26, 1899)

103 *PRO, FO, 407/152*, No: 3, p. 4 (Viscount Cromer to the Marquess of Salisbury, Cairo, July 1,1899)

104 *PRO, FO, 881/7510*, No: 29, p. 48 (Viscount Cromer to the Marques of Salisbury, Cairo, February 20,1900)

105 *BOA*, Fon Kodu: DH.EUM.KADL., Dosya No: 11, Gömlek No: 28, Tarih: H. 19/Ra/1329 (20 Mart 1911); *BOA*, Fon Kodu: DH.EUM.KADL., Dosya No: 86, Gömlek No: 43, Tarih: H. 22/S/1331. (31 Ocak 1913)

In the following decades, as in the first decade after the establishment of the Joint Courts, there had also been cases in the Joint Courts of enormous commercial ventures and very valuable properties.[106]

Similarly, the works that the Municipality of Alexandria had done were closely related to the prosperity of the city. Because the ratio of foreigners in the city was high, it also meant an intertwined relationship of interests. Naturally, these relations were also entering the jurisdiction area of the Mixed Courts. The decision of the Alexandria District Court in favor of the mixed courts in the case of debates over whether the Domestic Courts or the Mixed Courts would take the case for the Alexandria Municipality had also been approved by the Alexandria Court of Appeals. Thus, in the case of the Municipality, it was declared that the Mixed Courts were the sole authority.[107]

Until the 1900s, education in all branches of European law was only given in French in Egypt. Only students who are in favor of French and who have attended elementary and secondary education are eligible to enter the School of Law. All students in preparatory schools favoring the English were deprived of practice in law school and legal education in practice. It was decided to remove this disadvantage. In 1899 an English section was opened at the School of Law. Three English lawyers with the necessary qualifications were appointed to this school as a faculty member. In October 1899, 37 students registered with the school. Seventeen of these students were included in the English part and twenty in the French part. The students in the English part of the school would follow a French course for a period of 3 years to evaluate the work in the field of law. This 3-year education would be concluded with the entry of these students in French, both written and oral exam. A standard and authoritative commentary on Egyptian civil law was also being prepared in English.[108] However, an arrangement that changed the status of "Khediviate Law School" would be done in 1912. Accordingly, this school was being transferred from the supervision and supervision of the Ministry of Education to the supervision and supervision of the Ministry of Justice. The close relationship of the Ministry of Justice with the law

106 Mark S. W. Hoyle, "The Mixed Courts of Egypt 1886-1895", *Arab Law Quarterly*, Vol. 1, No. 5 (Nov., 1986), pp. 562.

107 Mark S. W. Hoyle, "The Mixed Courts of Egypt 1896-1905", *Arab Law Quarterly*, Vol. 2, No. 1 (Feb., 1987), pp. 58-59.

108 *PRO, FO, 881/7510*, No: 29, p. 54-55 (Viscount Cromer to the Marques of Salisbury, Cairo, February 20,1900)

education had many advantages that directly affected the law education. With this amendment, an upper council was established in the school. Two members of this council would form this commission for a period of not more than two years assigned by the chief executive of the appellate court, the chief prosecutor, the school principal and the Justice Ministry. The number of students in the school was 270 in 1912 and 55 students were granted diplomas.[109]

By 1891 the official judicial languages recognized by the laws in the Mixed Courts were French, Italian and Arabic. In February 1889, the Egyptian government was generally sent to the governments, suggesting that they were one of the judiciary languages recognized by the English. Only the approval of France and Greece remained, and other states had approved this proposal. As most of the judges were more familiar with French and Italian than English.[110] By 1892, judges in international courts spoke French no matter what their nationality, and tried to do the trial in French.[111] The official languages accepted in the mixed courts in 1898 were only French, Italian and Arabic. The exclusion of the English Language caused great damage to the interests of British and American plaintiffs. This issue was discussed in the British Chamber of Commerce in Alexandria. The costs and delays in translating legal actions into English harmed British commercial interests.[112] By 1905, English would be one of the official languages recognized by the Mixed Courts.[113]

As a result, the Mixed Courts have been involved in judicial proceedings in a variety of areas since its establishment. One of the most important areas of jurisdiction in this period, especially in a commercial community such as Alexandria, is the main commercial affairs, and new developments have been made in the field of law by making new arrangements in this area. Decisions were taken quickly and commercial

---

109 *PRO, FO, 368/809*, No: 1, p. 51 (Reports by His Majesty's Agent and Consul-General on the Finances, Administration and Condition of Egypt and the Sudan in 1912, Cairo, March 22, 1913)

110 *PRO, FO, 407/106*, No: 64, p. 67 (Sir E. Baring to the Marquis of Salisbury,Cairo, March 29,1891)

111 W. Fraser Rae, *Egypt To-Day* (The First to the Third Khedive), Richard Bentley and Son, London 1892, pp. 216.

112 *PRO, FO, 881/7158*, No: 116, p. 95 (Lord Cromer to the Marquess of Salisbury, Cairo, February 27, 1898)

113 *PRO, FO, 881/8553*, (Memorandum respecting Egypt, Printed for the use of the Foreign Office, Foreign Office,December 11, 1905)

privacy was important.[114] Although there is a need to extend the powers of criminal jurisdiction of the Mixed Courts by the Egyptian Government and the British Counselors, it should be noted that until the first world war Egyptian nationalists did not bear a particular hostility towards the Mixed Courts and court employees.[115]

Disappearance of the Mixed Courts

The convictions of these courts, which were seen as positive in the first place, also changed over time and were now condemned as institutions representing the hegemony of aliens on Egypt. In 1936 al-Musawwar's weekly newspaper described these courts as "a crime against humanity". In fact, these courts were established not to increase the efficiency of aliens, but to limit this effect, on the contrary. The courts could have survived with strange and changing coalitions of Egyptians and aliens, but in the 1930s such courts completed their mission with a coalition of Egyptian nationalists and the progressively influential bourgeoisie and the British government.[116] From the 1930s the Egyptian bourgeoisie emerged as a new political force. According to this new influential proprietor, the Mixed Courts and capitulations seemed to be a burden on the Egyptian economy. First of all, Egyptian trade leaders, capitulations and mixed courts, who did not have any foreign nationality, thought that foreigners brought foreigners to an advantage over the locals. Even when tax was levied on foreigners, the Mixed courts had been searching for the consent of the great powers. That was why as long as the capitulations remained, the Mixed Courts would remain.[117]

Before the removal of the capitulations, the Egyptian Government had recommended that criminal cases in consular courts of foreigners be transferred to the Mixed Courts and that these cases should be

114 Mark S. W. Hoyle, "The Mixed Courts of Egypt 1896-1905", *Arab Law Quarterly*, Vol. 2, No. 1 (Feb., 1987), pp. 70-72.

115 Mark S. W. Hoyle,"The Mixed Courts of Egypt 1906-1915", *Arab Law Quarterly*, Vol. 2, No. 2 (May, 1987), pp. 184.

116 Nathan J. Brown, "The Precarious Life and Slow Death of the Mixed Courts of Egypt", International Journal of Middle East Studies, Vol. 25, No. 1 (Feb., 1993), pp. 33-34.

117 Nathan J. Brown, "The Precarious Life and Slow Death of the Mixed Courts of Egypt", International Journal of Middle East Studies, Vol. 25, No. 1 (Feb., 1993), pp. 45.

transferred to the Egyptian courts in a transitional period. International conferences on capitulations in Montreux almost succeeded in obtaining whatever they requested. Almost none of the participants in the conference were willing to defend the capitulations and the Mixed Courts. With the support of the Egyptian government and the bourgeoisie, the capitulations and the coalitions advocating the Mixed Courts had not been able to tolerate much so that the Mixed Courts were quickly lost, leaving little trace behind them.[118] Officially, the Mixed Courts in Egypt were closed on October 15, 1949.[119]

Conclusion and Evaluation

In the Ottoman Empire, on which the Sharia and Common Law were based, we see that the European law started to enter the Ottoman legal system as a necessity of the contemporary conditions, in case of necessity of capitulations. In this context, in the Province of Egypt in 1875, there was a wide public support and hopes for the establishment of mixed courts. It can also be said that the European law (especially the French legal system) and its influence had increased gradually over the Egypt Khedive and the government through such courts. Because Egypt was financially in a very precarious period during the opening of these courts. Financially the situation of the country weakened the political influence of the Egyptian rulers. As a matter of fact, when the Mixed Courts started to work in 1876, the country had experienced economic bankruptcy. As a result, the Egyptian administrators had to accept the European control over the country by means of "De la Dette Publique". Even Khedive Ismael would be removed from the administration because he wanted to get rid of this economic and legal siege, although he was responsible for the country's economic downturn.

The definitions of the mixed courts concerning the Egyptians and the aliens were also problems to be clarified. In this context, Turks were

---

118 Nathan J. Brown, "The Precarious Life and Slow Death of the Mixed Courts of Egypt", International Journal of Middle East Studies, Vol. 25, No. 1 (Feb., 1993), pp. 47-49.

119 Jasper Y. Brinton, "The Closing of the Mixed Courts of Egypt", *The American Journal of International Law*

Vol. 44, No. 2 (Apr., 1950), pp. 303.

not regarded as foreigners because Egypt was a legitimate part of the Ottoman State. This same situation was applied to the other Ottomans, the nations living in the provinces for a while.

The fact that a large number of cases had been opened since the time of its establishment was also a sign of trust in these courts. In this context, the judges of the Mixed Court were trusted. Egypt's economic and financial stability within the process were also the main factors that increased confidence. But in the first quarter of the 20th century, the perception of trust in these courts began to change. The Egyptian bourgeoisie, which started to function as an effective force over the Egyptian government and Egypt, had by then started to evaluate these courts as a tool for the political and economic system of the European powers on the country. The cases in the mixed courts were transferred to the Egyptian courts and the Egyptian authorities at the international conference in Montreo agreed to almost all of their requests. Consequently, at the end of the first half of the 20th century, these courts were completely removed from the Egyptian judicial system.

Bibliography

State Archives of the Prime Ministry of the Republic of Turkey (BOA)

BOA, Fon Kodu: DH.EUM.KADL., Dosya No: 11, Gömlek No: 28, Tarih: H. 19/Ra/1329 (20 Mart 1911)

BOA, Fon Kodu: DH.EUM.KADL., Dosya No: 86, Gömlek No: 43, Tarih: H. 22/S/1331. (31 Ocak 1913)

The Puclic Record Office/The National Archives in England (PRO)

PRO, FO, 368/809, No: 1, p. 51 (Reports by His Majesty's Agent and Consul-General on the Finances, Administration and Condition of Egypt and the Sudan in 1912, Cairo, March 22, 1913)

PRO, FO, 407/106, No: 64, p. 66-67 (Sir E. Baring to the Marquis of Salisbury,Cairo, March 29,1891)

PRO, FO, 407/106, No: 64, p. 67 (Sir E. Baring to the Marquis of Salisbury,Cairo, March 29,1891)

PRO, FO, 407/106, No: 64, p. 69 (Sir E. Baring to the Marquis of Salisbury,Cairo, March 29,1891)

PRO, FO, 407/106, No: 64, p. 71-72 (Sir E. Baring to the Marquis of Salisbury,Cairo, March 29,1891)

PRO, FO, 407/119, No: 152, p. 110 (Lord Cromer to the Earl of Rosebery, Cairo, March 9,1893)

PRO, FO, 407/150, No: 142, p. 133 (Viscount Cromer to the Marquess of Salisbury, Cairo, February 26, 1899)

PRO, FO, 407/152, No: 3, p. 4 (Viscount Cromer to the Marquess of Salisbury, Cairo, July 1,1899)

PRO, *FO, 881/4509*, p. 3 (Summary by Lord Tenterden on the History of the Administration of Egyp 1840-81, Foreign Office, October 10, 1881)

PRO,FO, 881/4509, p. 18-19 (Summary by Lord Tenterden on the History of the Administration of Egyp 1840-81, Foreign Office, October 10, 1881)

PRO, FO, 881/5322, No: 174, p. 127 (Sir E. Baring to the Early of Rosebery, Cairo, May 13,1886)

PRO, FO, 881/6808, No: 7, p. 25 (Lord Cromer to the Marquess of Salisbury, Cairo, February 3, 1896)

PRO, FO, 881/6965, No: Inclosure in No 81, p. 57 (Further Memorandum on the Judgement of the Mixed Courts, December 2, 1896)

PRO, FO, 881/7158, No: 116, p. 88-89 (Lord Cromer to the Marquess of Salisbury, Cairo, February 27, 1898)

PRO, FO, 881/7158, No: 116, p. 95 (Lord Cromer to the Marquess of Salisbury, Cairo, February 27, 1898)

PRO, FO, 881/7510, No: 29, p. 40 (Viscount Cromer to the Marques of Salisbury, Cairo, February 20,1900)

PRO, FO, 881/7510, No: 29, p. 48 (Viscount Cromer to the Marques of Salisbury, Cairo, February 20, 1900)

PRO, FO, 881/7510, No: 29, p. 54-55 (Viscount Cromer to the Marques of Salisbury, Cairo, February 20, 1900)

PRO, FO, 881/8553, (Memorandum respecting Egypt, Printed for the use of the Foreign Office, Foreign Office,December 11, 1905)

Secondary Sources

Akyıldız, Ali, "*Tanzimat*", Türkiye Diyanet Vakfı İslam Ansiklopedisi, C.40, TDV, Ankara 2011, pp. 1-10.

Baer, Gabriel, "Tanzimat in Egypt--The Penal Code", *Bulletin of the School of Oriental and African Studies*, University of London, Vol. 26, No. 1 (1963), pp. 29-49.

Brown Nathan J., "The Precarious Life and Slow Death of the Mixed Courts of Egypt", International Journal of Middle East Studies, Vol. 25, No. 1 (Feb., 1993), pp. 33-52.

Brinton, Jasper Yeates, "*The Mixed Courts of Egypt*" Advocate of Peace through Justice, Vol. 93, No. 4 (December, 1931), pp. 254-255. http://www.jstor.org/stable/20681637 (Accessed: 23-06-2017 07:40 UTC).

Brinton, Jasper Y., "The Closing of the Mixed Courts of Egypt", *The American Journal of International Law* Vol. 44, No. 2 (Apr., 1950), pp. 303. http://heinonline.org/HOL/LandingPage?handle=hein.journals/ajil44&div=20&id=&page= (Accessed: 14-07-2017 11:47 AM)

Brown, Nathan J., "The Precarious Life and Slow Death of the Mixed Courts of Egypt", International Journal of Middle East Studies, Vol. 25, No. 1 (Feb., 1993), pp. 33-52.

Cannon, Byron D., "A Reassesment of Judicial Reform in Egypt, 1876-1891", *The International Journal of African Historical Studies,* Boston University African Studies Center, Vol. 5, No. 1 (1972), p. 51-74.

Gönen, Yasemin Saner, "*Hukuki Kapitülasyonlar ve Sonuçlari*", Osmanlı, C.6. Yeni Türkiye Yayınları, Ankara 1999, pp. 340-353.

Hanley, Will, *Foreignness and Localness in Alexandria (1880-1914),* A Dissertation Presented to The Faculty of Princeton University in Candidacy for the Degree of Doctor of Philosophy-Recommended for Acceptance by The Department of History, April 2007.

Hoyle, Mark S. W., "The Mixed Courts of Egypt 1875-1885", *Arab Law Quarterly*, Vol. 1, No. 4 (Aug., 1986), pp. 436-451.

Hoyle Mark S. W., "The Mixed Courts of Egypt 1886-1895", *Arab Law Quarterly*, Vol. 1, No. 5 (Nov., 1986), pp. 562-576.

Hoyle, Mark S. W., "The Mixed Courts of Egypt 1896-1905", *Arab Law Quarterly*, Vol. 2, No. 1 (Feb., 1987), pp. 57-74.

Hoyle, Mark S. W.,"The Mixed Courts of Egypt 1906-1915", *Arab Law Quarterly*, Vol. 2, No. 2 (May, 1987), pp. 166-184.

Hoyle, Mark S. W., "The Origins of the Mixed Courts of Egypt", *Arab Law Quarterly*, Vol. 1, No. 2 (Feb., 1986), pp. 221-230.

Hunter, F. Robert, "Self-Image and Historical Truth: Nubar Pasha and the Making of Modern Egypt", *Middle Eastern Studies*, Vol. 23, No. 3 (Jul., 1987), pp. 363-375.

Hunter, F. Robert, "State-Society Relations in Nineteenth-Century Egypt: The Years of Transition, 1848-79", *Middle Eastern Studies*, Vol. 36, No. 3 (Jul., 2000), pp. 145-159.

Karaosmanoğlu, Yakup Kadri, "Mısır'da Milli Şuurun Uyanışı", *Orta Doğu*, Year 1, Number 2, Ankara 1961, pp. 3-4.

Kutluoğlu, Muhammet Hanefi, "Kavalalı Mehmet Ali Paşa", *Türkiye Diyanet Vakfı İslam Ansiklopedisi*, C.25, Ankara 2002, s. 62-65.

Ortaylı, İlber, "Osmanlı Devleti'nde Kadı", Türkiye Diyanet Vakfı İslam Ansiklopedisi, TDV, C. 24, Ankara 2001, pp. 69-73.

Peters, Rudolph, "For His Correction and as a Deterrent Example for Others": Meḥmed ʿAlī's First Criminal Legislation (1829-1830)", *Islamic Law and Society*, Vol. 6, No. 2, The Legal History of Ottoman Egypt (1999), pp. 164-192.

Peters, Rudolph, "Islamic and Secular Criminal Law in Nineteenth Century Egypt: The Role and Function of the Qadi", *Islamic Law and Society*, Vol. 4, No. 1 (1997), pp. 70-90.

Rae, W. Fraser, *Egypt To-Day* (The First to the Third Khedive), Richard Bentley and Son, London 1892.

Reimer, Michael J., *Social Change in Alexandria Egypt 1807-1882*, An Unpublished Dissertation, Georgetown University, Washington, D.C, March 16, 1989.

Rumpf, Christian, "*Osmanlı ve Türk Hukukunda Avrupalılaştırma Hareketleri*", Osmanlı, C.6. Yeni Türkiye Yayınları, Ankara 1999, pp. 481-492.

Smith, J.V.C., *Pilgrimage to Egypt*,Gould and Lincoln, Boston 1852.

Şen, Murat, "*Osmanlı Hukukunun Yapısı*", Osmanlı, C.6. Yeni Türkiye Yayınları, Ankara 1999, pp. 327-339.

Tanör, Bülent, "*Anayasal Gelişmelere Toplu Bir Bakış*", Tanzimat'tan Cumhuriyet'e Türkiye Ansiklopedisi, C.1, İletişim Yayınları, İstanbul 1985, pp. 10-26.

Tignor, Robert L., *Modernization and British Colonial Rule in Egypt, 1882-1914*, Princeton University Press, New Jersey, 1966.

CHAPTER 4

MAJOR HALIS ATAKSOR'S BIOGRAPHY AND HIS ROLE ON APRIL 25 ANZAC LAND REMOVAL

Burcu Mercan

Summary

In this article, the biography of the 27th Regimental 3rd Army Commander Gazi Major Halis Ataksor and his participation in battle front because of Anzac landing on 25 April 1915 will be tried to be explained.

While this work was being done, it was benefited from documents and various sources from the archives of Serdar Hâlis Ataksor, the grandchild of Gazi Hâlis. In addition, it has benefited from the related part of Halis Ataksor's autobiography which he wrote his life from his birth to his death, from the diary he held during the war, from his own draw war sketch and himself photo album. In the direction of the information given by Battalion Commander Major Halis himself, the initial phase of the Çanakkale Land Wars will be tried to be elucidated and an attempt will be made to show how effective the first day's defense and strategies at the result of the war. The findings are expected to contribute to the biographies that academics study about them, and to the new work about the April 25 Anzac Landing.

Key Words: Dardanelles War, Major Halis Ataksor, 25 April Anzac landing

WHO IS VETERAN MAJOR HALIS ATAKSOR?

Halis Efendi was born in 1876 in Aydın. Ahmet Muhtar Efendi, the great scribe of director of the financial administration of a province, was appointed to Kütahya; therefore, he came to Kütahya at a young age. In 1881, he started primary education at Küpecik Mahalle Mektebi. He entered Kütahya Ottoman Junior high school in Hijri 1301 (1885-1886) and finished middle school in Hijri 1304 (1888-1889). Recognizing the necessity of language learning in this period, Hâlis Efendi began to learn French. The following statements, which we find in his special notes, the value he gives to language learning was remarkable:

'I started learning French because of my own needs. Neighboring women said to my mother that your son would be infidel.'

Subsequently, he began high school the newly opened in hijri 1305 (1889-1890). He was elected to the Kütahya Liva Assembly in hijri 1309 (1893-1894) and continued to Bursa Mülkiye high school. At the end of his six years of successful education there, he received a commendation and came to Istanbul, and started to Harbiye in hijri 1312 (1896-1897). In hijri 1314 (1898-1899) he finished Harbiye as an officer, who graduated with a superior degree. Right after his graduation, he joined the Balkan War. When he was in the 12th regiment of 1. Battalion 4. Company, he was promoted to first lieutenant. Meanwhile, Halis Ataksor made the adjutancy of Lieutenant-Colonel Ziya Bey and 8th Liva Commander Mirliva Ishak Pasha, Gâvur Ishak Pasha. He did the member deputy of Construction Commission and the clerkship of Martial Court.

In 1912-13 the Balkan War, he got wounded from his feet and eyes in the battle of Vize-Soğucak. After this, he was referred to as "Blind Halis". He was promoted to lieutenant in hijri 1324 (1908-1909). Subsequently of Balkan War was sent to the Dardanelles Front of World War I in September 1914. In the battle of Çanakkale, as the 27th Regiment 3rd Battalion commander, he was found in Seddülbahir. One of the hero soldiers in charge was Mehmet Sergeant who was from Biga. On April 25, 1915, Anzak, who went to Ariburnu, became one of the first commanders to fight against the soldiers.

On June 5, Halis Ataksor also played an important role in the Çanakkale battle, where the 31st and 32nd trenches of the 57th Regiment were captured by Anzac troops. The two Turkish trenches that were in Bombasırtı location (It is corresponds to the midpoint of the trenches, today there is the Quinn's Post graveyard in this area) and parallel to the western coast of the sea, from south to north, were captured by Anzac troops; however, no one, including the 57th Regiment Commander, had any information on this subject. In response to the news, which was sent to the Regimental Command, the Battalion and Regiment Commander reported that the trenches were not seized. After that four hours of uncertainty, Cpt. Hassan Efendi, still felt suspicious about the answer he received, made sure from the situation by listening to the trenches and made a plan for the removal of the trenches from the hands of the British forces. Captain Halis and three brave bombers (Corporal Hasan, Corporal Süleyman and Corporal Mustafa)[120] from the 27th Regiment 10th Company took back the trenches, and this prevented the division of the Turkish trench line into two pieces. The division of the trench line is very important in terms of the battle's course, because this initiative will cut off the contact between the Turkish troops. 27. Regiment commander Şefik Aker, in memoirs, speaks about him as "a very valuable and selective soldier".[121] Moreover, in the memoirs of Mucip Kemalyeri who is Commander of the 27th Regiment 12th Company, he said, "He was a very powerful soldier, and always talk about our regiment commander with respect."[122]

On August 8, 1915 Şefik Aker was appointed to the 19th Division Command, then Halis Efendi, who rose to major in June, became commander of the 27th Regiment. After Çanakkale battle, he was a Territory Inspector of Mardin during the National Struggle (1919-1913) and was found in Urfa, Diyarbakır and Siverek regions.

The intellectual personality of this commander who spent his life in battlefields of war is as striking as his heroism. He knows French, German, Arabic and Persian well. He began to translate the History of Herodotus, but because of his death, the translation did not finish. In addition, Hâlis Bey, who translated the Paris Commune, published articles about Komuk Turks on Ziya Gökalp's Küçük Mecmua. These articles were brought together in 1988 by his son Yilmaz Ataksor in latin letters and published in the name of Komuk Eli in the History of

---

120 History of the Turkish Armed Forces Ottoman Revolution Turkish War in the First World War Volume 5, Book 3 The Operation of the Dardanelles Front (June 1915 - January 1916), Gnkur. Press, Ankara 1980, p.567.

121 Aker, a.g.e., p.243.

122 Mucip Kemalyeri, How the Canakkale Spirit Was Born and the Battle of Azerbaijan (1917-1918), Baha Press, Istanbul 1972, p.46.

Diyarbakır.[123] Halis Efendi also had an artistic side at the same time. Today, his various drawings and black pencil studies are in the private archive of his grandson Serdar Halis Ataksor.

Major Halil Efendi retired from the army in 1925 and married Zekiye Hanim within a year. In the same year, he was awarded the Independence Medal by the Grand National Assembly of Turkey. Afterwards, he worked in Uşak Municipality to solve the infrastructure problems of Uşak. Halis Efendi has also made a significant contribution to the first asphalt paving of the Republic of Turkey, in Uşak.

After all these services, Halis Efendi was disturbed twice from his lungs and once from his kidneys. Due to his lack of money, he was treated first by the military, then his treatment expense paid by the Governor of Izmir. In 1933 he was sent to his eternal journey.

When Halis Bey died in 1933, there was no the Surname Law yet. But he likes the name 'ATAKSOY' very much and wants to be put this name on his grandkids. For this reason, in 1934 when the Surname Law came out, they had taken the successor ATAKSOY as a surname. Unfortunately, because of writing the letter R instead of the Y letter of the population servants, and his successors are still known as ATAKSOR.[124] On the other hand, in his tombstone is written his surname as ATAKSOY.

GENERAL LINES OF THE PROCESS THAT REACHS 25 APRIL 1915 ANZAC LANDİNG

The Canakkale front of World War I; is a front opened to invade Istanbul through the Dardanelles Strait of the Entente States, to defeat the Ottoman State and share its territory, to send aid to Russia, the allies of the Entente Bloc, to strengthen the Tsarist Russia against the Bolsheviks. For this reason, Britain, who wanted to enter the Dardanelles, believed that it could only be accomplished with naval battles. However, the defeat of the British on March 18, 1915, which it did not be considered, brought two new options: Either the British Navy would accept the defeat and be pulled back or put on the button for the black combat.

123 The subject of the work, Hâlis (Ataksor), Komuk Eli in History of Diyarbakir, Yay. Prepared by Yilmaz Ataksor, Çeltüt Printing Industry and Trade Co., Istanbul 1988.

124 Halis Ataksor, Komuk Eli in History of Diyarbakir, Yay. Prepared by Yilmaz Ataksor, Çeltüt Printing Industry and Trade Co., Istanbul 1988.

Admiral Robeck, who opted for the second option, told Lord Kitchener on March 20th that land operations were necessary.[125] On March 22, British Commander Ian Hamilton, commander of the United Kingdom, decided landing with the aim of seizing the coastal bastions. British Minister of War Lord Kitchener approved the decision, and Navy Minister William Churchill supported it. A single politician in the British War Council did not appeal. All the entente forces were sent to training in Alexandria. In addition, the New Zealand Division and the Gurka Nepal Brigade were also requested to the region by Ian Hamilton.[126]

On the 24th of March 1915, the 5th Army was established to defend the Dardanelles in the Ottoman wing, and the German Port von Sanders was brought to its head. According to Sandres' plan, the position of the Turkish army in Çanakkale until the 25th of April was as follows: Total of 6 divisions and total of 75 people including some forces as 2 Divisions in Saros and Bolayır; 1 Division in Arıburnu, Kabatepe and Seddülbahir; 2 Divisions from Kumkale to Beşike on the Anatolian side of the Bosphorus; 1 Division in Eceabat. The zone of the forces; were distributed as the 5th Division where the peninsula merged with Thrace; the 7th Division in Bolayır (Saros-Bolayır Zone); 3rd Division in Kumkale, 11th Division (Anatolian coast Zone) on Beşike coast; the 9th Division from the middle of Anafartalar to Seddülbahir, the north of 9th Division and the 19th Division (Maydos Zone) in Bigalı.[127] Apart from these, it was located the Independent Cavalry Brigade in the north of Saros Bay, the Gallipoli Gendarmerie Battalion was located in the mountainous areas, the Çanakkale Gendarmerie Battalion in the opposite coast of Bozcaada.

On April 25, the forces to land Arıburnu were 1st, 2nd, 3rd and 4th Australian and New Zealand Infantry Brigades. Other than these, artillery and portable sanitary organization would also be disembarked. Australian Infantry Brigade (4000 people[128]) as the precursor unity with the 1st Employment Division and half of the 3rd Field Hospital would land as three parts. The first part of 1,500 people landed at about 4:30 am.[129] The second and third parts with 2750 people and in the north

125 Ian Hamilton, Gallipoli Memories 1915, Örgün Press, 2006, p.38-39.

126 Hamilton, a.g.e. p.42.

127 Miralay Şefik Aker, Çanakkale Memories, Arma Publications, Istanbul 2005, C.I, p.189.

128 Robert Rhodes James, Gallipoli Operation, Belge Publications, 1965, p.143.

129 Aspinal Oglander, History of the Great War Çanakkale Gallipoli Military Operations, c.1, Arma Publications, Istanbul 2005, p.206-213.

11th Battalion being commanded by Captain Tulloch, from Fisherman's Dams to Conkbayırı; 9th Battalion in the South, to Kabatepe region; in the center, 10th Battalion commanded by Charles Leer, who encountered Battalion Commander Captain Halis Efendi, landed on the coast to reach Topçular Region[130]. The 12th Battalion was waiting as a caution battalion. Then the 1st and 2nd Australian Brigades would land at 5:00 pm and the sticker would be completed.

The Turkish union that opened fire against this landing of the enemy was two section soldiers assigned to watch the big and small Ariburnu coast. After the first conflicts, a command was given to the caution armies of the 1st and 3rd Battalion to devolve at 5:45 am in Maydos for the 9th Division[131]. Thus, the battalions mentioned were started the road to enter into conflict with the enemy.

The reason why the Anzac landing is met with such a weak force was that the 5th Army Commander Marshal Liman von Sanders thought that "Coastline surveillance is adequate"[132]. Prior to Liman Pasha, 9th Division commander Halil Sami Bey and Şefik Aker planned to prevent before the enemy landed on the coast. Mustafa Kemal also supported this idea. The reason is that although the enemy's weapons are as powerful as they can be, but they are not strong enough to damage the trenches.

25 APRIL 1915 THE ANZAK LANDING AND THE ROLE OF THE CAPTAIN HALIS BEY

At around 01.30 pm on April 25, A.N.Z.A.C[133] forces were placed in the destroyers from İmroz Island. At 3 o'clock, the three war ships were at a distance of two miles from the land. Leading troops realized that when they started to advance on the boat, they were dragging to a mile north of the planned export point. In this subject, some historians

---

130 The chain of Conkbayırı, Kemalyeri, Göktepe and Kavaktepe, which are known as Topçular crest, are known as Günsilsilesi by British.

131 The 2nd Battalion referred to here was attached to the 27th Regiment prior to the date of April 1, 1915, but was transferred to the 9th Division Command. See. ATASE Archive, Folder 5338, File H-10, Index1.

132 General Staff War History Presidency. War History Publications. Serial No: 3, Turkish Wartime in First World War 5.Cilt Çanakkale Front, Gnkur Press, Ankara 1978, p.9.

133 A.N.Z.A.C. is a word formed from the English initials of the Australian and New Zealand Corps: Australian and New Zealand Army Corps.

claim that Anzacs landing area was marked with red barges and these barges were dragged to north one mile by Turkish soldiers. Although the British placed the barges ahead of time in order to mark the export point; Captain Halis Ataksor, 3rd Battalion Commander of the 27th Regiment, ordered to drag these barges and place them to the north; however, it cannot possible to prove that with current documents. In addition, his grandson Serdar Hâlis Ataksor rejects also this discourse in person.

With such a deflection, the British forces, which set foot on the Ariburnu coast at 04.30 am, were in a rush and confusion. At the same day, the troops affiliated to the 9th Division were assigned to observe the region from the Azmakdere site in the Anafartalar Plain to the Çamtepe site in the south of Kabatepe.

The 27th Regiment, under the command of Major Şefik Aker, was emplaced as reserve forces at Eceabat (Maydos), Zeytinlik district; after a short time after midnight, in the region extending from Kabatepe and Palamutluksırtı, the 1st Battalion, 3rd Battalion and a machine gun division returned from the night drill. Shortly afterwards, the sounds of the ball from the west side caught the attention of the forces in Maydos[134]. For the first time, the sounds of the ball were coming from a different point, not from the entrance of the bosporus.

On top of that, the 27th Regimental Commander Şefik Bey, who heard the news that a landing was made on Arıburnu, immediately ordered his soldiers to be ready and waited command for movement order from 9. Division. The command at 05:45 was like this[135]: 'the copy

1. It has been understood that since half an hour the enemy has begun the attempt to shelter between Ariburnu and Kabatepe. 27. Regiment battalions in Zeytinlik and machine guns, mountain battery in Çamburnu now move commanded by Kaymakam Şefik Bey, which will block the performance of the enemy and absolutely repulse the enemy into the sea.
2. The army troops in Sarafim camp are about to take action.

9th Division Commander
Colonel Halil Sami"

134 Halis Ataksor, Çanakkale Report, Serdar Hâlis Ataksor, Timas Publications. Istanbul, 2008, p.120

135 ATASE Arşivi, Klasör 5338, Dosya H-10, Fihrist 1-2.

Transfer of Captain Halis Bey to the Front

After taking orders, Senior Captain Halis Efendi commanded the 3rd battalion and machine gun department passed to Mount Kakma and landed on the Ece plain. It would follow the direction Saddle point-Kavaktepe-Kanlısırt. The 1st Battalion commanded by Captain İbrahim Efendi would go to meet with the 3rd Battalion in Kavakdere region from Kabatepe road and would pass to Kemalyeri. The two battalions followed two different routes to prevent casualties in a possible conflict.

When Captain Halis and his soldiers crossed the Saddle Point and came to Ece Plain, there was heavy fog in the plain. This fog prevented seeing of the battalion the observation balloon and enemy planes in the air. Thus, the battalion was not affected by the severe navy shooting beyond the plain[136]. Then, a wounded soldier was seen on the way before he reached Kavaktepe. 27. Regiment Commander Şefik Bey learned from this soldier that the enemy was getting on the line of the Kanlısırt-Kırmızısırt[137]. Both battalions passed to Kemalyeri. The 3rd Battalion commanded by Halis Efendi turned the direction from Kemaliye to Merkeztepe. The reason for this was that the attack on Kanlısırt was dangerous because of attacks from the south. The 1st Battalion commanded by Ibrahim Efendi would also turn to the direction of Kanlısırt. For the 3rd Battalion reaching 165 Rakımlı Hill, an offensive order came from this region. However, the 1st Battalion was continuing to progress the southern slope of the hill. And Cebel Battery expected from Çamburnu district have still been on the road.

Meanwhile, three of the four gun in the hands of the 72th Battalion of Cebel and deployed in Kanlısırt were seized by the British. The only gun, was taken difficultly, was brought later to use 3rd Battalion from Kocadere[138]. With the 1st Battalion coming to the region, the first intervention to the British forces would be with a 1st and 3rd Battalion consist of 2,000 people, a ball and a machine gun troops[139]. It is worth

136 ATASE Archive, Folder 5338, File H-10, Index 2.

137 ATASE Archive, Folder 5338, File H-10, Index 2.

138 ATASE Archive, Folder 5338, File H-10, Index 4.

139 Murat Karatas, Canakkale Wars with Maps, Nobel Publications. Ankara 2007, p.37.

mentioning an important point here. The number of soldiers fighting in the Gallipoli battles is different in various sources. For this reason, the number have given is closer to approximately 2000 people.

Captain Halis Efendi is on the offensive

The 3rd Battalion which will attack at 07:55, will take these orders from Regimental Commander Şefik Bey[140].

1. The left side of the enemy is approximately on the back of Kılıçbayır (inclusive), and the right side is Kanlısırt (inclusive). Progressed part of the enemy has captured the brook (Çataldere and Çataldere's east part of Kanlısırt) which is in front of us and moves to the crests (Topçular Crest) upon it.
2. The First Battalion will attack on Kırmızı and Kanlısırt. The Third Battalion will attack the left side of the enemy from the Kırmızısırt (except).
3. The First Battalion will leave a division as precaution in my custody.
4. The artillery will be at 165 Rakımlı Tepe.
5. The Mechanic Rifle Division will be protective with their attack from the south of 165 Rakımlı Tepe.
6. I will command the situations about artillery and machine guns.
7. The battle weights will be send to Bigali ammunition with the ammunition send purpose by the detainment of the required amount and unlade of the others at here. The ammunition from Bigali will be kept behind the 165 Rakımlı Hill. The battalions will take their arsenals out of here.
8. The battalion's treatment center will be on the side of the road leading to the village of Kocadere, on the back of the 165 Rakımlı Hill.

Captain Hâlis Effendi, who attacked by the above orders, had drawn all the attention of the Anzac troops. Commander of the 1st Battalion, Captain Ibrahim, who took advantage of the situation, passed through Keklikderi and captured Adanabayırı and here The

140 ATASE Archive, Folder 5338, File H-10, Index 5-7.

Anzac repulsed by his forces. Meanwhile, the Anzacs were landing reinforcements against the lagoons of Kanlısırt with Kırmızısırt and the northern slopes. Immediately the gun and machine guns were turned in this direction to prevent reinforcement. When the Turkish military began to force on, 9th Division Commander Halil Sami Bey gave the following information to the Commander of the Regiment, Şefik Bey, by telephone[141]:

"Copy
At time 08:25

To district governor Şefik Bey
A quarter ago, the 57th Regiment from the 19th Division and Cebel Battery, moved your right side with the division commander.

9th Division Commander
Miralay Halil Sami"

As the British could not be landing reinforcement force, they alternatively tried to pass troops among Kanlısırt shrubs and from the creek path; however, for the second time they failed because of the Turkish gun and machine gun shooting. On the other hand, they could not go beyond Kırmızısırt. Meanwhile, the forces of Captain Ibrahim and Captain Halis Efendi captured İncesırt Zone. Then there were conflicts in İncedere valley and Çataldere. It was shot to this area from the British Navy.

Captain Abraham and Captain Halis, who had taken over Fundalıksırt, were heavily exposed to the British fire from Merkezepe-Gedik-Sivritepe-Kanlısırt. The capture of this region by the Anzacs meant that it was easy to proceed. For this reason, the influence of the two commanders and their soldiers on the situation of the war was important. The 1st Battalion forces who survived this pressure fired an attack against the British troops from Adanabayırı on the eastern slopes of Kanlısırt. A team of machine rifle divisions was sent as reinforcements to the attack troops. At the same time, the 3rd Battalion 8th Division Cebel Battery came from Çamburnu and was placed at 165 Rakımlı Hill. Captain Halis repulsed British on

141 ATASE Archive, Folder 5338, File H-10, Index 9

the north-western side of Fundalıksırt and in the Incebayır. A force of about 2,000 people, consisting of only two battalions, collided without allowing the enemy to get on. On the other hand, the 1st Battalion captured Çataldere and Karayörükderesi with the support of the machine gun division.

The British were moving from Kılıçbayır to Conkbayırı. Meanwhile, 3rd Battalion Commander Halil Efendi realized that the right wing was in critical condition. If the enemy passed the right flank, it would pass the Conkbayiri and reach the back areas from there and surround the Turkish troops. This would probably indicated that they would successfully complete the landing operation, because the 5th Army had no other forces in the region. After all, when there was no thought left anyone, I started to think about the men. Their aim was defending the region until the 57th Regiment of Mustafa Kemal command came the region. Until the 57. Regiments arrived, if the trenches were lost, Conkbayiri would have lost.

The one-and-a-half-unit force, under the command of Captain Halis was holding British soldiers in Merkeztepe and Bombasirti, on the other hand the force was under mutual fire from the 180-altituded hill of Kilicbayiri and Adanasirti. Turkish soldiers who could not move were getting closer to the Anzac soldiers 20-step distance because of the heather-covered structure of the land. Capt. Halil Efendi and the Turkish troops were waiting for the combat participation of the 57th Regiment under command of Mustafa Kemal in such a difficult situation. 27th regiment was having the golden value five and half hour time to the Turkish army which was passed from the landing of the enemy until the participation of lieutenant colonel Mustafa Kemal with the 57th regiment to the battle. Especially if the troops commanded by the Captain Halis had been disorganized over an hour from the departure of the 57th Regiment to the arrival of the region, the Anzac soldiers could easily advance on the peninsula. This expectation, which is critical for the future of the battlefield, can be said for the success of the 57th Regiment, which was made possible by the resistance of the 27th Regiment.

At the same time, these two battalions were the first hot encounter with British forces. This is why the results of waiting for the 57th Regiment were also severe. Mülazim-i Evvel İdris Efendi and Mülazim-i Sani Mustafa Efendi were martyred and the 3rd Battalion Commander, Captain Halis, was injured from the arm. When Captain Halis went to the 4th Division between Kesikdere and Kilicdere, he took two bullets from his arm and a bullet from his leg. The khaki color on the arm of the seriously injured Captain Halis turned red and blood was dripping from his fingers. He warned the young officer Mucip Efendi who saw this and get the medical sergeant immediately "Do not tell soldiers I am injured!" [142]. Halis, gradually exhausted, was unable to get up from his place. After that, he called Mucip Kemaleri that "Do not retreat from where you are. Only in this place you can send a reporter who will tell us that all of you are dead. I will send you reinforcements as soon as possible." [143] and then he was taken back to the front of the cellar [144]. Officers could not get rid of the boat while they were taking Mr. Halis' clothes. Then, it was understood that the bullet that peeled off the foot caused the bleeding and dried the blood and glued it to the boot. This boat was removed only by cutting it from the foot[145]. We can say for this injury that Captain Halis was not behind the cover, but was injured when he went between the company. Reason is only encouraging his soldiers.

Mustafa Vehbi Efendi, who was an account officer for not having an officer in the battalion, took command of the Battalion. Although it was inexperienced in this regard, he was able to keep the troops together until 57th Regiment revert to the battle area. But on the other hand, because the arsenal of Mr. Mulazım-ı Sani Ibrahim is exhausted, he began to retreat with his soldiers. Turkish troops were fighting with 12,000 British troops, despite the fact that the soldiers and the soldiers wounded hundreds with nearly 2,000 guns. Another highlight of these attacks is that these trenches, held on the first day, will not change until August 6th. These trenches, which were held under the command of Captain Halis and Captain Ibrahim, provided geographical superiority for three and a half months to Turkish troops.

Colonel Mustafa Kemal was transferred to the scene, the 57th Regiment started an offensive. [146] Then, the 27th regiment began attacking the slopes of the Kanlısırt, where three Turkish cannonballs were also deployed, with a heavily constructed land structure. Because the capture

---

142 Kemalyeri, *a.g.e.*, p.42.

143 Kemalyeri, *a.g.e.*, p.42.

144 Kemalyeri, *a.g.e.*, p.39-42.

145 This information has been transferred from Zekiye Hanim, the wife of Gazi Major Halit Ataksor, to his granddaughter Serdar Ataksor.

146 ATASE Archive, Folder 5338, File H-10, Index 13.

of Kanlisirt means the capture of Kirmizisirt. For this reason, Regiment Commander Sefik Bey gave that order: [147]

"From artillery
April 25, 1915
12.00

1. My heroic friends have been given many times to the enemy with the attacks they have done like lions, and they have taken captives and kidnapped them to the other side of Buyukdere.
2. The 57th Regiment inflicted the enemy in front of us on the right side of the heroic battle.
3. In order to pour the enemy into the sea, first we need to capture the Çamlısırt (Kanlisirt) and we are there to save our artillery who are crying in the hands of the enemy.
4. The 3rd battalion will give a division under the command of 1st battalion. With the rest of military force, the 1st Battalion's attack will be facilitated by the fire from the backbone. On the right side, will be taken action by contacting with the 57th Regiment. Additional orders will be given to capture the future ridges (Merkeztepe, Bombasirti).
5. The 1st Battalion will attack Kanlisirt. This will hold back and the gunners will save. There is no enemy on the top and east of Düzsırt in the north of this back, it is behind the enemy. This place will be occupied by the seizure of Kanlisirt.
6. after the guards of trenches that we had previously made on the western edges of the ridges, the enemy will be followed to the sea with fire, and if they are surrendered, their weapons will be abandoned and taken prisoner.
7. Artillery and machine guns will remain in the position and will protect the attack.
8. I am currently at the beginning of the battery and machine gun division.

27th Regiment Commander
District Governor Mehmet Sefik"

[147] ATASE Archives, Folder 5338, File H-10, Index 12.

From noon onwards, the three section of 1st Battalion and Capt. Hâlis' three sections started counter attack against Anzac forces deployed in Kanlısırt and Cemaldere. The hunter Turkish troops marched forward with the bayonet and the English began to retreat from the southern slopes. Then the enemy was pulled back from the eastern slopes. The Anzac troops, who did not give up easily, began to attack again to keep Kanlisirt. An hour later, Kanlisirt was saved by Turkish soldiers and cannonballs.

The battles continued as far as the evening. For this reason, Commander Mustafa Kemal, ordered to prepare for the night attack. The artillery was again placed in the Kanlısırt and Gedik Point. Meanwhile, the 77th Regiment was scattered. It is striking that Mustafa Kemal does not want to take this section when it is desired to be given to the 19th Division. The reason was that a large part of the 77th Regiment was made up of Arab soldiers. As a matter of fact, in a very critical situation these soldiers were scattered leaving the left flank of our troops defenseless and even opened fire on Turkish troops, assuming enemy soldiers. Having such an ally has been the greatest misfortune of Saib Bey's battle line.

When the night showed 02.30, 77th Regimental Commander Mr. Saib with a half-troop soldiers passed to Kanlisirt. Commander of the 1st Battalion in there asked Captain Mr. Ibrahim to withdraw his soldiers, saying, "Who is the biggest commander here?" [148]. According to him, it's reason was a thought that a possible attack could take place from the rear of the 1st Battalion. After all the struggles made throughout the day, Kanlisirt was evacuated with a forced retreat. The troops were pulled to the south of the Adanasırtı[149]. It is a great advantage of the Turkish army to make such a decision that Anzacs can not notice.

Conclusion

Definetely, not only sea battleship but also land battleship is won under difficult conditions and with great devotion on the front of Canakkale. The nine-month-long battle finally ended with the victory of the Turkish Nation in December. One of the heroes that provide these achievements is Veteran Major Halis Ataksor. In the battlefields of life, Mr. Halis attacked without fear against the Anzac troops who made the

148 ATASE Archive, Folder 5338, File H-10, Index 28.

149 ATASE Archive, Folder 5338, File H-10, Index 29.

First World War on the Canakkale front. We can learn this from the 27th Regimental Commander Şefik Aker, from the Mucip Kemaleri and from people who wrote about the memories of Canakkale.

On the 25th of April, the 3rd Battalion Commander, Captain Halis, and his soldiers who was on the way to the 9th Division Command, took offensive at 7.55 A.M. by order from Mr. Sefik with 1st Battalion after 2nd Battalion's attack and defend. All the struggles that day were made have also affected the outcome of the war in a great way. The reason for this is that the held trenches do not change hands from 25 April to 6 August. This gave a great geographical advantage to the Turkish army. His strategic moves show us both his courage and his superior ability as a commander.

When Anzaklar tried to exit Conkbayiri from Kılıçbayır, the right flank realized that there was not enough power against the enemy forces and that he intervened immediately became the first advantage that Halis Ataksor gained for the Turkish army on the first day of Çanakkale land battle. Because Conkbayiri's geography was a gateway to the implementation of British plans. So the conquest of Conkbayiri means that the enemy can comfortably enter Gallipoli, walk through the trenches and seize the Turkish trenches. At such a crucial point, Captain Halis, who sees that the army's ammunition has diminished and his power has been exhausted, has taken immediate control. There was a huge casualty to be avoided that night, which provided to continue the battle in favor of the Turks.

Halis Ataksor's second advantage for the Turkish army is the waiting period for the 57th Regiment. This process was best evaluated by Captain Hâlis Effendi, who appointed Mülazim Mithat Efendi and Mülazim Mustafa Efendi to form a buffer zone. A force of about one and a half units under the command of Captain Hassan managed to keep the enemy on line until the transfer of the 57th Regiment, which provided a great advantage to the Turkish army. If the Anzac soldiers crossed this line, the inner parts of the peninsula would have been seized. Because there was no other Turkish unity in the region. In this context, we are witnessing the heroism of the 27th Regiment before the 57th Regiment. The achievement of the 57th Regiment is influenced by the 27th Regiment.

As a result, the heroic commander who favored these critical moments in favor of the Turkish Army made great contributions to the success of the Canakkale Front with the successes it had shown. Veteran Major Halis Ataksor is one of our heroes who have not signed a single victory but also encouraged the spirit of national struggle at the same time. However, the contributions of the Turkish soldiers, who were thrown into the fire without breaking their eyes with all the other commanders, are indisputable facts.

References

Aker Miralay Sefik, Canakkale Memoirs, Arma Publications, 2005, C.I.

Ataksor Halis, Komuk Eli in History of Diyarbakır, Publication Prepared by Yilmaz Ataksor, Celtut Printing Industry and Trade Co., Istanbul 1988.

Ataksor Halis, Çanakkale Report, Prepared by Serdar Hâlis Ataksor, Timas Publishing Istanbul, 2008.

ATASE Archive, 27th Harp Ceridesi, Folder 5338, File H-10, Index 1-29.

ATASE Archive, 27th Harp Ceridesi, Folder 5338, File H-10, Index 1-29.

General Staff War History Presidency, Harp Historical Publications Serial No: 3, Turkish War at First World War 5.Cilt Canakkale Front, General Staff Publishing House, Ankara 1978.

Hamilton Ian, Gallipoli Memories 1915, Orgun Publishing House, 2006.

Karatas Murat, Canakkale Wars with Maps, Nobel Publishing Ankara 2007.

Kemalyeri Mucip, How the Canakkale Spirit Was Born and the Azerbaijan War (1917-1918), Baha Press, 1972.

Oglander C.F. Aspinal, History of the Great War: Canakkale Gallipoli Military Operation, c.1, Arma Publishing, Istanbul 2005.

Rhodes Robert, James, Gallipoli Operation, Document Publication, 1965.

www.halisataksor.com.tr

CHAPTER 5

BULGARIAN POLITICS OF RUSSIA DURING THE FIRST WORLD WAR IN THE RUSSIAN DIPLOMATIC DOCUMENTS

Yrd. Doç. Dr. Eray BAYRAMOL

The Balkans, one of the fields of World War I, have a geopolitical importance for the European States, the Ottoman State and also the Tsarist Russia. Owing to the fact that Bulgaria binds Asia, Europe and Africa to each other, it has attracted the interest of all states that want to have a say on the Near East.

The need to find raw materials, energy and new markets that came up with the Industrial brought the fact of competing with each other for industrialized countries. With this fact, England, Russia, Germany and the Ottoman State produced various policies on the Balkans. One of the intersection points of these policies was Bulgaria.

The Balkan nations under Ottoman sovereignty have declared their nation states with the influence of the French Revolution, and with the provocation and support of the states, such as Britain and Russia, that want to have a say on the region. Greece established in 1830; Serbia, Romania, Montenegro established in 1878; Bulgaria and Albania established in 1908 and 1912, respectively.

In the emergence of Bulgarian nationalism, Russia successfully used Orthodoxy and Slavism phenomenons. By the 19th century, Russia under the identity of the Orthodox patriarch had approached to the Bulgarians to benefit from them in the Balkans, and Russia benefited from the

Bulgarians in the War of 1828-1829 for the first time. During this war, a Bulgarian named Marcheh was in the service of the Russians. He supported the Russian army with 500 volunteers and then encouraged all Bulgaria to revolt. This was the first rebellion attempt of Bulgarians who then rebelled for independence in 1835. The rebellion, led by the Bulgarian merchant named Velche, was suppressed by the Turkish government. Another rebellion emerged in the vicinity of Niche. This rebellion was the greatest rebellion that happened before the Vidin Revolt, and it was remarkable in terms of the realization of foreign nterventions.

This uprising happened in 1841 spread to many parts of Bulgaria. Rebellion was a good opportunity for Russia for intervention to the Ottoman State. In a letter sent to the Ottoman Government,the Tsar claimed that the Bulgarians were oppressed under mismanagement of the Ottomans and this was the reason of rebellion. Russia declared the decision of sending an officer to the region to prevent the repetition of the incidents by detecting the problems and taking necessary measures. Thus, Russia made it clear that it was involved in Bulgaria matter. The biggest uprising in Bulgaria was the Vidin Rebellion, which began in 1849 and was suppressed in 1850. On those dates, the Panslavism movement showed a great improvement in the entire Slavic region through Russia. Russia was trying to spread the Slavic issue, reviving the racial and national events, with Orthodoxy to the whole Balkans. In applying this policy, the Bulgarians were chosen as the target nation. Russia incited Bulgarians for independence against the Ottoman State. In doing so they showed the Serbs as an instance.[150]

The Balkan states, who wanted to remove the Ottoman State completely from the Balkans, launched the Balkan Wars in 1912. The war ended on 10 August 1913 with the Treaty of Bucharest signed among Bulgaria, Greece, Serbia and Montenegro. Furthermore, the Treaty of Istanbul was signed between the Ottoman Empire and Bulgaria on 29 September 1913. Moreover, the Treaty of Athens was signed between Greece and the Ottoman State on 14 November 1913. With these treaties, the Ottoman State experienced great land losses in the Balkans.

150 Halil İnalcık, **Tanzimat ve Bulgar Meselesi**, Eren Yayıncılık, İstanbul, 1992, s. 16-43.

Macedonia and Western Thrace; was shared among Serbia, Greece and Bulgaria. Eastern Thrace was left to the Ottoman State. Thus, the Ottoman Empire lost all of its lands in the west of the Meriç River.

Since the emerging new situation would bring policies of the big states to a standstill on the Balkans, it was not accepted. For this reason, the Triple Entente Bloc, created by Italy-Germany-Austria, and the Triple Alliance Bloc, established by Britain-France and Russia, came face to face. The tension between these two blocs caused to the outbreak of the First World War.

As a result of these developments that took place just before the First World War, Russia began to look for an alliance with Bulgaria on the way to war. For this reason, some officials from the Russian Foreign Ministry have conducted various negotiations with Bulgarian politicians. Presence of Bulgaria, received support from Germany in the Balkan Wars, on the Russian side after exiting from German influence was crucial for Russia in the possible battle.

Russia built the Bulgarian issue on Panslavism. With the treaty in 1878, the Ottoman State rented out the island of Cyprus to England. It was interpreted as a move made against them by Russia. According to the Russians, Britain received a new direction for its politics in the Eastern affairs through this agreement. The movements of the liberation of Romania, Serbia and Montenegro from the Turkish sovereignty and the establishment of independent Bulgaria that was started by Russia after the introduction of Cyprus to Britain ended.[151] Russia, whose second failure on Bulgaria was the cooperation of Bulgaria with Germany in the Balkan Wars, did not want a third failure. Furthermore, Austria's secret treaty with Turkey in 1908 was about the protecting the status of Macedonia and restoring the Sultan's authority to this region, and also for making Russia ineffective in the Balkans. The treaty obliged Serbia and Montenegro to be impartial in the conflict between Turkey and Bulgaria. Moreover, as a result, the Austro-Hungarian state made concession agreements on Thessaloniki and its surrounding provinces.[152]

England was the other competitor of Russia in the Balkans. One of the reasons for the rivalry among Russia, England and Germany was

---

151 İ.Brusilovskiy, "Novoe Napravlenie Angliyskoy Politiki v Oblasti Vostoçnavo Voprosa", **Severnıya Zapiski**, Peterburg, Oktyabr-Noyabr 1914, s. 116-117.

152 Andrey Mandelştam, "Mladoturetskaya Derjava", **Russkaya Mısl**, Moskva i Petrograd, İyun 1915, s. 13-46.

conflicts of interest in the Straits. The British interests in India along with Iran and the Fertile Crescent were under Russian threat. For this reason, the states that compete on the Straits issue seemed to be England and Russia; However, later on, the influence of Germany started in the Eastern Question, especially due to its role in the Balkan Wars. Germany involved in the debate that the England and Russia were in. The Germans, supported by the Austro-Hungarian Empire, began to talk about population acquisition at the Bosphorus as to have a say in the Balkan affair. They brought the Baghdad Railway Project, from Anatolia to the Persian Gulf, to the agenda. The project of the British to reach the Fertile Crescent and India from Istanbul was not only under a Russian threat but also under a German threat. According to the Russians, although Turkey still seemed to be on the British side in those days, the Sultan blocked the way to India by locking the Straits and Dardanelles. Turkey began gradually entering the German orbit gradually due to the difficult situation it was in. When Britain threatened both Russia and Germany on the Balkan matter, Russia took the risk to abandon France that they were allied with at that time. Turkey, on the other hand, approached to Germany for the same reason. With the emergence of the German influence in the Ottoman state administration, the views of Russia and England on the Near East problem were separated. All alliances and agreements, involving Europe, were terminated. In accordance with the new point of view, groups were occurred among the states.[153]

According to the Russians, the aim of England in the battle between England and Germany for achieving superiority on the Near East in last 15-20 years was to establish a single caliphate by taking over Arabia and southern Syria from Turkey. It was the way of describing English politics by the Germans. This policy, by rooting in the Middle East, would become a shelter for India. For these reasons, England determined three separate strategies. The first one was to enter the Fertile Crescent via the Arabian Caliphate and to destroy Baghdad Railway of the Germans. The second one was to take over Syria. The third one was to have Armenia. Having Anatolian geography meant having the Fertile Crescent at the same time. England could not take the risk to enter the war for this purpose. For this reason, preferation of England was to share

153 İ.Brusilovskiy, "Vopros o Prolivah", **Severnıya Zapiski**, Peterburg, Oktyabr-Noyabr, 1914, s.115.

the Ottoman heritage; but Germany was not intended to be included in this division. The Russians thought that the hatred between England and Germany had emerged for this reason. According to the Russians, Germany chose the way of defending the Ottoman Empire against the Near East policy of England. The Bulgarian crisis in 1888 was regarded as a milestone of this policy of Germany. Fragmentision or disappearance of Turkey could have negative consequences for German imperialism. Germany wanted to expand independently from England, France and Russia. Otherwise, German culture and influence would not find a way to spread. For this reason, the Germans needed to give life to the detrited Ottoman state organism. If England, France and Russia had the opportunity, they would detach Germany from Asia via the Straits. For this reason Germany would try to protect the Ottoman Empire with all its power. If Istanbul is captured by someone else, Germany would lost its eastern and western fronts and would be defeated by the war.[154]

To prevent Germany's influence on the Ottoman Empire, Russian Ambassador Giers[155] appointed General Leontev to meet Enver Pasha. According to the telegram sent by Giers to the Russian Foreign Ministry on 23 July 1914, Russia proposed an alliance to Enver Pasha through General Leontev and declared that Russia could neutralize the Caucasus armies in the face of this alliance. Leontiev also offered a collaboration for the current situation in the Balkans if Turkey was to form an alliance with Russia. If Russia succeeded against Austria in the Balkans, it was stated that a peace treaty based on mutual concessions between the Balkan states and the Ottoman State could be done.[156] With this initiative, Russia was aiming to pull Bulgaria and the Ottoman Empire to their side against Germany.

Russia looked for ways to form an alliance with Turkey on the eve of the First World War. One of the reasons for this alliance search was the competition with Germany. For this purpose, General Leontiev continued to meet with Enver Pasha. It was understood from the telegraph, which Ambassador Giers sent to Foreign Minister Sazonov

---

154 İ. Brusilovskiy, " Germaniya i Blijnıy Vostok", **Severnıya Zapiski**, Peterburg, Oktyabr 1915, s. 195-202.

155 Giers; Russian diplomat. He was the Russian Ambassador in Budapest between 1902-1912. He served as Ambassador in Istanbul between 1912-1914. He was Ambassador in Rome between 1914-1915.

156 Tsarskaya Rossiya v Mirovoy Voyne, Tsentr Arhiv, Leningrad, 1923, No:628, 629. (Turkey Part No:9 and No:10.)

on 27 July 1914, that Enver Pasha was still at the same point in terms of alliance with Russia. There were members of government who could be strongly against a possible alliance with Russia, but; according to the embassy, there was hope for the alliance because the army was under the control of Enver Pasha. German and Austrian Ambassadors had a serious pressure on the government. In this meeting, Enver Pasha made concrete demands from Russia. According to this, Russia would withdraw from the Caucasus and give back most of the war zones to the Ottoman State. In addition to this, Russia would support the Ottoman State in the matter of Bulgaria. In exchange for it, Enver Pasha made a commitment to remove all German officers from the Ottoman army. The dismissing of the German officers was meaning that the German influence in the Ottoman State would be removed. Furthermore, the Aegean islands would be returned and a defense alliance agreement would be made with Russia for 5 to 10 years. In this way, according to General Leonteve, Turkey would have the opportunity to take revenge on its Balkan neighbors.[157]

Russians used the term "seriously ill" by referring to the difficult situation of the Ottoman State and they commented that Europe was waiting impatiently for this sick state organism to give its last breath and for this reason the Ottoman State was under constant pressure by Europe. According to the Russians, who indicated that only 30% of the Turkish population within the Ottoman State were Turks, despite this, the Turks always kept the effort of becoming a dominant nation. Nevertheless, the intellectual Turks tried to keep stand the Ottoman State with a constitution in a European form, but; according to the Russians, the same mistakes were repeated and the Turks continued to struggle to become the dominant power in the state and this caused some objections to arise. The Turks tried to suppress all national movements to consolidate their sovereignty. The Russians who expressed that the emerging new situation did not create positive results for the future of the state gave the example of Bulgaria to verify these claims. Military obligations of other nations were added to the Ottoman army, which was mostly composed of Muslims and Turks. Thus, the half of the army consisted of non-Turks. According to the Russians, the Turks could overpower other nations with the formation of the Ottoman army from Turks; but after this the other

157 Tsarskaya Rossiya v Mirovoy Voyne, Tsentr Arhiv, Leningrad, 1923, No: 650 (Turkey Part No:20.)

nations were also armed with the participation in army. Thus, the Turk dominance in the army decreased. Despite wearing military uniforms, Bulgarian Christians did not forget their landlessness and the accounts with the feudal lords, and Bulgaria was now a free state.[158]

Having achieved independence with the support of Russia, Bulgaria had to receive approval from Russia in all its future policies. Bulgaria and Russia discussed about what kind of attitude they would adopt against the position in the Balkans in the First World War. Russian Ambassador in Istanbul, Giers, brought this issue to agenda in the telegraph sent to the Minister of Foreign Affairs on 23 July 23 1914. According to the information given by the Giders, the Bulgarian Minister Plenipotentiary visited Giers and conveyed some of his thoughts about Bulgaria's political position. Minister Plenipotentiary was stating that it was time for Bulgaria to leave the Russian influence and orbit. According to the Minister Plenipotentiary, Bulgaria and other Balkan states should now be united; but according to Giers, the Serbs were still angry and doubter to the Bulgarians. On the other hand, the Bulgarians committed to be impartial in the current crisis and Giers talked about the possibility of setting up a Balkan Bloc against Austria; but, Giers also stated the need of being cautious and mentioned the possibility of an alliance between Bulgaria and the Ottoman State.[159]

On those dates, the negotiations between Bulgaria and Austria continued. According to the report sent to the Russian Foreign Ministry by the Russia's Bulgarian Minister Plenipotentiary Savinskiy[160] on 12 July 1914, the Austrian Minister Plenipotentiary was having often meetings with Bulgarian Prime Minister Radoslavov[161]. According to Savinskiy, the developing events were moving in line with the instructions of Austrian Ambassador in Bulgaria, Tarkovsky.[162] Radoslavov requested a detailed

158 Gortsev, "Gosudarstvennıy Krizis v Turtsii", **Sovremennik**, Peterburg, Avgust 1912, s. 286-287.

159 Tsarskaya Rossiya v Mirovoy Voyne, Tsentr Arhiv, Leningrad, 1923, No:631 (Turkey Part No:12.)

160 Savinskiy; Russian diplomat. He served as a director in the Russian Foreign Ministry in 1911. He served as Russian Minister Plenipotentiary in Stockholm between 1912-1913 and as Russian Minister Plenipotentiary in Sofia between 1913-1915.

161 Radoslavov; Bulgarian politician. He became Prime Minister of Bulgaria in 1913.

162 Tarnovskiy; Austrian diplomat. He served as Avustrian Ambassador in Bulgaria between 1914-1915.

explanation from Tarnovskiy on the situation of Bulgaria. If Austria did not give satisfactory answers about the current situation of Bulgaria, they informed to give a written warning to Belgrade. According to Savinskiy, if Austria was not active against the Serbs, Bulgaria informed that they would be impartial in all cases. Radoslavov reported in a meeting with the Austrian Minister Plenipotentiary that the Bulgarian military was in favor of a hostile attitude towards the Serbian side, and that their view on a war with the Serbs was positive.[163]

Bulgaria negotiated with Austria about the Serbian matter and this worried Russia. An agreement between Bulgaria and Austria on this issue would affect Russia's influence adversely over not only Bulgaria but all Slavic geography. For this reason, Russian Foreign Minister Sazonov wrote the reply to the Savinskiy's report without delay. Sazonov expressed his concern about this issue in his secret telegram sent to Savinskiy on 16 July 1914. According to Sazonov, Radoslavov's report that he would remain impartial about Austria-Serbia was an expected move. The reason of frequent meetings between the Austrian Minister Plenipotentiary and the King was Austria's promise of helping Bulgaria on the Macedonian Serbs matter. Although Austria and Bulgaria did not yet reached a consensus on this issue, they probably would reach a consensus in the future. According to Sazonov, if Austria attacked Serbia, Bulgaria would certainly send its insurgents on Macedonia. Radoslavov was pursuing the wait-and-see policy on impatiality matter. He would make the real decision after that. For this reason, Bulgaria had not made the final decision. Russia would not allow Austria to take any action that was not in line with the interests of Russia; nevertheless Austria attempted any movement, Bulgaria would still on Austria's side. According to Sazonov, this was the actual tactic of the Bulgarian King. Additionally, if Russia allowed Austria, Austria would have Bulgaria do the international "banditry". According to the Russians, this situation meant disastrous for Russia, because; in such a case, the prestige of Russia on the Slavic peoples would be irreparably damaged.[164]

In addition, Russian Foreign Minister Sazonov stated the demands of Russia from Bulgarian state in the telegram he sent to Savinskiy on 21 July 1914. Sazonov was demanding in this telegram to resolve

163 Tsarkaya Rossiya B Mirovoy Voyne, Tsentr Arhiv, Leningrad, 1923, No:141, (Bulgaria Part No:1.)

164 Tsarskaya Rossiya v Mirovoy Voyne, Tsentr Arhiv, Leningrad, 1923, No: 146 (Bulgaria Part No:2.)

the misunderstandings between Bulgaria and Russia and to restore the damaged relations. Sazonov, who was speaking of the necessity of establishing strong ties for the future national ideals of Russia and Bulgaria, knew that Bulgarian policies should take place in Russia's attempt and initiative. Bulgaria could have only achieved its national interests and the territorial integrity against Serbia in this respect. However, creating chaos in Macedonia and feeding these chaos by supporting anti-Serbs could push Russia to reposition Bulgaria's status. Such an attempt against Russia could break the link between the Russian and Bulgarian people forever. At the end of the telegram, Sazonov expressed his belief that Bulgaria would not forget the wills and advices of his own history, and that they would certainly not be betrayed to Russia, but to stand by Russia.[165]

Just after the threatened telegram sent to Bulgaria by Russia, Sazonov sent a new telegram to Bulgaria's Sofia Minister Plenipotentiary, Savinskiy, on 23 July 1914. In this telegram, his was giving some promises on to soften Bulgaria's hard-line manner on cooperation with Russia. According to Sazonov, the problems with Bulgaria were small problems which were not worth exaggerating. The only way out for both countries was to find other solutions other than the war. For this reason, Sazonov made some promises to Bulgaria. According to this, the region up to Vardar, including İştib and Koçan, would be given to Bulgaria. After victory, Serbia would commit to actualise this promise. Furthermore, according to Sazonov, Serbia seemed to abandon its old attitude towards the fraternity and cooperation of the Slavic nations. Serbia should not be sacrificed to this policy, but; it was still necessary to be vigilant against the possible destructive damages of Serbia.[166]

Savinskiy was conveying the information, which was received from Austrian diplomats, to the Russian Foreign Ministry in his report dated 27 July 1914. According to this information, Radoslavov was following insidious and treacherous policies against Russia in talks between Austria and Radoslavov. He was promising to be impartial against Germany and Turkey. If Russia submitted its commitments to Bulgaria in a formal way, Bulgaria could return from this mistake because Bulgaria had taken written commitments from Austria and Germany. According to these

---

165 Tsarskaya Rossiya v Mirovoy Voyne, Tsentr Arhiv, Leningrad, 1923, No: 1655 (Bulgaria Part No:4.)

166 Tsarskaya Rossiya v Mirovoy Voyne, Tsentr Arhiv, Leningrad, 1923, No: 1684, (Bulgaria Part No:5.)

commitments, Bulgaria would take Nish, Vardar and Thessaloniki along with Serbian territories in Macedonia. According to the Russians, the promises would not be actualised, but the Bulgarians were taking these promises serious. According to Savinskiy, Russia should immediately inform written promises about Bulgaria's future land acquisitions to Bulgarian government. These promises should off course be written in the general framework without privatization. According to the Russians, although Bulgaria was attracted to the charm of Austria, the Balkan block would definitely be established in the future. This was not only the determination of Serbia but also Greece and Romania. In order for this determination to take place, Russia should have surely made hard pressure on Bulgaria.[167]

Sazonov sent a report in the context of this policy to Savinskiy on 27 July 1914 and reported that Bulgaria needed to undertake anti-Serb opposition for Bulgaria to approach Russia. Such a situation could have very dangerous consequences for Bulgaria and on this basis an alliance between Bulgaria and Russia could be actualised. Nevertheless, if Bulgaria declared its impartiality against Turkey, Russia would have to step in and support Bulgaria's territorial demand.[168]

Sazonov reported on another telegram to the Minister Plenipotentiary of Sofia on 27 July 1914 that Bulgaria should make its decision as soon as possible. Because Russia's commitments to Bulgaria were being blocked by Turkey. If Bulgaria did not respond to the demands and committments of Russia, Russia would eject Bulgaria from allies. In the case of Russia being in Bulgarian side, Bulgaria would support Russia's Black Sea fleet. Moreover, if a war happened between Bulgaria and Turkey, Russia would meet with its allies Britain and France to take a committment not to attack Bulgaria.[169] Russia's demands were officially reported to the Bulgarian government. According to this, as long as Bulgaria maintained its impartiality, its territorial integrity would be maintained.[170]

---

167 Tsarskaya Rossiya v Mirovoy Voyne, Tsentr Arhiv, Leningrad, 1923, No:180, (Bulgaria Part No:6.)

168 Tsarskaya Rossiya v Mirovoy Voyne, Tsentr Arhiv, Leningrad, 1923, No:1768, (Bulgaria Part No:7.)

169 Tsarskaya Rossiya v Mirovoy Voyne, Tsentr Arhiv, Leningrad, 1923, No: 1771, (Bulgaria Part No:8.)

170 Tsarskaya Rossiya v Mirovoy Voyne, Tsentr Arhiv, Leningrad, 1923, No: 187, (Bulgaria Part No:10.)

The Bulgarian government informed in the response to Russia that it would maintain its impartiality. However, Savinskiy had doubts in this regard. Savinskiy expressed these doubts in the report sent to the Ministry of Foreign Affairs on 30 July 1914. According to him, Bulgaria was still implementing the wait-and-see policy. Therefore, he had doubts that the agreement proposed by Russia would be actualized. According to the Russians, the Bulgarian King would wait for Russia to gain victory in the war and shape his main policy according to the Russia's success in the war. Furthermore, the French Ambassador visited Radoslavov and convinced the Bulgarians to make a move together with Russia. If the Turkish forces attacked, they would be repelled. However, Savinskiy approached skeptical to the commitment of Bulgarians. Bulgaria could change its mind at the final stage and could take part in the Austro-Hungarian side.[171]

Sazonov informed the decision of the Russian government in his letter to Russian Foreign Minister, Savinskiy, on 2 August 1914. Sazonov stated that Russian politicians had long negotiations on the demands of the Bulgarian King from Russia and reported that there was a consensus on that Bulgarian King was not agree for an allience with Russia. Because the Bulgarian government was negotiating with the German banks on borrowing. Russia, along with France, had proposed to Bulgaria a loan contract with very mild conditions; however Bulgaria did not accept Bulgaria's offer. According to Sazonov, this was a very clear proof that Bulgaria was on the Austro-Hungarian side. Sazonov stated at the end of his letter that hostile actions against Bulgaria would now be reviewed and the strongest one between the two countries would live forever.[172]

According to Russians, who observed that Germany increased its influence in international political affairs at critical times, this was not an ordinary case. A deep political cause was underlaying the Germans' attempts and influence in the Balkans. The famous German sociologist Paul Rohrbach gave an interview to the Swedish newspaper and made observations on "the Near East way opening by Germany". According to the Russians, Paul Rohrbach's observations were pointing out a purely political program. German imperialism would spread towards Asia starting from the Balkans. Germany would gain significant acquirements

---

171 Tsarskaya Rossiya v Mirovoy Voyne, Tsentr Arhiv, Leningrad, 1923, No: 188, (Bulgaria Part No: 11.)

172 Tsarskaya Rossiya v Mirovoy Voyne, Tsentr Arhiv, Leningrad, 1923, (Bulgaria Part, Letter dated 2 August 1914),

by entering these regions and at the same time would open a wide channel for its cultural, political and economic impact. According to the Russians, Germany wanted to be "sun on the ground" with these attempts. The Germans took the first important step to these goals by making the Baghdad Railway concession agreement. Therefore, Germany could contact to Asia Minor and Fertile Crescent from Istanbul.[173]

Arising conflicts in Balkans, Anatolia and the Fertile Crescent caused the First World War. Just before the outbreak of the war, the conflict between the powerful states caused to look for various alliances. Bulgaria was one of the key countries of the Balkans. Russia, with the influence of nationalist politics over Slavic, thought that Bulgaria would be on its side. Germany, which had found its place in the world power balance, intended to supply raw materials and energy for its industry and obtain new markets, just like other states. The competitors of Germany in this issue were Russia, England and France, which had the same purpose. The way to new markets and raw materials was passing through Istanbul, the Straits and Anatolia via the Balkans. Russia made great efforts to establish the Slavic Union in the Balkans, but after Germany had taken Bulgaria to its side, Russia failed in this region for the third time. Russia's alliance search, which was reflected in Russian diplomatic documents, both with Bulgaria from the one side and with the Ottoman State from the other side was unsuccessful. This failure largely interrupted the future policies of Russia, then the Soviet Revolution took place and Russia left the First World War. In conclusion, the most highly aggrieved parties of the war were Russia, Ottoman State and the countries of the region.

References

Brusilovskiy, İ, "Novoe Napravlenie Angliyskoy Politiki v Oblasti Vostoçnavo Voprosa", **Severnıya Zapiski**, Peterburg, Oktyabr-Noyabr 1914.

Gortsev, "Gosudarstvennıy Krizis v Turtsii", **Sovremennik**, Peterburg, Avgust 1912.

İnalcık, Halil, **Tanzimat ve Bulgar Meselesi**, Eren Yayıncılık, İstanbul, 1992.

173 İ. Brusilovskiy, " Germaniya i Blijnıy Vostok", **Severnıya Zapiski**, Peterburg, Oktyabr 1915, s. 195-202.

Mandelştam, Andrey, "Mladoturetskaya Derjava", **Russkaya Mısl**, Moskva i Petrograd, İyun 1915.

Russian Documents

Tsarskaya Rossiya v Mirovoy Voyne, Tsentr Arhiv, Leningrad, 1923, No:628, (Turkey Part No:9)

Tsarskaya Rossiya v Mirovoy Voyne, Tsentr Arhiv, Leningrad, 1923, No:629, (Turkey Part No: 10)

Tsarskaya Rossiya v Mirovoy Voyne, Tsentr Arhiv, Leningrad, 1923, No: 650 (Turkey Part No:20.)

Tsarskaya Rossiya v Mirovoy Voyne, Tsentr Arhiv, Leningrad, 1923, No:631 (Turkey Part No:12.)

Tsarkaya Rossiya B Mirovoy Voyne, Tsentr Arhiv, Leningrad, 1923, No:141, (Bulgaria Part No:1.)

Tsarskaya Rossiya v Mirovoy Voyne, Tsentr Arhiv, Leningrad, 1923, No: 146 (Bulgaria Part No:2.)

Tsarskaya Rossiya v Mirovoy Voyne, Tsentr Arhiv, Leningrad, 1923, No: 1655 (Bulgaria Part No:4.)

Tsarskaya Rossiya v Mirovoy Voyne, Tsentr Arhiv, Leningrad, 1923, No: 1684, (Bulgaria Part No:5.)

Tsarskaya Rossiya v Mirovoy Voyne, Tsentr Arhiv, Leningrad, 1923, No:180, (Bulgaria Part No:6.)

Tsarskaya Rossiya v Mirovoy Voyne, Tsentr Arhiv, Leningrad, 1923, No:1768, (Bulgaria Part No:7.)

Tsarskaya Rossiya v Mirovoy Voyne, Tsentr Arhiv, Leningrad, 1923, No: 1771, (Bulgaria Part No:8.)

Tsarskaya Rossiya v Mirovoy Voyne, Tsentr Arhiv, Leningrad, 1923, No: 187, (Bulgaria Part No:10.)

Tsarskaya Rossiya v Mirovoy Voyne, Tsentr Arhiv, Leningrad, 1923, No: 188, (Bulgaria Part No: 11.)

Tsarskaya Rossiya v Mirovoy Voyne, Tsentr Arhiv, Leningrad, 1923, (Bulgaria Part, Letter dated 2 August 1914),

CHAPTER 6

HISTORY OF MODERN MEDICINE EDUCATION IN CHINA

Prof. Dr. Eyüp SARITAŞ

Abstract

Approximately with 4000 years of remarkably rich civilisation history, China has built and accumulated a substantial amount of medical knowledge since ancient times. Even though origin of the Chinese medicine goes back to 2000 years from now, it began to proceed as of the last century as far as history of medicine is concerned. As in the case with many other countries, China followed up closely with the western history of medicine teaching in the 20s last century, and since the mid 50s of the last century, it chose to adopt the history of medicine teaching it has so far built up. We make good efforts to provide elaborate information and offer analyses for the origin, development process of the history of medicine teaching from a modern perspective, as well as medicine teaching in China, Confucianist thinking and journals published on medical teaching in China.

Key Words: China, History of Medicine, Education

A. Beginning of the History of Medicine Teaching in China

As of the second half of the 19th century, new progresses were made in the history of medicine. The progress recorded in the history of medicine applies to the western medicine. Upon swift advancement of science and industry in western countries, history of medicine has become a significant branch of the medical science. In this 21st century, further works and studies on history of medicine have reached a level that cannot be ignored or disregarded. The history of medicine, employing quite an extensive point of view when examining humanity from biological, psychological and social aspects, has grown to become an academic discipline with its specific characteristics. History of medicine is a crucial scientific field of study that examines developments and phases of the medical science in a historical context, origin and emergence of the medical science, progress and rules of development.[174] Scientists that perform studies in medical science in China have been influenced by these progresses, and upon their personal efforts, history of medicine teaching activities were put into practice at couple of medical schools in China. Number of hospitals that followed and applied western medicine practices was quite limited in China in 1949 after establishment of the People's Republic of China. For instance, in 1929 with good efforts by Prof. Dr. Wang Jimin, National Judicial Medicine Institute of China was established and he was assigned to hold office as an academic member at the institute. As Wang Jimin started to hold office he created new course contents fort the history of medicine. In 1934, Li Tao Beijing Medical Institute was established, and history of medicine courses that were never taught before were taught. Prof. Chen Bangjian was invited to the Jiangsu state the same year, new courses, namely, history of medicine, history of diseases were opened for academic studies.[175]

According to Chen Bangjian, medical science constitutes an important portion of culture. History of medicine, on the other hand, is part of the cultural background. History of medicine explicitly reveals, with medical studies, the phases and progress of medical science. In other words, history of medicine employs the methods used by the science of history in explaining phases of the medical science.[176]

---

174 Bo Wei Kang, Zhongguo Yixue Shı (Chinese History of Medicine), Shanghai University of Traditional Chinese Medicine Press, 1990, p. 1.

175 Zhang Daqing, Yixue Shı Jiaoyu Zai Zhongguo: Lishı, Wenti Yu Zhanwang, (History of Medical Education in China: Historical Background, Troubles and Future Opinions: Zhongguo Kexue Shı Zazhı (Chinese History of Sciences Journal), Issue 4, 2007, p. 432.

176 Chen Bangjian, Zhongguo Yixue Shı (Chinese History of Medicine), Shangwu Yinshuguan, Shanghai 1937, p. 1.

Even though historical background of the Chinese medicine goes back to couple of thousand years, history of medicine teaching began in the 30s of the last century. Zhongguo Yixue Shı (History of Chinese Medicine) prepared by Tao Chısun makes the early educational materials in the field of study. The cited work was followed by Zhongguo Lidai Yixue Shılüe (An Overview of the History f Chinese Medicine in Historical Periods), written by Zhang Zanchen and published in the same year. Some of the other important works on history of medicine published in China is as follows:

-Dai Dafu, Zhongguo Yixue Shı Jiangyi (History of Chinese Medicine Course Book), Shanghai Medical Faculty Press, Shanghai 1935.

-Li Taosuo, Yixue Shıyao, (Outlines of History of Medicine). The book was published with the tile of "Essays on the History of Capital Chinese Medicine" as a course book in 1938, in 1940, it was republished by the Chinese Medicine Agency.[177]

In the 30s and 40s of the 20th century, the Chinese History of Medicine Society organised and held some seminars on the medical history at couple of universities in shanghai. For instance, at the medical history seminars held at the Medical faculty of Shanghai in 1937, medical scientists namely Wang Jimin, hu Mei, Wu Liande, Hai Shende, Yang Jishı, Hou Xiangchuan, Yi Buen ve Wu Shaoqing gave lectures. In 1943, the Chinese History of Medicine Society in collaboration with Chendan University organised seminars on the history of medicine. In 1947, Chinese History of Medicine Society lectured on medical history in Nanjing.

In the midst of the last century, it catches the eye that relatively more professional activities are performed regarding the history of medicine in China. In this context, the 3rd Academic Conference on the History of Medicine was held in Shanghai in 1950. During the conference, a Commission for Preparing Materials for History of Medicine was constituted, Ministry of Health Conference was organised in August of the same year and it was resolved that History of medicine is recognised as a compulsory course at all medical faculties throughout the country. In 1951, over 30 nation-wise commissions on medicine were established in China, and History of Medicine Commission is one of these commissions. In the same year, Medical Faculty of Beijing University,

177 Wang Jimin, Shı Nian Lai Benhui Gongzuo Baogao, (A Decade's Study Report), Yixue Zazhı, Issue 12, 1947/

Hefei Southeast Medical Faculty, Shanghai Tongde Medical Faculty, Shanghai and Military Medical Academy opened history of medicine courses.[178]

Towards the mid 50s, rooted modifications began to occur in establishing research studies and strategies for medicine in China. It is a fact that quite a number of oriental territories, including Turkey, followed up with and adopted technological advancements in western countries in many fields. In 1954, Mao Zedong, the founder and first president of the People's Republic of China criticised the policy followed by the Chinese Ministry of Health up until then, and expressed his opinion that "The Chinese medicine is not to follow the western medicine. The latter is to follow the first." To implement radical change anticipated by Mao, working groups were created and formed throughout the country just to make sure that western medicine adopts and follows up with the Chinese medicine. Inevitably, as the working groups started with their activities, systematic modifications were made in the history of medicine courses that were available at medical faculties of the time, hence the idea that western medicine relied on and followed the example of the Chinese medicine was taught. As of this time, Zuguo Yixue (national medicine) concept was created amongst and commonly used by the medical circles of China.

As a result of radical changes in medicine as mentioned above, the Chinese Ministry of Health established Chinese Medical Hospitals in big cities such as Beijing, Shanghai, Guangzhou, and Chengdu. Upon establishment of these hospitals, the Chinese history of medicine has become one of the indispensable and compulsory courses for the Chinese medicine. All 4 of the medical faculties mentioned here formed units for history of medicine. For instance, Prof. Dr. Deng Tietao created and chaired a unit at Gangzhou Medical School where he lectured on the history of medicine to the scientists engaged in other fields of medicine in 1965. After the 1st History of Medicine Elements Educational Programme held the Chinese Ministry of Health ended in 1955, history of medicine courses were made available at some of the western medicine faculties, as well. The work named History of Medicine, written by the Russian scientist B. Petrov was used as educational materials at the time when activities referred to in this study were realised. Medical education activities and initiatives ordinarily followed up with were substantially

178 Zhang Daqing, Yixue Shı Jiaoyu Zai Zhongguo, *ibid.* p. 433.

damaged at the time of Great Cultural Revolution; consequently a significant disengagement occurred in the history of medicine as in the case with other fields of studies of the time.

After the midst of the 50s, educational programmes were created in order to raise and provide education to postgraduate students in history of medicine as in the case with other medical disciplines in China. Even though research studies on the history of medicine made great a progress thanks to these initiatives in education were interrupted at the Great Cultural Revolution period. In the period of time after the Cultural Revolution came to an end, training programmes were created for postgraduate students in order to catch up with and raise manpower needed in the history of medicine teaching so that former educational level is resumed. For instance in 1978, a number of postgraduate students were provided with education at the Medical Research studies Institute of China. Student that participated in those educational initiatives graduated in 1981. Beijing Medical Institute, Harbin Medical University, Sıchuan Medical Institute, 4 military medicine universities, Heilongjiang Medical Institute of China held seminars on the history of medical teaching intended for students that were admitted for postgraduate studies in medicine.[179]

Towards the midst of the 70s, the courses that discussed social aspects of medical education were limited in number in China. Back in the time, political thinking was given more importance compared to social and political issues that concentrated on medical techniques at medical faculties and on services to protect health.

In 1983, a research group composed of volunteers of history of medicine was established at Harbin Medical Sciences University. The group helped a lot to pave the ground and lay the foundation of history of medicine teaching in Harbin territory. In 1989, the History of Medicine Research Center was established at Beijing University of Medicine, which held education seminars intended for postgraduate students for many years, and offered courses that enabled students to examine history of medicine from many different aspects.

After the 90s, improvements in the education system also influenced the history of medicine teaching, and over 50 medical schools throughout the country added to their curricula history of teaching courses taught with modern methods. Today, history of Chinese courses taught in

179 Zhang Daqing, Yixue Shı Jiaoyu Zai Zhongguo, *ibid.* p. 435.

modern means and methods are currently integrated with the education system of China not only on Chinese medical schools but also at western medical faculties.

B. Opinions on Social History of Medicine in China

Social History of Medicine has created, since the early 20th century, a sub-scientific research area of the social history profoundly emerging from the science of neo-history. This specific area is the oldest member of all sociological disciplines. Sadly, it has been substantially disregarded or otherwise omitted by research workers up until today. Scientists engaged in social history of medicine, which is considered as a quite new research for the history of Chinese medicine, gradually increase in number. Scientists engaged in the field interpret the history of Chinese medicine from a social history perspective, in other words, they employ research methods borrowed from the sociology history. As it will be recognised, social history of medicine is mostly correlated with the science of history, and adopted the research methods borrowed from the science of history.[180] Social history of medicine explains not only the lives and health of communities but also their social life in an anthropological proceeded from the corners to the axis of the social history in the course of time. Even though social history of medicine holds such an important place, it was not recognised as a scientific discipline until the first half of the last century.[181]

Since social history of Chinese medicine is and provides a new academic research field, an equally new research method has been required specific to the field. What needs to be highlighted in particular at this very moment is that there actually is no need to create or otherwise establish a new research method for this new field because social history of medicine relies on and developed from traditional sciences (i.e. medicine, sociology, history etc.). For this reason research method of the social history of medicine can be exercised and implemented based on the

180 Du Zhızhang, Guanyu Yixue Shehui Shı De Lilun Sıkao, (Opinions on Social History of Medicine), Shıxue Yuekan, (History Journal), Issue 2, 2006, p. 15.

181 Feng Erkang, Shehui Shi Yanjiu de Tansuo Jingsheng Yu Kaifang de Yanjiu Lingyu, (Spirit of Observations and Explicit Research Study Fields in Social History Research Works) Zhou Shıming-Song Dejin, Zhongguo Shehui Shı Lun, (Opinions on History of Chinese Society), Wuhan 2000, Hubei Education Press.

research methods of the conventional sciences referred to hereinabove. The research method, in the meantime, also covers the research method of traditional historical research studies as well as the historical research methods as is used in the western world.[182]

C. Medical Education in China and Traditional Chinese Philosophical Thoughts

History of China has attributed great importance to conventionalism for periods up until today. Traditional practices wisely transferred from dynasty to dynasty and generation to generation enabled enormous funds of knowledge. As in every sphere of life, traditional practices that are followed in China also apply to medical field. It however needs to be clarified at this point that not all branches of science has been treated equally important for economic reasons. History of medicine, which modernised at a relatively later time, sets a good example for that. History of medicine courses are shorter compared to other clinical modules whereas the course contents are much more difficult and individuals that perform works in the field are deprived of financial means needed for their studies. For these reasons, academicians that perform works on the history of medicine decrease in number on a gradual basis. Maximum efforts are needed to redress unfavourable conditions. At a time towards first quarter of the 21st century, research studies in medical science- which cover a much extensive area compared to other scientific branches- have come to reach a privileged position thanks to funds of knowledge up until today from the times of transition. Consequently, research studies on history of medicine are never to be disregarded if one wishes to have a profound understanding of the historical course of medical science since ancient times as well as its current position.[183]

There is a close relationship between the ancient Chinese medicine and traditional Confucianist codes of thinking. A number of intellectuals relied on Confucianist thinking system in their medical

---

182 Du Zhızhang, Guanyu Yixue Shehui Shı De Lilun Sıkao, *ibid.* p. 20.

183 Chen Liyun, Shılun Zhongyi Yishı ke Dui Suzhı Jiaoyu de Yiyi (Some Opinions on Context of Education for Improved Quality of Traditional Chinese Medical Studies), Shanghai Zhongyiyao Daxue Xuebao (Shanghai University of Traditional Chinese Medicine Journal, December 2000, Issue 4, p.3.

studies during historical periods. Thinkers mentioned here became specifically and remarkably well-known in the thinking spheres applicable to their time. In Confucianist thinking system, what constitutes the inner self is "Ren" (仁) and "Li" (礼). "Ren" means benevolence, "Li" means traditions. The two concepts have functioned to guide scientists of medicine in performing their profession. At the time when Confucianist thinking prevailed, code of ethics was vital for doctors. Doctors deprived of code of ethics were not allowed to perform the profession. As far as treatment of diseases is concerned, there was a direct and inseparable relationship between the techniques applied, doctors' mental well-being, attitudes at the time of performing their profession, thinking structure and any incorrect practices. For these reasons, scientists engaged in medicine in old times had to be equipped with theoretical knowledge and professional ethics when implementing a method of medical treatment. Sun Sımiao, a Chinese scholar of medicine, also the most well-known of the Tang Dynasty period (from 618 to 907), highlights in his work "Qian Jin Fang" that scholars of medicine were absolutely expected to put into practice what they have learned, and that they must have adopted the code of ethics in profession. According to him, this is the most important and nicest virtue that teaches and raises scholars in medicine.

In China, activities of raising doctors on funds made available by the state began at the time of South-North dynasty, whereas medical schools were opened during the reign of the Tang Dynasty. For instance, in 624, Tai Yi Zhı schools where doctors were being raised were opened. Curriculum of the school involved administration, mathematics, treatments and pharmacy courses.[184]

D. Journals on Medical Education in China

As a result of searches conducted, we have figured out that periodicals published on the history of medicine were quite limited in China. Journals in circulation on the history of medicine today are also very young and recent. Efforts have been made to provide general information about periodicals published on medicine in China. Activities

---

184 Wu Hongzhou-Cheng Panji, Zhong Yı Jiaoyu Fazhan Lishı Yu Tese (About the Development, Historical Background and Characteristics of Traditional Chinese Medical Education), Nanjing University of Traditional Chinese Medicine Journal, 2000 Issue 4, p. 186.

of publishing in medical sphere go back to 1792 at the earliest in China. The very first journal that was put into circulation under the name of Wu Yi Hui Jiang was not a periodical journal actually.[185] Following establishment of the People's Republic of China in 1949, more than 730 periodicals on medicine were put into circulation. Periodicals with a concentration on medical education are very few in number amongst these publications. The most important periodical amongst the journals was being published under the name of Yi Yu (Medical Education).

Yi Yu journal was put into circulation as a monthly periodical by the Chinese Ministry of Education Commission of Medical Education in Nanjing in the October of 1935. In 1939, head office of the journal was moved to Chongqing and issue 1 was published only that year. In 1941, the journal was put into circulation biannually, and the new issues are available at the National Library of China, Sıchuan State Library, and the 4th Military Library.

In the midst of the 30s in the 20th century, there were over 30 faculties that taught medicine and healthcare and that provided higher education than vocational schools in China. Many amendments occurred in medical education not only in China but also in the rest of the world. History of modern medical education does not go back to very old times in China. Yi Yu journal published very precious articles on condition of the medical education in China as of the first quarter of the last century, and provided very significant findings.[186]

In the light of the information obtained from the Yi Yu journal, in 1936 there were 33 medical schools around the country, 5 of these schools were national institutes, 2 of them were military medical schools, 7 of them were state medical schools, and 19 of them were private medical schools. Then again, number of students that studied medicine was 3616 that year, and there were 821 academic members teaching at those schools. In June of 1940, number of medical schools reached 30 around the country. Majority of the schools were seated in states Yunnan, Guizhou, Sıchuan, and Shaanxi. There were very few numbers of medical schools in states an regions such as Henan, Fujian, Jiangxi, Gansu, Guilin, Shanghai, and Hongkong. The journal continued publications for

---

185 Tao Yuan, Zhongguo Daxue Keji Kan Shı History of Scientific Publications of Universities in China, Xian, Shaanxi Training University Press, 1997, p. 33-34.

186 Wang Rui-Jiang Xiaomin-Tao Yuan, Woguo Yixue Jiaoyu de Kaishan Zhı Kan Yı Yu (Starting Point of Medical Education in China: Yi Yu Journal), Bianji Xuebao, 2002 Issue 5, p. 333.

a long time and it published articles predominantly on medical education, dermatology, psychiatry, external diseases, internal diseases, medical biology, pharmacology, microbiology and forensic medicine.[187]

Conclusion

Scientific activities on the history of medical education in China started in the late 20s of the 20th century. Scientific activities in the field began with personal efforts of a small group of scientists. Works on the history of medical education written by medical scientists, namely, Prof. Dr. Wang Jimin, and Prof. Dr. Li Tao, and Dr. Chen Bagjian, laid foundation of the history of medical education in China. Even though history of medicine in China that contains traditional treatment methods has a long historical background of a coup of thousand years, activities for history of medical education in China began only in the first quarter of the last century by following up with the educational programmes already in use in the western world. In the 50s, particular importance was given to open medical schools wherein treatment methods of Chinese medicine were applied on the one hand, and medical faculties wherein western medical education was applied were also opened on the other hand. These two different types of schools were not existent in the country before the People's Republic of China was established. As mentioned hereinabove, books on the history of medicine written by some Chinese scientists engaged in medicine were being used before those schools and faculties were opened. Before long, commission for history of medicine were formed at the medical schools of Chinese medicine and western medicine mainly in Beijing and in other big cities such as Shanghai, Chengdu, Guangzhou, Chongqing, and Zhengzhou, hence courses of history of medicine were made even more systematic.

Bibliography

BO Wei Kang, Zhongguo Yixue Shı (Chinese History of Medicine), Shanghai University of Traditional Chinese Medicine Press, Shanghai 1990.

187 Wang Rui-Jiang Xiaomin-Tao Yuan, Woguo Yixue Jiaoyu de Kaishan Zhı Kan Yı Yu, *ibid.* p. 334.

CHEN Bangjian, Zhongguo Yixue Shı (Chinese History of Medicine), Shangwu Yinshuguan, Shanghai 1937.

CHEN Liyun, Shılun Zhongyi Yishı Ke Dui Suzhı Jiaoyu de Yiyi (Some Opinions on Context of Education for Improved Quality of Traditional Chinese Medical Studies), Shanghai Zhongyiyao Daxue Xuebao (Shanghai University of Traditional Chinese Medicine Journal, December 2000, Issue 4.

DU Zhızhang, Guanyu Yixue Shehui Shı De Lilun Sıkao, (Opinions on Social History of Medicine), Shıxue Yuekan, (History Journal), Issue 2, 2006.

FENG Erkang, Shehui Shı Yanjiu de Tansuo Jingsheng Yu Kaifang de Yanjiu Lingyu, (Spirit of Observations and Explicit Research Study Fields in Social History Research Works) Zhou Shıming-Song Dejin, Zhongguo Shehui Shı Lun, (Opinions on History of Chinese Society), Wuhan 2000, Hubei Education Press.

TAO Yuan, Zhongguo Daxue Keji Kan Shı (History of Scientific Publications of Universities in China), Xian, Shaanxi Training University Press, 1997.

WANG Jimin, Shı Nian Lai Benhui Gongzuo Baogao, (A Decade's Study Report), Yixue Zazhı, Issue 12, 1947.

WANG Rui-Jiang Xiaomin-Tao Yuan, Woguo Yixue Jiaoyu de Kaishan Zhı Kan Yı Yu (Starting Point of Medical Education in China: Yi Yu Journal), Bianji Xuebao, 2002 Issue 5.

WU Hongzhou-Cheng Panji, Zhong Yı Jiaoyu Fazhan Lishı Yu Tese (About the Development, Historical Background and Characteristics of Traditional Chinese Medical Education), Nanjing University of Traditional Chinese Medicine Journal, 2000 Issue 4.

ZHANG Daqing, Yixue Shı Jiaoyu Zai Zhongguo: Lishı, Wenti Yu Zhanwang, (History of Medical Education in China: Historical Background, Troubles and Future Opinions, Zhongguo Kexue Shı Zazhı (Chinese History of Sciences Journal), Issue 4, 2007.

PART TWO

LITERARY STUDIES

CHAPTER 7

SYNOPSIS

Wang Chunyang

Abstract

Compared with other contemporary authors, Wang Zengqi is indeed one of a kind, which manifests in the phraseology, the characters and the structure of his novellas. In terms of phraseology, Mr. Wang uses vulgar (common) language to narrate stories of ordinary people, fusing his literate thoughts and the folk culture to present readers with the beauty of earthliness. When it comes to characters, Wang tries to apply Confucianist and Taoist thought to his masterpieces so that heroes and heroines unite the quality of tenderness with that of peripateticism. They treat others with a warm heart and show others their free will simultaneously. With regard to the structure, the author acts as a maverick. He weakens the existence of time and diminishes the plot as well as logic in order to build a random construction in accordance to average people's life, in which the storyline progresses unsystematically. All above reveal Wang Zengqi's willingness to embrace folk culture and it is this willingness combined with cultivated wisdom that brings us a poeticized world.

Key words: Wang Zengqi Novella Folk Culture.

Wang Zengqi is quite unique in contemporary literary circles. During his entire literary career, he always stood outside the mainstream and preferred using a style related to folktales, which shone in his later years. Astonishing works such as "Shou Jie" masterfully incorporating the "Genre Painting" style propelled his literary works to the top. Predecessors have done lots of valuable research on Wang Zengqi; from covering his life, his creating claims and his status in contemporary literary circles, however, there is a lack of discussion about the style related to Wang's novel, thus the "Genre Painting" style is the focus of this paper. From language to characters, from characters to structures, this paper tries to understand the relationship between Wang Zengqi's novel style and folk culture so that we can better observe the world painted by Wang Zengqi.

INTRODUCTION

Wang Zengqi is hailed as the "Lyrical Humanist" as well as "China's Last Unadulterated Scholar". Compared to other famous contemporary writers, Wang Zengqi's masterpieces are surprisingly little in number. In 1993, when he wrote a preface for "Wang Zengqi Collected works", he said: "With all my works put together, the first thing that I thought was 'So Few!'" However, the younger generation would exclaim: "So few! With so few works, Wang Zengqi established his status in literary circles! With so few works, he cannot be ignored by the world. This is the true meaning of 'So Few' ."

Generally speaking, Wang Zenqi's works are divided into three phases: 1940-1947 is considered as the first phase. Wang spent these five years in National Southwestern Associated University where he started working on a journal called "Wen Ju", consisting of poetry and novels. With enlightenment from literary masters like Shen Congwen and Zhu Ziqing and inspiration from like-minded friends such as Zhu Dexi, Wang Hao and Li Rong, this unique atmosphere awakened his potential. In 1944 Wang Zengqi left National Southwestern Associated University and then taught in Kunming and Shanghai. He spent his leisure time on his works including "Occupation", "The Toll in a primary school", "Lao Lu", "Revenge", "Green Cat" and "Wheelwright Dai". Back then Wang Zengqi was young and aggressive. Faced with the difference between his ambition and reality, he had a hard time fulfilling himself. The modernism of western countries also had an impact on him. The aforementioned factors combined resulted in his depression and a discontent with realitiy, for anguish on his own existence. However, the pastoral style in his works began to sprout during this period of time.

1961-1962 is considered as the second phase. The discussion of Wang's creation in this phase cannot be isolated from the general political atmosphere ranging from 1958 to 1976. From late 1950s to 1970s, China was politically in turmoil. A succession of political events such as the Anti-Rightist Campaign, the Great Leap Forward and the Cultural Revolution were initiated and the entire literary circle got involved. Wang Zengqi could not stay away from this. As a result, he was classified as a rightist in 1958 and then was exiled to Zhangjiakou in the name of getting reformed. He lived with this title till the year of 1960 when he got political rehabilitation, but his former job could no longer be restored to him. Therefore, in 1961 he was sent to a research station in Inner Mongolia and finished "Yang She Yi Xi" at the end of the year. In the following year, he published a short story collection named "Yang She De Ye Wan" which included "Yang She Yi Xi" "Wang Quan" and "Kan Shui". This is Wang Zengqi's only publication within the second phase. In 1966, the Cultural Revolution broke out. Due to him previously being labelled a rightist, he was imprisoned and suffered plight till 1968 when he was summoned by central government to improve some revolutionary operas. However, in the aftermath of Cultural Revolution, he was investigated on account of his contribution to the aforementioned revolutionary operas. He finally got his second rehabilitation in 1977. The atmosphere from 1956 to 1977 limited Wang Zengqi's creating, but it is said that "Misfortune might be a blessing in disguise". His experience during these 20 years affected his creations in his later years.

1979-1997 is considered as the third phase of Wang Zengqi's works. During this period of time, the Chinese government initiated the reform to open up China, and Chinese people could finally throw off the shackles of politics. Because of this, Wang Zengqi seemed to find himself again and once again became a maverick. With everyone else immersed in the mainstream featuring scar literature and introspection literature, Wang Zengqi was wandering in a world created by folktale novels . A succession of masterpieces such as "Shou Jie" "Da Nao Ji Shi" "Qiao Bian Xiaoshuo" and "Nue Mao" were published, introducing readers to the cordial world of Primitivism. Due to his experience of processing revolutionary operas during Cultural Revolution, Wang Zengqi showed an antipathy to deliberate, stylized creations and advocated for natural and real works. Revolutionary operas focus on highlighting positive characters, side-kicks and heroes. Wang Zengqi started going against this requirement. In his works, characters make their debuts one by one without logic or highlights, thus we couldn't tell who's the leading role and who's the secondary role, let alone spotting those omniscient heroes. In addition to that, the so called "Breaking News" or "Big Event" is no longer the main focus and works behind the scene, sometimes serving as a background. Instead, average people's trifles and gossip are the consistent plotline. Thanks to this deep insight of his opposition to mainstream thought, Wang Zengqi can exhibit himself so properly. To some extent, we can accredit this feat to his plight in the second phase.

Since the reform to open up China, there has been an increase of research on Wang Zengqi. Among them we can find some biographies telling the story of his life, such as "Lao Tou Wang Zengqi" by his descendants, "Biography of Wang Zengqi" and "Wang Zengqi De Chunxiaqiudong" by Lu Jianhua and "Wang Zengqi Lun" by Gao Yuanbao. This research is great help in keeping Wang Zenqi's life experiences, thus they laid a firm foundation for subsequent studies. Apart from the biographies mentioned above, there are also some other research specialized in the comparison between Wang Zengqi and other contemporary writers. Through these comparisons, researchers hope to find the answer to the relationship between Wang Zengqi's individuality and the generality of the era in which he lived. For example, there are "Harmony and profondity are both beauty – Stories of Wang Zengqi and Lin Jinlan" by Zuo Wei, "Comparison between Wang Zengqi's short stories and Lu Wenfu's short stories" by Luo Jiang and "The Mission impossible to complete – Research on Lu Xun, Wang Zengqi and Yu Hua's revenge theme novels" by Xia Yongwei. Also, there are some studies attempting to analyze Wang Zengqi's literary language style, like "Hutong Wenhua – Yuyan Yishu Si Pin" by Jia Xiaohong. There are studies focusing on Wang Zengqi's temperament and interst ("The Genre Painting in Wang Zengqi's Short Stories" by Lu Xiaoxia). Lastly, there is research focussingon Wang Zengqi's spiritual realm, for instance, we have "The Buddhism in Wang Zengqi's short stories" by Peng Cong. Generally speaking, Wang Zengqi is admired by the younger generation and is thought to have blazed a trail in the literature of new era. However, criticism does exist. In "Shi Zuojia Pipan Shu" edited by Zhu Dake, there is an article named "Peng Chu Lai De Fo Ye – Wang Zengqi" by Xu Jiang. In this article, Wang Zengqi is described as a conservative camouflaged as a pioneer and a liar under the guise of humanity. It ended with the conclusion that Wang Zengqi is far from a top-level literary master". But the purpose of this article is to peel away the holy halo around Wang Zengqi and speak against the idea of raising Wang too much. In terms of Wang Zengqi's literary achievements, it gives a high comment instead of a denial. In the meantime, we find that all of the studies above put their focus on a single aspect or only a part of Wang Zengqi and there are not many comprehensive studies. This left some room for further studies and hence this paper is trying to analyze Wang Zengqi's short stories from literary language style, characters' temperament and story's structure feature in order to attain a comprehensive perception on Wang's short stories.

"HUTONG CULTURE"
Say what the folk say. Do what the folk do

The literary language used by Wang Zengqi in his works is quite unique, specifically speaking, it is tightly connected to folk life and abundant with a flare of folk culture. It depicts philistines in the perspective of philistines. In Wang Zengqi's stories, there is no hero, no big event and no dramatic conflict. Everything is indifferent to fame or gain, like a stream, familiar to every reader, as if the reader were listening to a passerby telling his own story. This outstanding nature and uniqueness is called "Genre Painting Style" – a style opposite to jumping on the bandwagon, a style concentrating on life that the author knows and a style featuring inner cognition. Without superiority from mainstream literature and the elusive narcissism from literati, what remains is the common experiences and thoughts that Wang Zengqi shared with countless tin-pot characters. When readers are roaming in Wang's stories, they would not actively attempt to grab onto the so-called main idea, instead, they would just chew on those sweet scenes between Ming Hai and Xiao Yingzi or lament in the misfortune of Shi Yizi and Qiaoyun or look for secrets among Hutongs in Beijing. The representation of this language style should be Hutong Wenhua (Hutong Culture).

"Hutong Wenhua" is a foreword Wang Zengqi wrote for his photographic collection "Hutong Zhi Mo" (meaning the decline of Hutong). This article was written in 1993 when China was transforming from a planned economy to a market economy. With the transformation undergoing, brand new matters and ideologies flooded into China.

Beijing, as one of the first batch of cities initiating transformation, was the earliest to embark on this process. However, what came with the curiosity was the conflict between the new and the traditional. With the animosity fermenting, a number of traditional items, among which the Hutong was a symbol, were threatened by new items and gradually went into a downfall. Wang Zengqi is considered as a veteran Beijing'er who spent years living there, despite the fact that he was actually born in South China. He had deep love for Hutongs. Seeing Hutongs going into downfall, this veteran Beijing'er felt great lament and this great lament brought us "Hutong Wenhua".

"Hutong Wenhua" is about Hutongs, but it's also about the deep culture developed around Hutongs, including both material contents and spiritual contents. This article starts with the characteristic layout of Beijing which renders this city the look of tofu. What follows tofu is the way to cut tofu, from the aspect "cutting" parts of a city, the "cuts" are Hutongs. Subsequently, the author lists six bases on which Hutongs are named, containing counting, celebrities, industries, shapes and lastly some reason unknown to us. Then the author depicts Hutong's general look, ranging from composition, status in Beijing to daily sceneries. After that, Wang Zengqi turns from Hutongs to Hutong culture. Hutong culture is composed of three parts: first, autarky or self-sufficiency. People living in Hutongs are attached to their native land and unwilling to leave it. Even a decaying house would be regarded as a fortune worth lots of money. In addition to this provincialism, people are also egocentric and indifferent to others' problems. Second characteristic of Hutong culture is to easily get content with status quo. Wang Zengqi uses Wotou (Chinese cornbread), pickled radish, soy preserved radish, stinky tofu and cabbage served with dried shrimps as examples to symbolize this psychology, which is quite precise. Last but not least, tolerance. Hutong culture often revolves around "rolling with the punches" and "knowing one's place". Tolerance is also accepted as the essence of Hutong culture. At the end of "Hutong Culture", Wang Zengqi points out the deteriorating condition of Hutong which results from the bandwagon of market economy and closes the whole article with a "Goodbye, Hutong.", leaving readers feeling lost and despondent. In terms of emotion and thoughts, Wang expresses his nostalgia for Hutong and Hutong culture. It is inevitable to see tradition dying away but tradition contains sentiments of generations. Seeing those things going extinct, people always feel helpless. Maybe this helplessness is the mood in which Wang Zengqi finished "Hutong Culture".

"Hutong Wenhua" reflects two of Wang Zengqi's preferences on literary language: First up, say what the folk say, do what the folk do. Second, write for the sake of literature.

Say what the folk say. "Hutong Wenhua" which contains a wide range of words available only in Beijing can be used as a template for Beijing accent, such as "Yao Er Jin Ji Dan (means give me one kilo of eggs)" "Huan Tou (a kind of tools used by barbers to attract clients) and "Jing Gui (tools used to make sound)" for daily life and "Nuo Wo'er (move away)" "Po Jia Zhi Wan Guan (a decaying house is still a fortune worth pots of money)" "Chu Jiefang (to socialize in one's neighborhood)" "Sui Fenzi (to give relatives or friends a kind of whip-round for both good and bad things)" "Dao Ge Xi Huo Dao Ge Nao (to congratulate or to show sympathy)" for the explanation of Hutong culture. Both are featuring typical Beijing accent. It is familiar for Beijing local residents and quite fresh for Non-Beiing readers as well. This style is not restricted to "Hutong Wenhua". In "Ji Mao (Chicken Feather)", what Wang Zengqi used to describe Wen Sao crying for losing chickens are "Za Ge Yao (Why)" "Wo Na Lu Hua Jiya? (my barred plymouth chickens)", which is not even Mandarin but a kind of local dialect. In "Shou Jie" there is "Da Wang (let a buffalo play in a mud)", "Ge Dang de (a kind of song for famers)" and some bawdy couplets like "Niu'er Sheng De Piao Piao De, Liang Ge Nai Zi Qiao Qiao De" which means there's a beautiful girl with a voluptuous chest. It is not exaggerating to say that Wang Zengqi's works are an encyclopedia for folk dialects. This language proves Wang Zengqi's knowledge on folk life and folk culture. It is this knowledge combined with an endeavor to restore the real folk life that brings the author and the reader closer. That's why readers often feel that they are reading something written by an old friend.

Thinking of the folk culture potrayed in Wang Zengqi's works as a tree, "say what the folk say" serves as the trunk above the ground whereas "do what the folk do" works as the root buried deeply in the soil. "say what the folk say" alone is not enough, as we can imagine a Chinese learning English and ending up being very fluent is still easily perceived as a language learner when he talks to native speakers. The fundamental reason to this is that he can't think as the native do, thus his sentences don't fit in native speakers' patterns, which will give him away. However, the gap between literature and the folk could be even wider than that between Chinese and foreigners. What makes Wang Zengqi one of a kind is that he as a member of the literates crossed this chasm and experienced the folk life and carefully deduced what average people would think. This attitude and effort reflects in his works as he could become whoever he was writing. "Hutong Wenhua"cites some sentences from "Ba Yue Jiao Yang" to depict Beijing local residents' philosophy of knowing one's place. One of them is "Dang Le Yi Beizi An Shan Liang Min (means be obedient for his whole life)" showing the speaker's innocence while the other is "Liang Dian Hai You Bangzi Mian Jiu Xing (so long as there is still corn flour sold in grain shops)" which is a local way to comfort the speaker and his friends. With these expressions in the article, readers wouldn't feel anything is unrealistic as it fits within the potential pattern in readers' mind. There are some other works like "Ba Qian Sui" in which Wang Zengqi described a process of assessing horses. First, we can read some basic skills such as knocking teeth, pinching a horse's hip and walking it around. Following up is the trump card: suddenly wrenching at the reins downward. This move is very useful to test livestock's stamina. While reading these sentences, readers wouldn't feel anything unnatural either. Readers would consider that Wang Zengqi isn't a writer but someone who is from a family feeding horses for several generations. This is precisely "do what the folk do". Without attentive observation of folk life, it is out of the question to tell the process of assessing horses this vividly. Those tones and miens reflected by Wang's literary language are part of each character and correspond with average people in real life.

The second characteristic reflected by "Hutong Wenhua" is "write for the sake of literature". Simply put, Wang Zengqi attaches importance to both verbalism and rhetoric when writing short stories.

Wang Zengqi is, essentially, a member of literate with a deep love for folk culture, which means we can still sense the existence of a traditional literati in Wang's works. In "Hutong Wenhua" there are mandarin sentences like "Ge ren zi sao men qian xue, xiu guan ta ren wa shang shuang" (meaning egocentric and indifferent to others' problems), "Zhi shen shi wai" (meaning don't get involved in others' issues), "Leng yan pang guan" (meaning sit on the sidelines) and "An fen shou ji" "Ni lai shun shou" (both meaning know one's place). At the end of "Hutong Wenhua" Wang Zengqi quotes "Xi feng can zhao" "Shuai cao li pi" "Man mu huangliang" and "Hao wu shengqi" to describe the dreary and dismal scene of decaying Hutong, taking both elegance and fluency into account, connecting ancient language and contemporary language. The qualities implied by these sentences are exclusive to his works. In "Hutong Wenhua", Wang Zengqi subtly combines his literate emotion with folk life, making elegance and vulgarity dance seamlessly. However, the combination of elegance and vulgarity cannot go without a precondition that the author has a firm foundation of elegance. The rule of the combination complies with elegant culture. Thus, Wang Zengqi is an authentic literatus.

In addition to verbalism, rhetoric is the other element which can reflect an author's literary accumulation. Faced with the same material, an average person would often end up with a description in the style of a repetitive journal account while a literatus would figure out how to make his depiction vivid and catchy and even reach a higher realm. This usage of literary language symbolizes the essence of literate. Take "Hutong Wenhua" as an example, we find 2 characters of Wang Zengqi's manner of writing: the first is sentences with a simple structure, photographs with terse language. "Beijing cheng xiang yikuai da doufu, sı fang sı zheng. Chengli you da jie, you hutong. Da jie, hutong dou shı zheng nan zheng bei, zheng dong zheng xi" means Beijing City is like a tofu, very square. There are streets and Hutongs in downtown. Streets and Hutongs go according to either the north-south line or east-west line. These are indeed very brief sentences, however, with these short sentences, Wang Zengqi gives readers a quite clear glimpse of Beijing's layout. This is proof showing Wang Zengqi is well grounded in literature. The second is a straightforward style of writing which means the author can build a scene within a few sentences. When writing about how quiet a hutong could be, Wang Zengqi instead of sentences like "so quiet that you can hear a needle falling on the floor", uses three images: Huan Tou (a kind of tools used to attract clients), Jing Gui (tools used to make sound) and the piccolo of a blind soothsayer of all whom serve as a foil to the quiet environment in Hutongs. Moreover, Wang uses "Xi feng can zhao" "Shuai cao li pi" "Man mu huangliang" and "Hao wu shengqi" to describe the dreary and dismal scene of the decaying Hutong. Despite the simple nature of these descriptions, readers are able to feel the sad emotion, just like a poem from Ma Zhiyuan: 枯藤老树昏鸦，小桥流水人家。 (Over old trees wreathed with rotten vines fly evening crows, Under a small bridge near a cottage a stream flows.) The third is diction. The words in Wang Zengqi's works are just right for his purpose. For describing Beijing residents' philosophy that leads them to easily get content with status quo, Wang Zengqi uses Wotou (Chinese cornbread), pickled radish, soy preserved radish, stinky tofu and cabbage served with dried shrimps as examples to symbolize this thought. When it comes to cabbage served with dried shrimps, there is a "嘿" (similar to wow) serving as finishing touch. It cannot be omitted or replaced. Without this "嘿" or having it replaced by other expressions like "This is nice" or "Great", the unique taste would disappear. "Cabbage served with dried shrimps, 嘿! " as if a real Beiing'er getting content with his life were standing right before us. With this one character, Wang Zengqi conveys the essence of folk life and leaves us an immense space to image.

The aforementioned traits are illustrated with "Hutong Wenhua" as an example. However, they are not restricted to "Hutong Wenhua". Readers can feel them in other works from Wang Zengqi's.

DA NAO JI SHI
Figures filled with humanity and tenderness

Da Nao Ji Shi (A Tale of Big Nur) tells a romantic story between a tinsmith Shi Yizi and the daughter of a porter Qiao Yun. From this story, we can see that Wang Zengqi pursues characters full of vivid details, with humanity and tenderness. In terms of characters' development, Wang Zengqi has his unique method: first is by endowing them with nice qualities, such as being polite and valuing justice higher than material gains. This can be seen from the businessmen working on the west of a steamship company as they work from day to day and treat people with good manners. As do the tinsmiths who work diligently and conscientiously and mutually help each other to make up what other lacks. The hero of this story, Shi Yizi, is obliging. Even though the old tinsmith had warned him of misconduct of those girls living in the east of their village, he would still go and help them. When Qiao Yun's finger was cut by a reed, he would suck out unsanitary blood for her. When Qiao Yun fell into water, he would go save her without any hesitation. When Qiao Yun lost her virginity, again, Shi Yizi bore Liu Haozhang's cruel beating for her. These are all proof of the aforementioned qualities. In addition to Shi Yizi, we could spot these qualities in other characters (Ming Hai and Doctor Wang Danren) from his other works as well.

The second methodology is to depict characters full of vivid details and humanity and tenderness. Wang Zengqi gives his characters a mental attitude full of passion. We rarely find any character trapped in moping or looking at his shadow and lament his lot even though a majority of them are average people. As a tinsmith, Shi Yizi is industrious and frugal and treats every task with seriousness. Abandoned by her mother when she was very young and then suffered from her father's disability, Qiao Yun still shouldered the burden of taking care of her whole family. These are typical examples of exerting oneself constantly, a kind of quality which readers can feel from these characters even though the author seldom mentions it.

The third method to write characters full of vivid details used by Wang Zengqi is integrating the attitude of reconciling oneself to one's situation into those characters. When Huang Haijiao was dumped by his wife, when Qiao Yun lost her virginity, neither of them gnashed the teeth in anger or abandoned themselves to desperate crying. Instead, both of them dealt with these unfortunate issues with perfect composure. Indeed, the attitude of exerting oneself constantly played a role, they would not be so calmed without the quality of reconciling oneself to one's situation. Plus, when reflecting on behaviors of other characters like Cartwright Dai, Ba Qiansui and Chen Xiaoshou, readers can note beyond the unperturbed attitude a realm in which the author can handle a butcher's cleaver skillfully and reach the unification of the material world and his inner spiritual world. To clarify characters' temperament, it is necessary to take Confucianism and Taoism into consideration. As a member of the Chinese literate, an affection for Confucianism and Taoism is inevitable. Wang Zengqi himself confessed that he was more affected by Confucianism. He said he liked Zeng Dian's (one of Confucius most famous students) thoughts which featured ultra-utilitarian. He appreciated poetry of Song Dynasty too, especially those by then Confucian scholars because they gain pleasure by observing all in the universe. Thoughts like "the benevolent loves others" and "In hard time, try to seek self-development while in success, try to let others be benefited" from Confucianism had a deep impact on Wang. He even praised himself as a Humanist of Chinese style". That's why the characters written by him would implement those thoughts above. Being polite and valuing justice higher than material gains, exerting oneself constantly are perfect symbols of those thoughts. Apart from Confucianism, Taoism had some effects on Wang Zengqi as well. The attitude of reconciling oneself to one's situation we found in the characters is the proof of Taoism's effects.

SHOU JIE
A Unique Organization of Folk Life

In addition to literary language and characters, the oirganization of Wang Zengqi's short stories is peculiar as it is not based on logical chronological order. Take "Shou Jie" as an example, it starts with "It's been four years since Ming Hai became a monk." What's following up is not either the reason why Ming Hai chose to be a monk, nor the process of how he became of monk. Instead, it is the environment that follows up. After the environment, the author suddenly jumps back to things before Ming Hai became a monk. With this "chaotic" narration, Wang Zengqi gives a brief account of a scene to readers. When finishing this story, readers have an idea about Ming Hai's destiny, on surroundings of An Zhao Zhuang (a place). This manner of writing which is not fair to be judged only by logic is similar to our daily life in which everything seems to be messy but is marching forward step by step. Thus, in this article, this unique manner of writing is called "life's logic". Hereinafter "Shou Jie" will be used as a representation to illustrate this style.

"Shou Jie" is a representative work in Wang Zengqi's third phase of creation. As is said in the foreword, during this period of time, the literary circles were entering a situation in which all flowers bloomed together, and all thoughts contended for attention. The Chinese people could throw off the shackles of politics. Under these circumstances, it is possible to create a masterpiece based on the principle of returning to oneself. Additionally, the shift of Wang Zengqi's mentality was another significant factor. Wang Zengqi once said: "There is no rule forbidding us from writing life before the liberation (the year of 1949). Since it is allowed to discuss history in novels or short stories, it should be allowed to discuss the old society (China before 1949). It is necessary for today's people to review life in the old society and to find the difference in attitudes between us at present and us back then. In a nutshell, "Shou Jie" symbolizes the emotion of a Chinese person living in the 1980s.

In terms of the content, "Shou Jie" tells the story of how Ming Hai became a monk and how he fell in love with the heroin Xiao Yingzi. "Monk" and "Love", two concepts forming a paradox by put together, can only live in harmony with each other in Wang Zengqi's literary world. Ming Hai was chosen to become a monk so that he could make a living. He followed his uncle to Bi Qi An (a nunnery) in An Zhao Zhung (a villiage). Before being initiated into monkhood, he had to learn some essential skills . During that period of time, Ming Hai got to know Xiao Yingzi, who lived nearby. They developed a positive relationship and Xiao Yingzi's mother, Zhao Daniang, adopted Ming Hai as her son due to his versatility. Thus, Ming Hai had a very righteous reason to frequently visit Xiao Yingzi's residence. Apart from seeing Xiao Yingzi, Ming Hai would also give a hand helping her family do farm work. Consequently, their relationship further improved. When it was time that Ming Hai was going to be initiated into monkhood, he went to Shan Yin Temple accompanied by Xiao Yingzi. At the end, on their way back to An Zhao Zhuag, Xiao Yingzi expressed her love by asking "What do you think of the idea of me being your wife?". This moment is the most beautiful scene in this story. In terms of thoughts, "Shou Jie" goes against serious revolutionary themes and styles. Through this story, Wang Zengqi advocates to restore secular beauty, to restore what is really happening in folk life. That's why in his works, we can read monks gambling, killing livestock and even getting married. Wang Zengqi displays an authentic folk life and endows this life with poetical beauty with literary methods.

As for the way he organizes his short stories, Wang Zengqi himself once made it clear that the character of organizations is "casual". But this casual style requires the author to be well-grounded in literature and it also needs to be elaborated with painstaking effort. The effort is not for conflict, suspense or coincidence. On the contrary, the effort is used to downplay those aforementioned concepts. Wang Zengqi argued against Maupassant and O. Henry and thought they had played with organization for their whole lives and ended up fooled by organization. They left their novels with obvious artificial traces. What Wang Zengqi accepted was Chekhov's style featuring casual plots and the unexpected. He tried to overcome the wide gap between short stories and poetry and to use his own works to implement his ideas. As a result, his works are filled with a natural organization with which everything goes randomly. It goes when it should go, it stops when it must stop. It is also acceptable to say Wang Zengqi's short stories were prosified and more like a folk life model, which can be interpreted in terms of timeline and plot.

The timeline of Wang Zengqi's works is always indefinite or vague. Generally speaking, timeline is a very noticeable element in a novel or short story. It could either be an exact year like "1921" or some historical event like the "May Fourth Movement". However, we can rarely find a distinct mark of time in Wang Zengqi's works. Readers are very likely to forget time while reading his stories. In "Shou Jie", "It's been four years since Ming Hai became a monk. He came here at the age of 13. " is the start. When reading this, we know it's about the time and the background, but we could not answer the exact history background if asked. This is one case. There's another case in which readers would be given a collective time, such as solar terms, seasons or some religious ritual. In "Shou Jie", Wang Zengqi used "Spring Festival" "Time for threshing grain" or "Ming Hai went to Shan Yin Temple to get initiated into monkhood" to mark the timeline. Additionally, in "Jian Shang Jia", Wang Zengqi narrated Ye San's life with "Begging of Spring...sold the green radish...when apricots and peaches were ripe...Around Dragon Boat Festival, loquats...Double Ninth Festival is approaching, sold paris...After entering winter..." Those like "Begging of Spring" "Dragon Boat Festival" and "Double Ninth Festival" are social time with some special events. This arrangement promotes the unification of plots and characters and results in an indefinite timeline. Wang Zengqi intended to indicate that characters can only exist in a stream of time and cannot rend time apart. According to him, highlighting time could only sever time and is not real folk life. Thus, it is inadvisable to stick out time.

In terms of plot, Wang Zengqi's short stories don't go according to a normal logical plot. There are vast text depicting sceneries in daily life. In "Shou Jie", readers can reflect an amount of details about Ming Hai's family and Xiao Yingzi's family's daily life, including how Ming Hai decided to become a monk and how Xiao Yingzi's sister prepare for dowries and how farm work is done etc. This kind of description is quite common in Wang Zengqi's other works as well. The narration of Ye San's daily life and the sketch of landscape surrounding the big pond can both serve as proofs. The depiction of sceneries are always the body of Wang Zengqi's short stories, making plots like narrations interspersed with flashbacks and thus downplaying the plots. But this is exactly the results Wang Zengqi sought for. The depiction of scenery is utilized to build an atmosphere or sentiment and to hint at the development of plots indirectly. They are part of Wang's organization. Taking "Shou Jie" as an example, the portraying of customs in An Zhao Zhuang, the painting of local people's life both drop a hint that the morality and ethics in this place that differ from main stream society. Because of this arrangement, readers accept these alternative customs subconsciously when reading those depictions. Therefore, when the scene in which Xiao Yingzi asks to be Ming Hai's wife pops out, it doesn't arouse suspicion and instead displays the beauty of folk culture. This is the consequence of Genre Painting's effect to rationalize illogical plots. Meanwhile, this style also fits with folk life's pattern which contains both undisciplined manners and fixed progress marked by collective events. Wang Zengqi's works consist of both undisciplined depictions and fixed plots based on narrations interspersed with flashbacks.

Conclucion

To sum up, Wang Zengqi's short stories are unique in terms of literary language, characters' temperament and story's organization. First is "folkilization", meaning phasing out the glory of main stream and revolution literature and bring characters, events, morality and emotion back to real folk life and regard them part of life in order to exhibit a remote utopia full of love and individualities. As a result, characters, events and mental activities are consistently vivid and cordial. The author is no longer a preacher from high above, readers are no longer disciples begging for mercy. Their relationship is transformed to equal two parties. Folkilization is the key point that makes Wang Zengqi's works unique. Second is "aesthetization", displaying the beauty of secular life instead of secular life itself. In average people's eyes, it's taken for granted to be secular, while only a literatus could discover the beauty hidden in daily life's routines. Wang Zengqi's portray of Cartwright Dai working, of Xiao Yingzi wrenching chufa, of Ba Qian Sui selling rice and of Wen Sao feeding chickens, are filled with a sense of harmony. This is the consequence of folkilization and aesthetization combined. Folkilization is to aesthetization, what unprocessed jade is to craftsmanship. With these two seamlessly working together, Wang Zengqi brought us a world of "Genre Painting".

Bibliography

Wang Zengqi, Wang Zengqi Masterpiece-Absolution, Huaxia Publishing House, 2008.

Wang Zengqi, Wang Zengqi Collection, Jiangsu Pulishing House, 1994.

Gao Yuanbao, Wang Zengqi Theory, Fudan University, 15. 082009.

Zhang Fengwei, The Influence of Wang Zengqi's Early Life on His Creation, Dongbeı Normal University, 2013.

Xu Mingming, Zengqi Short Stories Creation, Shanghai Foreign Stdies University, 2013.

Zhu Dake, Ten Writers Critical Book, Shaanxi Normal University Publishing House, 1999.

Wu Jicı, Hutong Cultural Language Taste, Jiaoyan Tiandi, 2001.

Yang Hongli, The Aesthetic Statement of Folk life- On Wang Zengqi's Novel Stylistics, Beijing University Publish House, 2008.

CHAPTER 8

HOMELAND LITERATURE IN THE CASE OF PALESTINE AND REFLECTIONS OVER TURKEY

Sultan Şimşek

Summary

Modern Palestinian literature in the early stages of its development was in line with literary movements in other Arab countries, then it has changed its face in 1948 when the Palestinian lands were invaded by Israel. In this occupation movement, a number of tragic events such as the expulsion of various Palestinians from their own lands, the mass killings in some Palestinian villages, the putting of confronters in prisons, and the forcible issuance of an Israeli identity card to the Palestinians in the area where Israel has settled in the settlement area have caused great suffering in the spirit of the Palestinian people. This event, which is called "*nekbe*"("*catastrophe*") in the history of Palestine, has caused a series of aggressive attacks, massacres and psychological pressure. The great sufferings and tragic events that have taken place have manifested themselves in literary works such as poetry, novel, story and theater in Palestinian literature, and has set the stage for the emergence of literary diversity in Palestinian literature, such as exile literature, dungeon literature and homeland literature.

After 1948, almost all Palestinian literati has started to talk about their aspiration of return back to their occupied homes and their promised land, then expressed their right to return back through their literary works. They have written eulogium, novels and stories, and tried to counter the chain of catastrophes that the nation underwent from the literature field. However, the continuation of Israel's presence in the region and its continued pressure on the Palestinian people and the fact that the large Palestinian population has settled to the places where they migrated in this period led to forget the new generation the right and the consciousness of return and then the normalization of occupation, so literary works focusing on the idea of returning to the country began to be written. Palestinian literary scholars have established literary associations aiming at raising awareness on this issue, and these associations have begun to show literary activities in every corner of the world. These literary activities, organized by Arabic literati, have started to be performed in our country in recent years.

In this work, information about the activities of homeland literature of Palestine which has characterized and edited in the migration environment and representatives of homeland literature in Turkey is given. While preparing the study, articles and poetry books, novels and stories related to the homeland literature were examined and interviewed with Palestinian poets who acted as representatives of this literature in Turkey. Despite the abundance of literary works in this area, it has been seen that there are few scientific knowledge studies on the area during the study. Witnessing and researching living Arabic literature is very important in terms of releasing a document about today's world to the next generation. Perhaps the literary activities carried out by the Arabic literati in our country, which has been heavily immigrated from the Arab countries, are the footsteps of a new kind of sectarian literature in the future. From this point, our study gains a different point of view.

Key words: Homeland, Literature, Palestine, Reflection

Introduction

Modern Palestinian literature changed its face in 1948 when the Palestinian lands were invaded by Israel, in the early stages of its development, it was in line with literary movements in other Arab countries.[188] In this occupation movement, a number of tragic events such

[188] This research has been prepared in the form of a book section by expanding the declaration of "Reflections on the Palestine Homeland Literature and

as the expulsion of various Palestinians from their own lands, the mass killings in some Palestinian villages, the putting of confronters in prisons, and the forcible issuance of an Israeli identity card to the Palestinians in the area where Israel has settled in the settlement area have caused great suffering in the spirit of the Palestinian people. This event, called "*nekebe*" ("*catastrophe*") in the history of Palestine, has led to a period of conflict that is full of day-to-day attacks, massacres and psychological pressure. The great sufferings and tragic events that have taken place in Palestinian literature have manifested themselves in literary works such as poetry, novel, story and theater, and they have been used in Palestinian literature as exile literature (edebu'l-menfa), dungeon literature (edebu's-sucûn) resistance literature (edebul mukaveme), homeland literature (edebu'l-avde) as the basis for the birth of literary diversity.

After 1948, almost all Palestinian literati men began to talk about their aspirations and their return to their occupied homes and expressed their right to return through their literary works. They have written eulogium, novels and stories, and tried to counter the chain of catastrophes that the nation underwent from the literature field. However, the continuation of Israel's presence in the region and its continued pressure on the Palestinian people and the fact that the large Palestinian population has settled to the places where they migrated in this period led to forget the new generation the right and the consciousness of return and then the normalization of occupation, so literary works focusing on the idea of returning to the country began to be written. . Palestinian literary scholars have established literary associations aiming at raising awareness on this issue, and these associations have begun to show literary activities in every corner of the world. These literary activities, organized by Arabic literati, have started to be performed in our country in recent years.

While preparing the study, articles and poetry books, novels and stories related to the homeland literature were examined and conducted written and verbal interview with Palestinian poets who acted as representatives of this literature in Turkey and the other countries. While we use the information we obtained during these interviews, we refer to the literateurs we interviewed.

---

the Reflections in Turkey" which was presented orally by the Migration and Human Symposium in Eastern Literature in Istanbul on 21-22 November 2017.

I. Nekbe Incident, 1948

In order to understand the homeland literature,it is necessary to understand the historical periods of Palestine which led to the birth of this literature. Palestine, who saw the domination of Persian and Roman empires before common era, and the Byzantine empire in common era, was dominated completely by Muslims in the period of Khalifah Umar Ibn Al-Khattab in the year 637. After Mercidabık Battle in 1516, Ottomans, in the period of Sultan Selim the Stern, dominated Palestine. And throughout the four centruies, the territories which is called Arz-Palestinian became a part of Ottoman's by divided into Gaza, Jerusalem, Nablus and Safed districts. [189] But the Jews have lived for centuries desire of to live in this region. For the first time in 1799 Napoleon put forward the idea of establishing a Jewish state on Arab lands. British Foreign Secretary Balfour's declaration that is written on behalf Zionist Jewish Associations who wanted to make Palestine their homeland claimed that the British Government was warmly welcomed this idea, but there would be no harm to the fundamental rights and freedoms of other religions' members on November 2, 1917. In this period, 90 percent of the Palestinian population was Arab. The Jews had a property equivalent to 2 percent of the Palestinian land. With this declaration, the Jewish immigration to the Palestinian territories started from various European countries with the support of the United Kingdom. Jewish settlements began to be established in the Palestinian territories. Palestine, which was exposed to the British occupation since 1917, was given to the British mandate by the Cemiyet-i Akvam in 1922. After the Second World War, the Jewish population that has migrated to the region has started to increase. When conflicts between the Arabs and the Jews become inevitable in 1947, the administration passed to the United Nations. The United Nations offered to divide Palestine into Arabs and Jews, and Jerusalem to be an international territory. The Arab people objected to this offer, yet they couldn't prevent Israel to declare itself as a state on May 14, 1948. In 1967, the Arab-Israeli War began when Israel declared the inclusion of East Jerusalem where the majority of Arab population live, on its territory. After long political complexities, in 1974 the Palestinian issue began to be ruled by the Palestinian Liberation Organization. On September 16-17, 1982, Israel's attack on Palestinian

---

[189] M. Lutfullah Karaman, "Palestine", DIA,c. XIII, s.89-103, İstanbul 1996 .

refugees in Lebanon's camps changed the balances in the Middle East. In 1988, the PLO unilaterally declared its independence. In 1993, at the end of the Oslo and Cairo agreements, a political structure emerged under the name of the Palestinian National Authority. While this structure tried to institutionalize itself in one region, it tried to maintain diplomatic relations with Israel from the other side.[190]

The incidents of 1948 Nekbe[191], which caused the birth of 5 homeland literature in this whole historical process, are a turning point that unforgivably inflicts the soul of the Palestinian people. At this time mass massacres were made on the Arab people, and the Palestinian people recounted this incident with the expression of nekbe (نكبة), which meant great catastrophe. In this period, the Palestinian people were forced to leave their homes and villages, and people who were torn from their lands were forced to live in exile camps in the border regions.[192]

The occupation of Palestine by Israel in 1948 has changed sociologically and affected the population growth rate and the structure the Arab population living in Palestine. After this incident, the cities were emptied and the population density shifted to the villages. The vitality in the cities where are central of the cultural, literary and political activities of the Palestinian society has trailed off.[193]

II. The Birth and Historical Process of the Homeland Literature of Palestine

Literature to homeland of Palestine is one of the currents such as exile literature (edebu'l-menfa), dungeon literature (edebu's-sucun) and resistance literature (edebu'l mukaveme) which are included in modern Palestinian literature. The great sufferings of 1948 and beyond flowed

190 Karaman, p. 99, Nurullah Yılmaz, Biogrophy of Palestinian Poet Mahmud Dervis, Erzurum: Fenomen Publishing 2013, p. 3-4.

191 For a detailed history of Palestine see Hüseyin Özdemir and Others, Palestine in Ottoman Documents Istanbul: Ottoman Archives Department Publication No: 102, 2009; Ilan Pappe, Modern Palestinian History, Translated by: Nuri Plumer, Phoenix Publishing, 2007.

192 Adil Estâ, Edeb'ul avda ve edebu'l-âidîn: Suâlu'l-itilaf, Defâtiru'l-eyyam, 31.03.2015, Access Date: 08.10.2017, http://www.al-ayyam.ps/ar

193 Gassân Kenefâni, "Palestinian Literature", 1968, Journal of İştirâki, Translator: Journal of Affiliates, Date of Access: 10.09.2017, https://istiraki.blogspot.com.tr/2016/04/filistin-edebiyat.html.

from the mind and heart of Palestinian literary people into poetry, stories and novels. Thus, from the time when the Palestinians were expelled from their lands and started to live in the camps, the homeland literature began to exist. The common characteristic of these literary works within the context of the the homeland literature is that it depicts the events of 1948 and beyond, encourages people to resist injustice and strives to keep the country and territory alive.

The main feeling in the literary works of Palestinan people who were expelled from the large territories of the country boundaries and felt the great feeling of sadness was the this sadness and dream of turning back to homeland. In 1967 defeat, the pain grew even bigger. The Palestinian people witnessed their withdrawal from their homeland. Then, in the Palestinian literature, the concepts of resistance to the enemy, resistance and struggle began to dominate. In other words, the movement of resistance literature became clear in Palestinian literature. At this time, however, the notion of return continued to take place in literary works within the scope of resistance literature. Bilateral agreements made in the years to come have settled well into modern Palestinian literature as a turning point in ignoring the right of Palestinians who were forced to leave in 1948. The conversion has become an active literary space with a new spirit of good news.[194]

Palestinian literary figures gave literary works about return to homeland before they came out as a phenomenon. Many Palestinian writers have paid attention to the concepts and words of "the turn" and wrote letters on the return to try and reveal the identity of being Palestinian.

There are writers heading in poetry, storytelling, novelty and theater. From 1948 to the present day, events related to Palestine continue to preserve the revival of revival literature as it does not diminish with certain periods.

First, dozens of Palestinian literary figures like Hashem Rashid, Hasan al-Buhayri, Abdulkerîm al-Qarîmî, and Ğassân Kenafani were portrayed the map of the return almost literally. And dozens of writers such as Mahmoud Dervis[195], Selim al-Qasim, Velid Seyf and Ibrahim Nasrullah continued to walk on this path. For this reason, we see that the homeland literature is revived in exile, difficulties, troubles and emigration, and when freedom is achieved and efforts to return turn out.

194 From the written interview we made about Cihad er-Rajabi on 10.10.2017.

195 For details, see Nurullah Yilmaz, Palestinian poet Mahmud Derviş Hayatı Literary Personality Works, Erzurum: Fenomen Publishing 2013.

III. Identification of the Homeland Literature of Palestine

> It is possible to define the homeland literature as a literary movement, not as a school formed in Palestinian literature, that's because the effects of the events of 1948 has continued until these days. It is like a huge archive reflecting numerous works of the homeland literature and the historical process through these works. The poet Muhammad Rabah describes the return literature as follows: *"It is a literary tendency that insists on the right to return, rejects the division of the country's dismissal, mocks all kinds of catastrophic and imposture agreements, and thinks that the ultimate solution of the Palestinians' problems will be realized by the refugees returning to their promisedland."*[196]
>
> According to Muhammad Tevekkelnâ, one of the homeland literature poets, the homeland literature is as follows: *"Homeland literature is the name of the corpus which includes prose texts, theater works and poetry, interested in Palestinian people to Palestine where is the homeland of the Palestinian people."*[197]

The homeland poetry, since its birth to these days, has emerged to motivation of protection rights and values. The politicians did not approve the signatures they put on behalf of the people. The Palestinians, who had been forcibly removed from their land, reacted to this situation by being more attached to their lands and living with the happiness of the dream of reunion. Homeland literature is like a mirror reflecting this mood of the people.

Suleyman Isa, one of the literary poets of the homeland literature, says the poem through a small child standing in the streets of one of the refugee camps:

Palestine is my home, the way of my victory
My country is still love in my heart
And an honorable melody on my lips.[198]

---

196 From a written interview with Muhammad Rabah on 10.10.2017.

197 From a written interview with Muhammad Rabah on 15.11.2017.

198 Suleyman Isa, Palestinian Dârî, http://www.sulaimanalissapoet.org/tfl-felasteen.html, Access Date: 09.10.2017.

In the context of the homeland literature of Palestine, there is longing, suffering and a criticism against silence the injustices and abandoning the society. However, it as an optimistic and positive structure since the happy ending with the return to homeland is imagined. Homeland literature tells to the Palestinians that their homes are waiting for them, although others have them now, the traces of their father's grandfathers are still there. [199]

The homeland literature has the purposes of defending the identity of the Palestinian people and keeping the national memory fresh by putting the right of the Palestinian people to the problem of survival as a result of expressing the right claim and turning it into an ideal of returning to the houses inhabited by the inhabitants. It encourages the Palestinians to pursue their past perverted rights. Because forgetting history means destroying a nation. Despite the fact that it mentions Palestine's sorrowful truths, it feels hopeful. It is possible to see this characteristic in the following line of the poem by Semir Atiyye of the homeland literature poet, written in the book of Risâletu'nin al-kuds:

"We will polish the struggle on the way to Jerusalem. Next we will leave our own ballad for the next day to cheer the ballad of birth. We will not leave a place for pain in our hearts. There will be no place where wears mourning in our hearts."[200]

IV. Where to Return?

What exactly did homeland literature say when it took the return action to the main axis? It is possible to answer this question in two ways when the literary works related to this field are examined. First of them: To be driven from Palestine, or those who are forced to leave in any way, are entreated to return. The second is: to mention about before 1948 and the years that occupation has not begun yet. For example, Mahmud Derviş mentions Palestine before 1948 in two eulogium named Mahattatu'l-kıtar (Train Station) and Talaliyyetu'l Berve (Berve Ruins). Murid Bergûsî (born 1944) Durûbun Cemîle (Beautiful Paths) and Fâruk Muhammed Vâdî (born 1949) speaks of Palestine before 1948 in his poem Usfûr'ş-şems (Sun's Sparrow). Their systemic occupation, which

---

199 From the written interview we made about Cihad er-Rajabi on 10.10.2017.

200 Abdulganiyy et-Temimî, Risatletun mine al-majd al-aksa, Damansk: Beytu Palestine li'sh-shi'r 2009, p. 5.

had begun in 1948 in their homeland, is the reason for their inability and their insurrection. Some of the writers who returned to Palestine after declaring mutual peace after the Oslo Agreement in 1993 continued to write about the concept of return, but some of them have stopped writing in this regard and have begun to deal with different issues. While Halil es-Sevâhirî (1940-2006) did not continue to write about homeland literature, Reşad Abu Shawir went from one exile to another to continue writing. Some of Palestinian literati had lived in childhood. For example, Khalid Dervish is among them and he talks about these days in his book The Death of Small Sufin. Some wrote articles referring to events between 1948 and 1967. For example, instead of writing about the events of the day after the return to home, Yahya Yehlef wrote about refugee camps and Jerusalem under siege in İrbid after 1948. Again Mahmud Şakir mentions before 1948 in his works. After returning home, they did not just write about returning stories and current affairs around them, but they expanded the subject line of their works. Adil Esta expresses that the returnees should be evaluated within the context of literature of returnee, not the homeland literature.[201]

V. Symbolic Implications of the Homeland Literature of Palestine

The literature of revolution which we can define as a literary movement in Palestinian literature has its own specifics, contents, words, descriptions and dreams.

The most obvious symbol of homeland literature is mifah namely key word. Those who had to leave their homes took the keys and the deeds with them. And one day they hope to show their deeds and return to their homes with their keys. Abdulganiyy et-Temîmî begins a poem on the divan called Risatletun min Masjid al-Aqsa:

My house's key is still on
I'm still embracing the memories of my country[202]

---

201 Adil Estâ, Edeb'ul avda ve edebu'l-âidîn: Suâlu'l-itilaf, Defâtiru'l-eyyâm, 31.03.2015, Access Date: 08.10.2017, http://www.al-ayyam.ps/ar

202 Abdulganiyy et al-Temimi, p. 17.

In almost every literary work, It is possible to encounter words which takes up the main theme of return to home, "âidûn / returners; we will return /avdetu'l- gurebâ; the return of foreigners; mea'l-âidîn, teşerrud/ being homeless. İnnenâ le âidûn / We will definitely return, which is located on the divan of Aarhidu'l-ave (Return Songs) of Aaron Hashim Rashid, is a nice example to this:

"We Will Definitely Return"
We will return, return, return definitely
There will be no boundaries, sieges and castles
Shout out to O! Those who fall apart their home
We will definitely return
We will return our homeland, plains and mountains
Beneath the pride, battle and fight banners
Brew with sacrifice, brotherhood and loyalty
We will definitely return

Homeland literature also uses the instruments used in exile and dungeon literature. It tries to enlighten the dark days of the Palestinian's exile and prison days with the dream of return to homeland. That is why the words of muhayyem / camp, hayme / tent, sicn / dungeon, kuyûd / handcuffs are frequently encountered in this kind of literary works.

VI. Academic Studies on the Homeland Literature of Palestine

However, no serious scientific researches have been done yet, and in universities, master's and doctoral theses are given about homeland literature recently. It is known that a doctorate thesis is prepared in France, yet; no information about this thesis can be reached during our research. And some literature researchers seem to have concentrated on this trend in recent years. Adil Esta is one of the writers who has been writing on homeland literature for the last five years.[203] Also in the book er-Rivâyetu'l-Palistiniyye ve'l-Menfâ belonging to Salih Abu al-Isba; The information about the subject is given in the works of al-Kıssat al-kasrira

[203] Adil Estâ, Edeb'ul avda ve edebu'l-âidîn: Suâlu'l-itilaf, Defâtiru'l-eyyâm, 31.03.2015, Access Date: 08.10.2017, http://www.al-ayyam.ps/ar

fi'l-ardi al-muhtelle of Subhi al-Shaqaqrai and Mevsat al-alba al-Palistin of Al-Hadr al-Ceyyusi.[204] Return literature has already been examined under the title of a chapter in research on Palestinian literature much until today.

Jihader-Rajabi expresses that despite the abundance of literary works in this area, these works are not enough subject to scientific and literary researches: *"Studies and scholarly researches are inversely proportional to the volume of the corpus of the literature. There is little work that does not match the influence of this literature on the cultural struggle."*[205]

VII. Important Novels of Homeland Literature of Palestine

VII.I Gassân Kenefânî In his novel "Aidun to Hayfa", which was first published in 1969 like the other Palestinians who have suffered a homeland and are angry with injustice, and have always dreamed of returning to their homeland. He refers to the 1946 Nekbe incident, as well.

VII.II. Such literary works that have been put forward in the historical process within the context of the homeland literature are also present in today's Palestinian literature. The novel *"Destinies: Holocaust Concerto and Nekebe"* written by Rabaî 'el Medhûn was awarded the Universal Arab Novel Prize in 2010.[206] The writer was the first Palestinian writer to be awarded a prize in this class thanks to the prize given to Holocaust Concerto. Holocaust is the name of the genocide that systematically performed by Nazi Germany before and after World War II. It consists of three main sections and a result section corresponding to the sections of the concert. This novel starts with four different stories that ask questions about Nekbe Incident and collate all together. The novel is the story of the Palestinians who have been forced to stay in the country for Israeli citizenship, as well as those who have been sent to exile and who are looking for a way to return. The novel begins with the story of Ivana, a Palestinian

---

204 From a written interview with Nirdîn Abu Neb'a on 10.10.2017.

205 From the written interview we made about Cihad er-Rajabi on 10.10.2017.

206 Adil Estâ, Edeb'ul avda ve edebu'l-âidîn: Suâlu'l-itilaf, Defâtiru'l-eyyâm, 31.03.2015, Access Date: 08.10.2017, http://www.al-ayyam.ps/ar

Armenian who married an English doctor before 1948. Ivana, who flees to London with her daughter Juli in the case of Nekbe Incident, wants her daughter to burn her body while she is in her deathbed, and hurl half of the her ashes to the Thames River, the other half of the her ashes to old Akka. The daughter does what her mother says and goes to Palestine with her husband and they are captivated by the Palestinian cities, so the events continue in chains. This is one of the novels that expresses the passion and desire of a Palestinian to return home. It is a decent example with regars to show us the scars of a person's soul who have been forced to flee from homeland, and although she couldn't return her country, she wants to hurl her ashes to her homeland, which indicates the hope of return to homeland.

VII. III. The Babu's-shems "The Gate of the Sun", which was written by Ilyas Hurî and published in 1998 on the 50th anniversary of the Nekbe Incidents and entered among the best 100 Arabic novels, is one of the works within the scope of the homeland literature. In this romanized series of sequential stories, the writer tells the story of those who went to the first exiled life after 1948 and their return attempts at home. Those who are sent to the first exile will escape from the camps and return to their ruined villages, to the their homes that the others stay. But they are beaten and fired again from there. They are killed at the borders of Israel and neighboring Arab countries. Yunus al-Assad, the novel's hero who is secret-insurgent and a man in love, strides through mountains as well as valleys between Lebanon and Palestine over the thirty years, then he comes together with his spouse whose name is Nebile in a cave where the name of the sun given. Numerous boys and girls are born. He sees them as a bond that does not break off between those who live in exile and the survivors in the country. This novel influenced the people living in Palestine, a group of Palestinians who challenged the 1967 Israeli Settlement Plan gave the name of the Babu'sh-shems that they established at the entrance of Jerusalem.[207]

207 Risâletu Elijah Hûrî ibas al-Shams, al-Jezira, al-Ahbār al-fenn, Access date: 18.09.2017, http://www.aljazeera.net/news/cultureandart/2013/1/12/

VII. IV. Another example is that Jihader-Rajabi's "I Will Never Die In Vain" (Len Emute suden). This novel was awarded first prize by the Islamic Arabic Literature Association in 1993. The Roman Palestinian hero, Vâil, leaves his family to live a more comfortable and happy life by questioning the life circumstances in Palestine and the environment in which his family is living. His brother Ali cannot succeed if he wants to turn his way. *"After setting up a regular life in New York, I will take along my mother, she will be happy, and I will fulfill her dreams. She will never cry again and she will be happy, always. Hunger will not feel even. Believe me. Together we will live a very beautiful life without tears, weapons, death and sad things "* [208] And he makes a long trip to America to set up a new life with American Jean, who he is in love with. With this conversation with an elderly woman during the journey, he experiences complex and profound emotions in his inner world. He realizes how much he loves his family and his country. He feels a great longing for his homeland before reaching America. When he arrives at the airport, he watches the live broadcast of the movement on one of the screens there. And he sees that one of the two Palestinian youths tortured by Israeli soldiers is his brother Ali. And instantly he decides to go back, saying, "I will not die in vain." However, he is already weak because of his heart disease and dies there before return back. This story is one of the most striking and important works of homeland literature.

VIII. Poetry Divisions of the Homeland Literature of Palestine

Dozens of poets such as Gassân Zuktân, Zekeriya Muhammed, Yahya Berzak, Mahmud Derviş, Mahmud Şakir, Cebrâ İbrahim Cebrâ, Halil Sevâhirî, Faysal Hurânî, Murîd el-Bergusî,Yahya Yahlef, Fâruk Vâdî have written poetry about homeland literature. Some of the poets

[208] Jihad al-Rajabi, Len Emute Suden, Riyadh: Ubeikan 2013, p.117; Ceyna Kılınç Abdelmotaleb, Palestinian literary critic Cihadar-Rajabi's review of the novel "Len Emute Suden", Unpublished Master Thesis, Istanbul University, Theology Faculty, Istanbul 2016, p. 72.

includes eulogium in their collected-poems which has a lot of topics, but they did not write a separate collected-poems on this topic. For example, we can give the poem of Fî intizâri'l-âidîn (Waiting for Rotarians), which is located on the first volume of Mahmud Dervis's al-A'mâlu'l- ûlâ poem. In this poem Dervish says:

"O our mothers wait in front of your door, we return.

This is not the time as they imagine.

Wind is blowing while the sailor is coming..

And the stream is beating his ship. "[209]

Some of them wrote collected-poems which had a complete return theme. Some of these collected-poems are:

1. Ali Haşim Rashid, Madhavan al-Awwa, 1960.
2. Harun Hashim Rashid, Enashidu'l-avde, (Amharic in Arabic, Translated from Arabic into English: Kerme Sami) Amman 2011.
3. Semir Atiyye, Nezîfu'z-Zikreyât, Dımaşk: Muessetu Filistîn li's-sekâfe 2006.
4. Semir Atiyye, Dîvânu'l-avde (The Return Poem Anthology / 100 poems), Damascus: Tecemmu'ul-avdeti'l-Filistini 2007.
5. Hasan ez-Zerîkî, Ahlâmu'l-avde, Beirut: Dâr al-hiyât 2011.
6. Muhammed Tevekkelnâ, Avdetu'n-nusûr, Damansk: Beytu Palestine li'sh-shi'r 2011.
7. Abdulganiyy et-Temimî, Risatletun mine al-majd al-aksa, Damansk: Beytu Palestine li'sh-shi'r 2009.

The writers and poets who give literary works related to the return to Palestine are not only Palestinians. Other Arab countries also have poets writing on homeland literature. For example, Muhammad Tevekkelnâ Syrian, Muhammad Mahmoud ez-Zebûrî and Abdullah Berdûnî Yemen. In addition, the Syrian poet Nizar Kabbani's Ya Kudsu / O Jerusalem poem is one of the poems that find fame in this regard.

---

[209] Yilmaz, p. 258.

O Jerusalem, my city
O Jerusalem, my darling
Tomorrow, the lemon will bloom tomorrow
Green hyacinths and olives will rejoice
And the eyes will laugh
Passager pigeons to return
To their lily homes
And children will back to play games

Return literature can be written not only by literary figures in the limelight or the dwelling but also by poets living in Palestine. In his poem Tevfik Ziyâd Cisru'l-avde, he call to his friends from far away from their home:

My friends with my eyelashes
Sweep your way back with my eyelashes
And I take your wounds to my bosom
I pick up the road's thorn with my eyelids
I build return bridge with my palms on two shores
I grind hard rock with my palms
And from my body…

VII. Reflections of the Return Literature in Turkey

In the last years, Arabic literary scholars who have put literary works based on prose in the form of prose have been continuing their literary activities under the leadership of "Association of Palestinian Poem and Return Culture". Association based in Istanbul. It is the first association that has designated Palestinian poetry and poets outside the borders of Palestine as a field of study. This organization, which defined itself as an association officially opened in May 2009 for the purpose of organizing literary and cultural activities in Turkey, defined its fields of activity as literary and artistic activities. He is interested in poetry, novels, short stories, theater texts in the field of literature and in the field of arts, cartoons, fine arts, calligraphy, naht art, music and songs. The Association outlines its objectives in the following articles:

1. Work on to bring out the role and works of artists and litterateurs about home-coming.
2. Strengthen literary and artistic communication among the performers in this field.
3. To communicate and collaborate with different cultural experiences.
4. Free printing of Palestinian literature, Arabic language and various cultural publications around the world.
5. To explore young talents, to work to improve them and to introduce collecting.
6. To effectively process subject turnaround in the Palestinian, Arab world and world-wide.[210]

Highlighting literary activities since 2009 are:

1. A meeting was held twice in Istanbul, one in 2014 and another in 2016, under the name of International Form of Home-Coming Literature and Arts.[211]
2. Seven poetry books and one storybook published. These are the following works:
   Halil Ahmed, Vamadat, Damansk: Beytu Palestine li'ş-shi'r 2011. 2011
   Hasan ez-Zerîkî, Ahlâmu'l-avde, Beirut: Dâr al-hiyât 2011.
   Yahya Muhammed Berzak, al-'Amâlu'ş-şi'riyyeti'l-kâmile I-II, Damascus: Beytu Palestine li'sh-shi'r 2011.
   Muhammed Tevekkelnâ, Avdetu'n-nusûr, Damansk: Beytu Palestine li'sh-shi'r 2011.
   Abdulganiyy et-Temimî, Risâletun mine al-majd al-aqsa, Damansk: Beytu Palestine li'sh-shi'r 2009.
   Hasan al-Emrani, Tehtefî et-Tuyur lakin temûtu, 2010
   Semir Atiyye, Eğāridu't-tufûleti'l-mukaddese, Beytu Palestine li'sh-shi'r 2010.[212]

---

210 Visam Hasan el-Bas, *Palestinian Return Culture and Poetry Association Brochure*, Damascus 2014.

211 From the verbal interview we made with Palestinian poet Semir Atiyye, Director of Palestinian Return Culture and Poetry on 10.09.2017.

212 Visam Hasan el-Baş, Palestinian Return Culture and Poetry Association Brochure, Damascus 2014.

3. Culture and art meetings were organized in the name of Revâku's-sakâfî three times in 2015-2016 and 2017 in Istanbul. These meetings were carried out in the context of sharing some of the works of the literati, evaluating the concepts of return literature in which the listeners also participated and in the context of cartoons and photography exhibitions[213].
4. Poetry nights and seminars exceeding 100 in various countries and cities have been held since its establishment. Sarajevo, San'a, Damascus, Sharjah, Dubai, Cairo, Istanbul and Antalya are among these cities.
5. One of the most prominent literary projects of the association is a project to introduce one of the Palestinian poets in every month for 5 years in the form of a poet returning to the country and to introduce their literary personality and poetry. This study is a source for researchers and a cultural study for those who are not researchers but interested in literature.
   The project aims to introduce a multi-faceted Arab poet who has been writing Palestine, diaspora, immigration, exile, homeland return, homeland love and longing for months between 2012 and 2016, both inside and outside Palestine. The association regularly published information, photographs, pictures and poems about poets from their own social media accounts without interruption every month. This project, which started in May 2012, introduced Yahya Muhammad Berzak (1929-1988) as a poet of the month[214]. Initially called 'poeth of the month' at first, then the project was named 'return poetry' because it contains more integrity with the content of the project. And in 2013, Moroccan poet Hasan al-Emrani (d.1949) was first introduced as a poet returning poet. From May 2012 to September 2016, sixty leading poets were introduced and in fact a foundation for a modern period mucemu'l-saara book was laid.

---

213 From the verbal interview we made with Palestinian poet Semir Atiyye, Director of Palestinian Return Culture and Poetry on 10.09.2017.

214 For more information and poems, see Yahya Muhammed Berzak, al-'Amâlu'ş-şi'riyyeti'l-kâmile I-II, Damascus: Beytu Palestine li'sh-shi'r 2010.

The Association officials say that their next projects will identify and introduce writers and poets in Turkey who give literary works about Palestine, Jerusalem and Masjid al-Aqsa.

Conclusion

It is interesting to note that despite the large number of literary texts within the scope of the return to homeland existing in modern Palestinian literature, this field is left untouched by scientific inquiries.

Literary activities in Palestinian literature are one of the most vivid examples of contemporary Arabic literature. It is thought that the homeland literature with rich works in each of the novel, story, theater and poetry types will maintain its place and update in Palestinian literature for many years in keeping with the conditions that bring forth this literature.

Witnessing and researching living Arabic literature is very important in terms of releasing a document about the next generation. Perhaps the literary activities carried out by the Arabic literati in our country, which has been heavily emigrated from the Arab countries, are the footsteps of the other mehter literature in the future. From this point of view, we are in a different perspective.

References

Abdulganiyy et al-Temimi.

Abdulganiyy et-Temimî, Risatletun mine al-majd al-aksa, Damansk: Beytu Palestine li'sh-shi'r 2009.

Adil Estâ, Edeb'ul avda ve edebu'l-âidîn: Suâlu'l-itilaf, Defâtiru'l-eyyam, 31.03.2015, Access Date: 08.10.2017, http://www.al-ayyam.ps/ar

Adil Estâ, Edeb'ul avda ve edebu'l-âidîn: Suâlu'l-itilaf, Defâtiru'l-eyyâm, 31.03.2015, Access Date: 08.10.2017, http://www.al-ayyam.ps/ar

Adil Estâ, Edeb'ul avda ve edebu'l-âidîn: Suâlu'l-itilaf, Defâtiru'l-eyyâm, 31.03.2015, Access Date: 08.10.2017, http://www.al-ayyam.ps/ar

Adil Estâ, Edeb'ul avda ve edebu'l-âidîn: Suâlu'l-itilaf, Defâtiru'l-eyyâm, 31.03.2015, Access Date: 08.10.2017, http://www.al-ayyam.ps/ar

Ağrakrak, Mohammed and the Commission, Arabic Competition Activity Texts 2010-2014, Istanbul: Akdem Publications 2015.

Asst. Assoc. Dr. İstanbul University, Faculty of Theology Arabic Language and Belief Instructor, email: sultan.simsek@istanbul.edu.tr

For a detailed history of Palestine see Hüseyin Özdemir and Others, Palestine in Ottoman Documents Istanbul: Ottoman Archives Department Publication No: 102, 2009; Ilan Pappe, Modern Palestinian History, Translated by: Nuri Plumer, Phoenix Publishing, 2007.

For details, see Nurullah Yilmaz, Palestinian poet Mahmud Derviş Hayatı Literary Personality Works, Erzurum: Fenomen Publishing 2013.

For more information and poems, see Yahya Muhammed Berzak, al-'Amâlu'ş-şi'riyyeti'l-kâmile I-II, Damascus: Beytu Palestine li'sh-shi'r 2010.

From a written interview with Muhammad Rabah on 10.10.2017.

From a written interview with Muhammad Rabah on 15.11.2017.

From a written interview with Nirdîn Abu Neb'a on 10.10.2017.

From the verbal interview we made with Palestinian poet Semir Atiyye, Director of Palestinian Return Culture and Poetry on 10.09.2017.

From the verbal interview we made with Palestinian poet Semir Atiyye, Director of Palestinian Return Culture and Poetry on 10.09.2017.

From the written interview we made about Cihad er-Rajabi on 10.10.2017.

From the written interview we made about Cihad er-Rajabi on 10.10.2017.

From the written interview we made about Cihad er-Rajabi on 10.10.2017.

Gassân Kenefâni, "Palestinian Literature", 1968, Journal of İştirâki, Translator: Journal of Affiliates, Date of Access: 10.09.2017, https://istiraki.blogspot.com.tr/2016/04/filistin-edebiyat.html.

Harun Hashim Rashid, Enashidu'l-avde, Jordan 2011.

Jihad al-Rajabi, Len Emute Suden, Riyadh: Ubeikan 2013, p.117; Ceyna Kılınç Abdelmotaleb, Palestinian literary critic Cihadar-Rajabi's review of the novel "Len Emute Suden", Unpublished Master Thesis, Istanbul University, Theology Faculty, Istanbul 2016.

Karaman, p. 99, Nurullah Yılmaz, Biogrophy of Palestinian Poet Mahmud Dervis, Erzurum: Fenomen Publishing 2013.

M. Lutfullah Karaman, "Palestine", DIA,c. XIII, s.89-103, İstanbul 1996.

Risâletu Elijah Hûrî ibas al-Shams, al-Jezira, al-Ahbār al-fenn, Access date: 18.09.2017, http://www.aljazeera.net/news/cultureandart/2013/1/12/

Suleyman Isa, Palestinian Dârî, http://www.sulaimanalissapoet.org/tfl-felasteen.html, Access Date: 09.10.2017.

Tevfik Ziyad, *Cisru'l-avde*, cf. http://www.adab.com/modules.php?name=Sh3er&doWhat=shqas&qid=472

This research has been prepared in the form of a book section by expanding the declaration of "Reflections on the Palestine Homeland Literature and the Reflections in Turkey" which was presented orally by the Migration and Human Symposium in Eastern Literature in Istanbul on 21-22 November 2017.

Visam Hasan el-Bas, *Palestinian Return Culture and Poetry Association Brochure*, Damascus 2014.

Visam Hasan el-Baş, Palestinian Return Culture and Poetry Association Brochure, Damascus 2014.

CHAPTER 9

EFFECTS OF ŞEHRNÛŞ-I PÂRSÎPÛR'S STORY NAMED AS TEMPERATURE AT THE ZERO YEAR ON THE IRAN'S CULTURE AND CIVILIZATION[215]

Arş. Gör. Saniye Simla ÖZÇELİK[216*]

Abstract

Iranian woman story authorship began to give products after a while from male writers. Although the first essays in 1920s were followed by the male writers, also works which describe women's inner world appeared in the generation after the Second World War, Iran's female storytelling gained a unique identity and significantly improved in terms of quality and quantity in 1990s.

In this study, after giving information about the life, literary personality and style of Şehrnûs-i Pârsîpûr (b. 1946) which has started to give work since 1970's years, the attitudes and the impressions of the writer has tried to been examined against the social transformations and the traumas by handling the story called "Temperature in the Zero Year" and it was tried to reflect the effects of these people on culture and civilization of Iran at that time. In the context of the story of Şehrnûs-i

215 The study was presented at the 1 st International Congress of Mardin Culture and Civilization (7-10 December 2017).

216 * İstanbul Üniversitesi Edebiyat Fakültesi, Fars Dili ve Edebiyatı Anabilim Dalı, simlasimla06@hotmail.com

Pârsîpûr's "Temperature in the Zero Year", Iran's culture, lifestyle and social fluctuations in the modern era has been looked by perspective of women and at the same time, the effects of pre-revolutionary and post-revolutionary censorship on literary works and culture have been observed.

Key words: Iran, Revolution, Temperature in Zero Year, Şehrnûs-i Pârsîpûr, Culture and Civilization

Literature of nations emerges as a reflection of social and political structures. Experienced social and political changes and developments most clearly reflect themselves through literary works.

Another dimension of the relation between literature and culture comes out in the content of literary work. The artist deals with a number of subjects in his work, no matter what age, sect, tradition or sense of art and these issues, whether directly or indirectly, refer to the affairs of that community, its status and life; it presents the harmony and contradictions of this life, the distress or the hope in a structure with care (Çetişli, 2001: 23). Thus, the work bears the signature of the person and period that create the text.

The Islamic Revolution, which was declared in Iran in 1979, has also been influential in the field of culture and art as well as being influential in the social and political arena.

"The Iranian Islamic revolution is undoubtedly one of the most important events of the 20th century. The Iranian Shah who have one of the most powerful armies in the world had to abandon the country and new government, under the leadership of Ayatollah Khomeini, that the clergymen are at the forefront is establishing. The most remarkable features of the event are the involvement of all layers of society, being called as "Islamic Revolution" and being of that clergymen are at the position of leadership in not only process of preparation but also after occurrence of the event." (Onat, 1996: 31).

As in all post-revolutionary periods in the world, after the Iranian Revolution, the government has also dominated cultural production in order to consolidate its power. In culture and art both the revolution and the conditions brought by the war caused that Iranian artist has approached their own culture. Since 1979, many important Iranian intellectuals have continued their literary activities abroad by abandoning their countries due to internal disturbances and oppression (Sülün, 6).

In this period, the literature was created by authors who had to leave the country after the revolution created a movement in itself. After the 1979 Revolution, Persian literature acquired qualities that are so distinctive as to be able to speak of the beginning of a new literary period. In this period, the Iranian authorship preserved its ties with tradition and directed new writing techniques and new themes. The change in worldview of the generation who came from political and economic profits of the revolution, Iran-Iraq war and the period, of course, caused the literary sensitivities to change. Writing against idealistic dogmatism and stereotypical experiences rather than stereotyped norms constituted the most important occupation of the writers of the period. The writer no longer claims to be spokesman for every segment of society and felt responsible for more writing. This tendency can be interpreted as a result of the political and social conditions of the period. (Mîr Âbidînî, 2005: 92).

In the early years of the 1979 Revolution, the writers attempted to write day-to-day discussions and newspapers, but they could not find necessary peace and focus to create creative works. The literary works of the period were generally devoted to describe the struggle of the people and to describe the corruption of the Shah regime. For example, in his famous novel Keleyder, Mahmud Devletâbâdî described the characters of the story as the products of a turbulent social environment. (Mîr Âbidînî, 2005: 93).

According to the Iranian literary historian Hasan-i Mîr Âbidînî, there were two main trends in the history literature of this period: some writers were inclined to identify developments in society rather than creating novelty in writing and they gave more importance to social relations of heroes than their psychological state. These writers who felt obliged themselves to observe and describe all life dimensions were worried about increasing the documentary direction of their works, whether they were Devletâbâdî who worked in the countryside, Ismail Fasih who wrote the city life, or Ahmed-i Mahmud who wrote the first war fiction. The second group of authors has paid more attention to language and style in their stories than social concerns. Among these group writers, authors such as Abbas Marufi, Cafer Müderris-i Sadıki, Muhammad Muhammadali, Şehriyar Mendenipur and Riza Culayi can be referred. The most important feature of these writers was to have a different world view and to focus on new writing styles in writing. It is also necessary to mention the female story authorship and the female authors as a distinctive literacy movement in these years. Female writers such as Golî-yi Terakkî, Şehrnûþ-i Pârsîpûr, Gazāle Alizâde and Mûnîro Revânipûr have dealt with the problems of Iranian society with a feminine perspective and have created the worthiest works of these years (Mîr Âbidînî, 2005: 93-94).

Şehrnûş-i Pârsîpûr is also one of the female artists who best show the suffocating atmosphere that is felt intensely in her own country.

Şehrnûş-i Pârsîpûr came into the world in Tehran on February 17, 1946 as a daughter of a father who was from Shiraz and and was judge and of mother who was a Tehranian mother. In 1352/1973 he graduated from Tehran University Department of Sociology. She was one of the first women to be admitted to the university. In 1346/1967 she married famous director and screenwriter Nazar Tevva. She had a son of this marriage for seven years and was divorced in 1352/1973 (Özkan, 2011: 56).

She graduated from the Social Sciences Department of the University of Tehran in 1973. Later, she studied at the Sorbonne University of Paris in the Department of Chinese Language and Culture between the years of 1976-1980. She returned to Iran after a few months of the Revolution in 1980. When she was twenty-eight, she wrote a novel which is considered as her first novel, Seg, and Zemistân-i Bulend (Dog and Long Winter). She also produced the Zenân-ı Rustyai (Peasant Women) program on Iran National Television. But in February 1975, she resigned from television as an objection to the arrest and execution of some writers. (Özçelik, 2016: 36)

Şehrnûş-i Pârsîpûr as a story and novel writer is considered as a head in the history of modern Iranian literature. Her broadcast range is quite extensive. Besides the imprisonment memories, she has a novel, eight stories at the long story form, a story compilation (Âvizehâ-yi Billûr), a collection of related narratives (Tecrübehâ-yi Âzâd) and a child story (Tupek-i Kırmız). The sum of these works exceeds almost four thousand pages. Her works have a considerable extensiveness of content as well. In them, political novels, historical novels, philosophical novels are also seen. She has not been foreign to women issues, and she has traced these problems in her all works, and she devoted her collection of stories called Zenân-i Bedûn-i Merdân to this problem. She even wrote a science-story, namely science fiction novel, called Şıvâ. (Özçelik, 2016: 38)

In 1976, she came out of Iran with his son, firstly to England, then to France. In this country she moved away from the problems of Iran and wrote her novel "The Simple and Small Adventures of the Wooden

Soul" but did not press for some reasons and only twenty years later she published in abroad. So she did not show any activity since she was in France during the Iranian Revolution. (Özçelik, 2016: 36)

When we look at the works of Şehrnûs-i Pârsîpûr, it can be said that, while not being indifferent to social events, she looks from a different perspective, especially on the eve of the Revolution, during the Revolution and after the deep social shock, it can be thought that Pârsîpûr symbolically describes the "suffocation" environment on the eve of the Revolution, marking the "Zero Year" mark in the story which is named as Temperature in the Zero Year which take part in story collection named as Âvizehâ-yi Billûr, a story which was written in 1977, 2 years before the Revolution.

The story of Şehrnûş-i Pârsîpûr's "Germâ der-Sâl-e Sefr" (The Temperature at the Zero) is a five-page story on pages 45-50 of the Âvizehâ-yi Billur story compilation (Tehran, 1977). The Zero Year has received this name because it came true in the southern climate, the hottest region of Iran, and to emphasize the time stagnation of the work.

The story is told from the language of the first hero, a sixteen-year-old girl. The stagnant life in the port city, known for its scorching heat in the south of Iran, and the escape plan of the girl's family, always delayed, are explained. During this stagnant environment, the conflict of the narrator with adventurous brother and his father was attempted to be reflected in moments of return to the past. The observations which came from the fact that Pârsîpûr went to Tehran in the early youth years and lived there for a while manifested themselves in realistic description of the story.

The main theme is a timeless temperature, as appearing from the name of the story. A port city which has damp and hot air in the south of Iran and near Bender Abbas[217] but not mentioned as place, a summer day as time were chosen.

In the story of Temperature at the Zero Year, the condition of narrator girl with her mother at home wearily because of climate, the narrator's observing of the workers at wharf and the narrators' desire to escape to the faraway climates with her brother were told. The conflict of the episode was actually based on the dilemma of going to and staying in the sweltry environment:

---

217 Bender Abbâs: The city which is the administrative center of the Hürmüzgan province of Iran.

We were at the crossroads, my mother, warmth and crossroads. Mom was said "It's better this.", "Man is sitting at the beginning of his own life, of course there is warm; however, your life is in your environment, your carpet is there, your table and chair is here, and your house enclosed you. Moreover, does it will last until the end of the world?" I knew that I would last until the end of the Sun month, not until the end of the world, but we had three months until the end of the Sun month ... (Pârsîpûr, 1977: 47).

In the last part of the story, in the other summer, again the mother's tiredness and the desire to leave there are mentioned. Due to the temperature, they decide to leave their place of residence.

> *The next summer my mother said, "We're going,", "I'm tired". She was picking up her suitcases, she said it to be sure, and sat on the suitcase. We looked at him and I thought he was going to cry now; however, I just heard his pale voice. Then, "True, human is at the beginning of his own house, carpets are there, the rooms are around him, but there is also warm, do you know?"*
>
> *I knew this, so we went. (Pârsîpûr, 1977: 49).*

The Story of Temperature at the Zero Year can be considered as a situation story like most of the works of Pârsîpûr. The oppressiveness of the unbearable warmth creates the structure of the story. All events are randomly ordered around this axis.

The timeline in the story's narrative are followed a linear development, but the time in the developmental phase has become disconnected and intertwined to revive the ambiguity of the story.

The story begins on a summer morning when the narrator is sixteen years old, explained in the past time mode, continues with the representation of the stifling moist nights on wide time mode, the narrator's routine interests are listed. Somewhere, her brother's involvement in the story with the capture of a theft accusation that we do not know if it's real on the pier, their talks about plans to work on a ship while they are drinking their father's beer and observations on the pier is told as the present time story seen. At the end part, her mother decision to leave on the next season is again presented as simple past tense. Thus, the repetitive and tedious life that the author wants to describe is presented in a favorable style. The whole line of events is actually presented as the curtains of the continuing disturbance of the temperature.

At the entrance and the end of the house, the house environment, roof tops and pier scenes were chosen. The place descriptions were not given much space, and the actions are given superiority. The place descriptions had not been given much space, and the actions had been given superiority. The only place description had been shown as her mother' inconsistent reason for staying in that environment is that "people have their own house, their carpets are there, and their rooms are in their environment". Permanent feeling that connects people to the place had not been created.

Because of situation story, people's description had taken less importance in this story. We understand the narrator's gender indirectly is in the midst of the story when she says that she wants to join a sailor and escape from these places:

After all, when there was no thought left anymore, I started to think about the men. I was tired and feel old. I was feel like I was rotting. I was going in front of the mirror and taking off my clothes. I was looking at my sweaty body; I was like the acne on my forehead. I was pitying myself under the light of the light bulb. Then I turned off the light to keep only warmth without light. Therefore, I was thinking about Benderians' men, and whole men in the world at the entrance of the door. When they came from far away, I said to myself, "he jumps in his arms, and I tell him to take me with him." Wherever he takes us; we go to the mountain; we could rent a cottage that in front of it has a swimming pool or a fountain or two or three cold climate trees - or anything-; we could hug each other; we could be partner. (Pârsîpûr, 1977: 46-47).

Two young characters of the story is slightly portrayed indirectly through dialogue. Especially, due to their talk on the roof, it was reflected indirectly that they have tendency to leave the environment they are in, and they tend to go somewhere indefinitely.

In the lower layer of story, the mother symbolizes the conservative past, and despite all the difficulties she prefers to stay at the side of "her ware", while children are dreaming of getting rid of this environment as soon as possible, with an innovative understanding. In the end, the mother also uses her disgust to get rid of this sweltering situation instead of the passivity of every year.

Instead of being loyal to the unity of space and time, in the style of narration, we are constantly witnessing the changing of the scenes according to the events. The narrator who witnessed the events reflects how events are without subjecting the events to too much internalization, even if she is in the center and influenced by the flow of the story. The external reality is transmitted without intervention. And she has shown a careless approach without much comment.

> *I was feeling. I was feeling a lot of things, but I was listening quietly. It was some kind of chatting friendship. It was like a disaster, that it was lost, in the heat and in the silence, it is like the window taken around the glass. I was feeling these, and I kept my feelings so that he would not understand it. I was carelessly. I was careless to not lose him, I was trying to not give him an opinion that would cause hurt him and go away. (Pârsîpûr, 1977: 49).*

Mutual talks are mostly happening between the two brothers and they are made up of indefinite dreams based on real escape, which they want to realize. Although the whole story is a monologue, it has been given the expression of the outside world without mentioning about internal talk. In dialogues and the text of the speech, it had not been taken places any different styles of speech and oral features.

The reader had been involved in the events by the first singular narrator, he/she was able to have direct knowledge of the environment and living environment. Naturally, the reader has been included in the story as much as the narrator picks and reflects the events, and sometimes he/she has the dilemma of watching the event. The events are arranged in an indefinite fashion to describe the ambiguity of the ambience, and no conspicuous sequence of events has been observed.

One of the methods that reflects the depressing main atmosphere of story is repetition. At both the beginning of the story and the end, the feeling of tiredness is expressed:

Prolog: At that summer I was sixteen, my mother tired at the end...

Epilog: At the next summer my mother said, "We are going.", "I am tired now"...

The relationship between mother and father and two boys and girls, they create the main characters of the story, was symbolized in the author's naturist approach. While the father represents the state and power in a sense, the mother is the representative of the people condemned to the situation. The intergenerational conflict we have encountered in many of Pârsîpûr's novels has been taken place on in this story. A boy who is dissatisfied with the current situation and wants to get rid of the harsh climate is accused of illegal activity (here it is theft) and is subjected to violence by his father who represents authority. Female characters are always passive. The girl is bewared about acting although she is joining her brother, and she reacts the situation silently:

> *I do not know. He was saying that and nervously tilted her head. He felt in love with the sea and wanted to believe, even more, his buddy ran from Benderabbas to here. I was feeling. I was feeling a lot of things, but I was listening quietly. It was some kind of chatting friendship. It was like a disaster, that it was lost, in the heat and in the silence, it is like the window taken around the glass. I was feeling these, and I kept my feelings so that he would not understand it. I was carelessly. I was careless to not lose him, I was trying to not give him an opinion that would cause hurt him and go away. Then he came with me less and he was going with his buddies. (Pârsîpûr, 1977: 48-49).*

The only way of salvation and dreams of the girl is again limited to hope from the male dominant understanding:

> *Therefore, I was thinking about Benderians' men, and whole men in the world at the entrance of the door. When they came from far away, I said to myself, "he jumps in his arms, and I tell him to take me with him." (Pârsîpûr, 1977: 47).*

Women's desperation is also a natural result of geography:

> *We thouht that we could go together and be a crew on the ships. Then, my brother was sadly shaking his head:*
>
> *- You cannot come, can you come?*
>
> *- I said no. He would shake his head again:*
>
> *- It can be well understood with you. (Pârsîpûr, 1977: 48).*

Bender, which is the place that constitutes the fateful environment of the story is a door that symbolizes the oppressive environment of the geography on the one hand and a shore that humans live, as well as a geography that opens up with challenging expeditions to another world.

Conclucion

The "zero year" in Temperature at the Zero Year can be symbolized as re-change (reset) of the calendar in Iran from 1975 on those years. In the story, the temperature that is dominant everywhere can be thought of as a heavy and stifling atmosphere of the 1970s due to the political pressures of the Shah regime. The social transformation that is taking place, the political pressures of the regime and the suffocation atmosphere that it implements also cause human desire to break away from this oppressive environment and escape. But, like the story tells us, the purpose is quite uncertain and unpredictable. The author tries to attract attention to the fact that there is no healthy and distinctive choice in the against the present situation with an intuitive power that is not in the ideological and utopian intellectuals that have been fascinated by the chaotic environment of that period and the excitement of transformation. When everyone is in alliance against unwanted reality, the utopia sought was quite uncertain and it exactly partakes of a "nâ-kucâ-âbâd" (an unknown homeland where it is) in the name of Persian appropriately.

In his subsequent works, he focuses on the unhappiness and hopelessness on the distopia and utopia that will reveal by the bored community who is the "knowing what s/he does not want" but "do not know what s/he wants". The escape of external realities and looking for utopia beyond the ocean has created the fate of the next generation, like a prophecy of Pârsîpûr, from the adverse heavy conditions of "natural" climate. The zone who cannot change the conditions of his own geography, suffers from sudden revolutions, and succumbs to reality, had to escape from the stagnant time and inconvenient place of his captivity. Even, the new generation, symbolized by the face of his brother, made it an ideal.

References

ÂBİDÎNÎ, Hasan-i Mîr, (2005), Dâstân and Dâstânnevisi, Mecelle-i Ferhengî-i Buhârâ, Issue 19.

http://www.aftabir.com/elibrary/item/, Access Date: 09.10.2017

CETISLI, Ismail, (2001), Literary Movements in Western Literature, Ankara: Akçağ Publications.

ONAT, Hasan, (1996), Shiism in the Twentieth Century andnthe Iranian Islamic Revolution, Ankara: Public Service Research Foundation.

OZÇELIK, Saniye Simla (2016), The Storytelling of Şehrnish-i Parsipur, Master Thesis, Selçuk University, S.B.E, Advisor: Assoc. Dr. Ali Temizel, Konya.

OZKAN, Emine, (2011), Leading Female Writers of Contemporary Iran Short Story Literature, Unpublished Seminar, Seminar Advisor: Assoc. Dr. Abdüsselam BİLGEN, A.Ü.S.B.E, Ankara.

PÂRSÎPÛR, Şehrnûş-i (1977), Âvizehâ-yi Billûr, Tehran: Rez Publications.

SULUM, Ebru Nalan, (Undated), An Analysis in terms of Cultural and Visual Aesthetics on Shirin Neshat and Ipek Duben.

http://www.academia.e. Access Date: 17.11.2017

CHAPTER 10

BALKAN MIGRATIONS AN EXAMINATION OF THE NOVEL AND OF OUR REALM

Ramazan TOPDEMİR

Abstract

Our realm in the novel, are subject to the political upheaval in the Balkans that took place during migration events. I. after the Declaration of constitutional monarchy against the Ottoman Empire Greek, Bulgarian, and with the instigation of Armenians of Russia are rebelling. The Ottoman state left to live in this mess of a hard time.

Rumeli an Turks suffered injustice, their suffering, and they had lost the territory our land it was. Awakened the nationalism of minorities, lost their lands, their partnership with the enemy causes us to rumeli. The author, Ali Bey and his family leave their land to Istanbul and discusses the lyrical expressions of the settlement. The author, Ali Bey, his family is missing and he tore lands 'our land' expresses. Our realm of the Ottoman Empire in the Balkans as the last piece that is missing is rendered.

Acting to subvert the power of the Sultan, enemies, receive the support of local collaborators. Those who are fighting for freedom to come to criticize the author. Don't know who you serve these people's struggles. The Ottoman Empire, the events in the novel who is the hero of the Father, Son Rifat, Ali and even leads to a difference of opinion. Father Rifat, given new rights for minorities in the country, Turkish traditions, language, religion, comes under pressure against removal.

The real owners of this land, the Turks have the same rights as it would be unfair to the minorities, he says. However, with the pressures of the western world, where most of the ceremony has been lost are highlighted.

Key Words: Migrations, The Balkans, Date, Country, Land

I-Balkan migration and an examination of our realm of the novel

(Sevinç Cokum, 1978) the case in the time of the novel in 1897 Turkish-Greek war and the war of independence in 1923 with the acquisition of starting with the ends.

The novel, The Year of the collapse of the Ottoman Empire in the Balkans and the political confusion tells. After the first Constitution in the Ottoman Empire, and both internal and external turmoil ensues.

Who are the heroes of the novel: Ali Bey, his wife, Mrs. Lady, kids, Pink, Rebel, Rifat and they spend a modest life with verse. The environment of peace begins to deteriorate as the children grow older. Big girls, Pink, goes to come to Skopje. Asiya is married to an officer grandfather is from Thessaloniki.

Ali Bey rifaat's only son to go to military school if she is the first girl can't have a problem then. But some officers also take action against the Sultan Ali Bey Rifat and sad to be in this group and it Angers both. That depends on loyalty to the Sultan. The events that occurred after the Declaration of the second constitutional monarchy of Ali Bey is going to break down. Boy, you sure makes the wedding.

Soon it turns into a battle of confusion in the Balkans. Rifat goes to the front. Ali Bey Konagi is invaded by the enemy, and Ali Bey is killed. Zeynep Gülsüm Lady, bride, girl taking the verse to rebel and migrate to Istanbul with their grandchildren. On the road rifaat's wife, Zeynep is kidnapped by the enemy. Rifaat's father-in-law consent of the teacher, her daughter's die of remorse.

The groom Edhem Rifat Bey, Balkan War, I. World War in Tripoli and has been involved in the front. Pink due to her husband's attitude, by staying in Skopje, the family falls apart.

It'll be a year from now. Gülsüm Master succumbed to his son's longing is overcome by the disease that was captured and died on the front.. rifat.

Father and mother to his three children to rebel. Qur hosts that are behind you and your days of being carefully looked at in front of Enver Bey had fallen in a sad way because the man she loves, house cleaning, laundry works to ensure livelihoods are increasingly. Thus the fall of an empire, you are presented with the tragedy of a family.

Gülsüm uncle Hashim basis of the largest parent and their children. The mansion of his uncle Hashim came to life at the mansion is a joy and it is seen that the day. Remember when father's Mansion, rifat reverts to the status of the past days:

"Uncle Hashim as well as Dec. Then baskalasird mansion. Like the accumulated day design love, joy holiday, holiday preparations would begin. Gülsüm Ana would be all rosy. Turn around and press the pastry with a rolling pin opened at the top of the marble players, and emits inceltird thoroughly. Gülsüm is leading in rumeli which was known as soft. Gülsüm Mother of a girl to marry in that mansion should learn a thing or two from. Stunt or no doubt that it would be." (s.8)

Blessing Aunt, ninety-three of poverty of the war years, who came to visit his grandson, to teach him a lesson by telling pink:

"The good old days, said the aunt. We we haven't done all the dowry. Hard combat your waist. Pasha when I got masters, my dad was right. Your mother was very unfortunate. Was thrown a little out of hand for him."(s.19)

Old Sajida Still, due to the invasion of the enemy, regretting remembering the old days when we had to leave the farm in the chairs:

Now, everything remained in my memory. Laughter, fun, carefree days went so far. Sometimes the taste of the fruit in the garden was shared, and sometimes sit under the cherry trees. (s.188)

When psychology is mentioned Ahmed the war of independence will change immediately. Ahmet, his father, remembering Ali Bey; remembers wistfully of bygone days:

"After being promised from a distant father, Ahmed's eyes work out sometimes. That timid look was gone. In front of the window, grinning. Further away, the sea, was engaged in passing cars and trams from the road, his feet slipped and by removing the tip of his neck." (s.240)

In the spring go to the front of the soldiers with a connection is established between the changes in the sky:

"Spring has arrived. She withdrew from the window, the darkness of winter. The color of spring in bunches in music were appearing. In heaven ... the Battle had begun." (s.50)

"Stunted bushes and dried thoroughly. Returning type from Blue to purple, the color the colors in the evening they threw thorns on the field now. But as far as I can see the sky was blue. Autumn blue.."(p.88)

Uncle rifat Hashim brain interpreted that with the decline of the winter season is full of despair at the moment hometown:

"Snow began to eat again. Beyond the whiteness of the church, multiplying the difficulties appeared with the gray walls. He kept glued to the window in the gloom of a dark winter."(s.144)

Social is handled at the time of the wedding ceremony :

"The bride was placed on the horse, everyone on the girl's forehead, the gold shining on his chest, admiring the gilt embroidered dress. Then the glow disappeared. He stood in a cloud of dust between the drum and sound the horn. There's a picture of children the joy of heaven. Palms was kinali, as always." (s.55,56)

Asiye with Rifat's wedding, joyous ceremonies can be done with:

"Rebel all over her wedding to the joy of it was covered. Comes in bundles, bundles, was going. Was preparing for a great toy. Wrestling being held in the square, the riders were racing. (s.71)

II-Figures in the novel of our realm

The total of our realm in the novel twenty-five hero. Twenty of them-one male, four are female. Male Heroes: Rifat Ali Hashim, Uncle, Cevat Bey, Ethem Bey, Hoca Ali Riza, The Father Hiristo, Gain, Mustafa, Niyazi Bey, Hoca Ali Riza, Hiristo, Gain, Mustafa, Citation Sergeant, Hilmi Bey.

Ali Bey, a member of a prominent family. Gülsüm married for love with a lady. This love ended with the death of Ali Bey. Gülsüm Ana, the children's mother and Father has made.

Female Heroes: Main Gülsüm Kerim, To Rebel, Nadya Main, Sajida Still, Nuriye Nanny, The Lady Simile, Zeynep, Murvet Had The Blessing Of The Aunt.

Gülsüm mother's daughter; and the Qur asiye, the people you love to get with demands. Rebel with a Qur'an to his wife when he loses in the Balkan wars, and settles himself next to Gülsüm Mother continue to struggle for survival.

Our realm, Ali Bey, Mrs. Ana's husband, rifaat's father. Respected around the Ottoman is the brain. From Abdullah Bey Ali Bey who is the Son of the rich families of the region, the land is very high. The Sultan is a figure with respect to the state. Ali Bey, killed during the Balkan wars.

Ali Bey, hard and solid against children is recognized as a figure. Rifaat's father, Ali Bey, rifaat's son, to deal with the land, goods and property to take care of his desires. Rifat also want to be a soldier. Ali, he doesn't know the precise structure of the son to the military profession : "Ali Bey Rifat's military didn't seem eager to go to school. "If I go away, water the soil, one per property of water required. Flood both our son, crazy boy. Placed under orders to obey don't know what.'

There was an insurmountable distance. The courtyard stentorian voice, immediately filled the audience rifat retained when the emphasis was. Primary school was the day when it will begin to kacivermis mansion. Away alder was there, behind him was hidden. On the day that the mother was causing the bleeding, the teachers would send to the samsa. He was laughing coach." They will put you to falaka." Her disappearance, about the mansions of the people that was freaking out it was obvious.

Nuriye Lady Dada yeldirmes he pulled onto his back, he kept running around. Then the coach appeared. He rode his horse. Come and rifaat found. You love his big hand and extend a thought. What's the benefit of running bre?" he said. You'll learn from that big turbans teacher. Sitting on a sheepskin elif ba you'll learn. You are the Son of Ali Bey. You can't hit the stick."(s. 8, 9)

With Gülsüm Ali Bey who is the Son of rifat Rifat, deals with matters of State at such a young age. Rifat Soldier achieves success by participating in war. Gülsüm Main words of flattery introduces her son: "you stop in these places and who can I craft it? Titretirs sharp like the cold of the high mountains to tourists. Battal Gazi learnt, himself already a hero would want to know. Sunca officers and bandit would come take care of you, huh? From rumeli of the Ottoman Empire survived the leg will be saved. I was told that the main Gülsüm. The heavens seemed to amount to this sound. Duali nice words. Calling, loving, a sound that combines..." (p. 7)

Rifaat is highly efficient private lessons from instructor's consent: "consent rifat instructor that summer and how he used to When they would sit outside the window on the bottom... of course, the teacher would laugh at or something that would tell Rifat's ediverird mention his own childhood. Thus bezip child was bored. Sometimes, a little wooden house. Rattlesnake kacismal left the chickens through the gate, ladies adviye him heartily, open outside of school whether it is sparkling, buttermilk, brought a lesson two little Zainab asked to enter the common room, when blocked cry, then could not bear to be seated in a corner, all of these liked.

He stumbled across a day time table went. Mushroom soup with red pepper on the beam where the sequence was drunk. Rifat wasn't hungry. But they will kasiklamal appetite with their soup, and in the meantime, stop by and taking a look thanks, settling, made me forget toughness. If a table with baklava, lamb armed with the fries though, Hoca Riza could hear the whole request." (s.27)

Officer, Rifat, the Turkish people of the situation of his father Ali Bey explains: "when we live together brings the promise of equality between us. However, we see the persecution. We make our voices anyone. The big States he's blaming us. We have to wonder if these mansions were looted.Informal in a land that does not pass our verdict.What we want is equality here, dad. Plant peace in our land we can live in our village without fear. I've seen nice unmarked graves in the border villages. Nice rundown abandoned houses wiped out, I saw minarets, the sound of the adhan.

Our people who migrated in the way I saw them."We're running away from gangs," they said. How our provision is said to have still passed? Here are to whom it was abandoned? Hungry, tired, jaded Soldier. Macedonia vows to pig farms and fed on a gang who can handle? Rampant Domination of foreign police these places, ownership can be mentioned?"

"This country is going, dad, you don't understand. The green of the meadow, the fruit of the tree solid foundation of this mansion nails, thin water flows. Fool you don't let your spinning mill. Informal, tremble like it used to be no it doesn't make the name of Ali Bey. Let your eyes be opened. Take a good look at. Investigators and officers foreign commissioners, Governors in rumeli and the game they played for hand in hand. Ali Bey, who cares anymore?"(s.105, 130)

Gülsüm Master, who is the wife of Ali Bey in the war of the sufferings and tribulations we learn that Mrs. Ana live. Her husband, with the killing of Ali Bey settled in Istanbul. Gülsüm Main' grandchildren, took me to the fountain when Mustafa Bey encounters with the heroines of the novel ruscuklu gain. During this encounter, we learn to gülsüm mother's life adventure. The narrator expressed the situation: "Mustafa Bey..she scolded the kids around before they gain fountain. Guys settle down and away he heard a dent in.

Obviously it's not coming from rumelia. Long they're extending their hands into the water, and another of them laughing. From the green of the wide Plains, were plucked from the flower. As in there carts to navigate through the forest to arrive at the water's edge to enjoy, they've already lost. Been weird he hears every awakening, every time. Urkuntu collapsing with the darkness they must meet. John caught his eyes. While walking as if in pain. Color, waste, put on a loose tunic. A belt at the waist. Lean over and gripped her shoulders.

'Where Are you from and I'll see what is your name?

Ahmed has come and gone because of fear. These big brown eyes added to the pain of love in bluish aklan. Gülsüm based on came close to the main crutch. The man asked again. 'Name deyeme you're not gonna tell me?

'His name is Ahmed, he said Gülsüm Ana. My granddaughter. Asked the gain with respect with the looks.: 'I suppose you're right from rumelia? His gaze took in the old woman's sunny corner of the yard. Accustomed to pain, trouble had become resigned to. Sun, behind Istanbul and the Balkans..

'We're not swinging our arms in our hands! We have our land taken away. Teddy's face fell a shadow on the gain. I sighed. 'We also ninety-three immigrants we need. When we started I was very young. 'Where do you come from? We ruscuklu..' (p.218, 219))

III-Places of our realm in the novel

The events in the novel takes place in Thessaloniki and Skopje, of our realm. The hero of the novel, Mikhail, a time they remain with friends during the Balkan wars in the church. The narrator briefly describe the internal environment and the external world of the church: "hot, sultry wind was blowing. Grilesmis the clouds, and leave the shadows of the hills they were walking. Michael now sitting on the stone steps, he was thinking about what Nadya's mother said. 'Bangers Hristo has made a dwelling place of the house of Allah.' Arrivals outside of here days of the month was dying.

The monastery is now a place of peace wrapped up in himself not exactly. Often at night, the sound of footsteps echoing inside the building would go far into the stone walls. Sleep between voices that was heated. Heard the howling and gnashing of trees in big storms, they would disappear under blankets most of the kids in the dorms. The rains caused was resolved when the ice was heated cagilti of the seas, also from here. Flashes of intermittent rain before the iron barred window was now shining on."(s.39)

Iclal Gülsüm mother's daughter heroines of the novel of the ladies home, was on the verge of Lake Ohrid. Iclal Lady evening step out onto the balcony, come through the market from the Market Watch. The narrator, expresses the plight of the artisans and the people of Ohrid: "the long lace dress lady lake and looking thoughtfully into the lake from the balcony.. iclal he should be. The boats slowly come and pass. Sometimes an umbrella alien women. Are sinking their heads under the branches. Sometimes it's the recession that parcalayiverir a shotgun. A bird was shot down.

Went to the mall. Heat in a dealer shop they would have a shelter at the entrance of the shadows. He sat on some benches or coffin the egg. Under the big elm tree coffee was always full. There hookah and tea and slowly drank it. The path where is located the mosque and the bazaar was always crowded. Previously, these soylesirl would laugh at the mall. Especially their banter with Abraham Albanian Niko felt endless. When you go to necmi Ibrahim Efendi Mosque once hid the master's shoes. On exit Necmi disgruntled Master, he's been looking for their sandals."(s.81)

Gülsüm Ana's little girl because of the Balkan war is separated from the ancient lands of icons'an forget. Even enters into the dreams of the places mentioned:"after I woke up from the dream that wouldn't let go easily. Vardar on the coast large, yellow flowers were in bloom. Qur leaves were falling as I receive them. The Vardar water blurred. Qur running into the station. A train come and go quickly, from the front. The station is empty. Then with a pair of away from a car is coming. Gilded ornaments in the sun is shining. The driver of the car of Enver Bey.

Koran he wants to run in that direction. The feet is weak. Yelling. 'Where Are you going?' Enver Bey, 'Away! I'm away! Too far...'he says." (s.153)

Karim, who lives with the aspirations of the old lands, the boundaries of reading poetry expresses in a chat environment owned by Turks: "... and then began to read. Turan mentioned in the verse poem that stagnant to the face in a flurry of Confusion lines are added. A fluttering like water.

'Oguz Han. This is it my heart that he inspired.' Then the impetuous waters retreated. Re-away from and walked away.

"What...what is my country to the Turks Turkistan, Turkey

Homeland is a country and great sentences: Turan"

'Your aunt when you read this poem, I immediately looked at a time sit at the piano and the keys stopped. Tense fingers seemed stiff. I said it's not in that key called. That, however, it is felt." (s.156)

The hero of the novel, Rifat, by participating in the Balkan war, the front line runs to the front of for many years. Rifaat's father, which is the Abode of Skopje and its surroundings we see being taken away by the enemies. The narrator of Turkish soldiers fighting heroically adhered after they experienced the moment that is how it works: ".... Trenches are excavated, piled up sandbags, placement of the ball are compounded by the difficulty in a sudden rain. Horses neighing to get their wet skin glowing eye.. a downpour. Like smoke drifting rain. Rifaat's words remembers. 'You're a shadow.. a shadow in a uniform..'

Across Groups, the old Bulgarians, Montenegro, shkoder was beating with balls... ball sirb crezut click Serial hot. If they can hold on to kocana in here, together with the left wing of the western Army, the Serbs think that they will be pushed back. Now dalgalanis behind every hill a red color, a kaynayis will appear.

'The seas of hope,' said Ethel. 'Land which can be hard, Sirb, would easily droop bridle, would have been unthinkable. Montenegro to proceed all wouldn't mind.'

Rehorses neighing. 'It is to enter into the fire... but when you spend time in the White Tower..' he didn't pay any attention to these words. To rebel 'Mother doesn't know what he said ill his son. Indulge it.' He was saying. 'Enter into the fire..' not angry, tired.

In the morning, jumped out of the tent with the cannon balls. Just come out and so they were. Rain bukmem waist, which the Bulgarians. Not knowing what to do... some hectic movements from the soles of collected a pile of mud preventing it from running in wet soil. Then defeat Kumanova surprising, devastating news.. whereas the Serbs sprayed said and stood. So they went away from the big square. Reasons and brings down a load of your shoulders. It is a pain in the beginning .

Then he heard the sound of your own balls and pulled his head into his hands. 'The children were at the door of the mansion.. in the lap of the Mother of the dawn. Big, they were looking at me with fearful eyes. Suddenly, it had all started to cry saying murvet. "I couldn't hold back my baby. When was the last time I saw them?' Qur murvet came and hugged him. He wasn't fussy never.'

The sound of gunfire stopped. There was a long silence. Staff officers gathered, leaning on the maps. 'Bulgarian exceeds passages. Bulgarian breaks the gates.' Ethem inside the head is buzzing. The Gatling sounds comes close. Colonel, the usturumca is talking about. 'If the path is interrupted sirb usturumca Union, we also istip here we will be able to provide based on the Bulgarians.'Well, he says.

We got to catch up to kumanova Skopje we got to catch up. The slender minarets of Skopje, Skopje Yesil ties, fountains, rose-scented wind, different shades of green. Come on out the blue dome of the sky the way will go hand in Skopje..?'

Then heard of the trench exceeded. Yenilis they don't want to believe it. Back from the dead, balls, bags, tops in the back ground.. dirt mixed blood. Behind smoke. Now officially renamed the kingdom of Yugoslavia, Skopje what.. what.... Sait Pasha gives the order to withdraw. Shadows... in uniform' are on their way to gracko. The monastery there.. a new hope." (s. 182-183)

The heroines of the novel Gain Ruscuklu Mustafa Bey, Mrs. Ana fountain's descendants when they misbehave, scold them. The situation interfere with Mustafa Gülsüm create the main topic of conversation that took place between the Gain Turkish territory. The narrator expressed the situation: "she scolded the kids around earnings before Mustafa Bey fountain. Guys settle down and away he heard a dent in.

Obviously it's not coming from rumelia. They are extending their hands into the water, another long laughter. From the green of the wide Plains, were plucked from the flower. As in there carts to navigate through the forest to arrive at the water's edge to enjoy, they've already lost. Been weird he hears every awakening, Every time. While walking as if in pain. Color, waste, put on a loose tunic. A belt at the waist. Lean over and gripped her shoulders.

'Where Are you from and I'll see what is your name?

Ahmed has come and gone because of fear. Added to the pain of love in these big brown eyes bluish the whites. Gülsüm based on came close to the main crutch. The man asked again. 'Name deyeme you're not gonna tell me?

'His name is Ahmed, he said Gülsüm Ana. My granddaughter. Asked the gain with respect with the looks.: 'I suppose you're right from rumelia? His gaze took in the old woman's sunny corner of the yard. Accustomed to pain, trouble had become resigned to. Sun, behind Istanbul and the Balkans..

'We're not swinging our arms in our hands! We have our land taken away. Teddy's face fell a shadow on the gain. I sighed. 'We also ninety-three immigrants we need. When we started I was very young. 'Where do you come from? We ruscuklu..' (p.218 - 219)

The main gain with Mustafa gülsüm from rumeli to worry about suffering the consequences of the departure burned, he continued: "mother, mountains, plain, desert separated us. I couldn't get to the Balkans, I don't know what you are about. At the end of summer we went to Edirne. The ruins of Edirne. In Edirne lingered. We saved her life. You're right, I don't know. The ships in front of me now. In awakening each of the blue sea and the ships. This heroic moment. We are born again. At night a lieutenant hymns reads, boom, you're in my thoughts. Starting from where can I explain? Tripoli I received a wound in my hip. Aches from time to time. But the Balkan deeper wound main. Copy from each other, many years. Rumeli like a dream. She Gardens, is a dream that binds." (s.230)

IV-Conclusion in the novel and the perspective of our realm

The novel is written from the dominant perspective of our realm. We want to give a few examples of showing respect to the viewpoint of Rome: "The teacher of Persia was not one to be feared at all. Smiling, loving, and understanding, the Minister's shoulders sunken, the one with the white goatee. Both heap rifaat he had a friend now. Output can run crazy in school, fountain head, and his friends could squirt water. In that big mansion, however, you could laugh with a groom by a younger brother koco'anic verses. Sometimes he was angry Koco. From the brain of this young man was no different." (s.8)

As seen here the novelist gives us information about himself in the third person from the perspective of the judge rifat. The teacher, you're running crazy in the exit of the school, games from a perspective that sees and knows everything their sakalastik describes.

"Uncle Hashim as well as Dec. Then baskalasird mansion. Like the accumulated day design love, joy holiday, holiday preparations would begin. Gülsüm Ana would be all rosy.

Turn around and press the pastry with a rolling pin opened at the top of the marble players, and emits inceltird thoroughly. Gülsüm is leading in rumeli which was known as soft. Gülsüm Mother of a girl to marry in that mansion should learn a thing or two from. Stunt or no doubt that it would be." (s.8)

Here, too, with the arrival of Uncle Hashim the author, gives information about the activity at the mansion. While you're at it sees everything in a way that uses the dominant perspective.

There is also a noteworthy point here. He is also a novelist himself, because she is a woman that have given more detail about women's work and more information. There are many instances of this in the novel. This also could hide it was shown that a woman's perspective of her in the novel.

"Small gold stone was poured with water. When it is passed to the second compartment, women, Pink suzdul minutely. Behold, judging by how many girls of marriageable age, so Plump, skinny, couple, you got me, how do you figure? Aisha the girl's hair with a soft towel could be installed on small asiye. Eyes, was caught in the beauty of pink. Her skin looked like white marble. Gülsüm big Lady sit on the sofa, opened the parcel and brought to silk and velvet. Ivory was taking the time to brush his long bushy hair. Meanwhile, a track Gülsüm ladies coffee." (s.12)

Here, too, the author by using the dominant perspective in bath women tell me what happened. Gene describes himself by being a lady novelist, more extensive processing:

"Night Rifat had calmed down anyway. Mother was sitting out there. There were three windows. Window covers type was inserted when pushed in the sun. Lace curtains opens, the smell of the flowers was unconscious. On three sides of the room were covered with Cedars. Didn't have much Luggage. Selected elaborate drapes, mattresses, rugs, Bursa catman, a large brass brazier, wall cicim few goods, crystal chandeliers and large wall clock rifat is located niches where these rugs harmony of colors in embroidery.. sometimes the rushes, thought he was amazing, not in niceties. Sometimes a bird in the honeymoon phase, is it from the garden to the garden fly, sometimes the way it would have reached a desert yellow amber. The power of your fingers to move over and she lay the fabric Skopje, dersaadet, Crete 'Big to Asia.' (s.15)

Here the author is describing where he lives with his mother rifaat dominant perspective when we see that it gives everything in a location that knows what he's thinking.

"Spring has arrived. She withdrew from the window, the darkness of winter. The color of spring in bunches in music were appearing. In heaven ... the Battle had begun. They were seen more to the front The troops now on the road. Tirhala, Yenişehir, Golos it's true." (s.50)

Here too, the judge time from the perspective of the author, Spring, Fall and winter tells us that went. Again, who knows everything in the way of a position from the start of the war the common soldiers to tirhala, Yenişehir, heading towards Golos he tells.

"Snow began to eat again. Beyond the whiteness of the church, multiplying the difficulties appeared with the gray walls. In the gloom of a dark winter kept glued to the window. Then the car from the window of apartment buildings, without the customer, profitable tea gardens, quickly walking, two people dressed in black have come and gone. The horses slowed, the shaking is over.""It was warm in there. Hashim Bey away from the window, Hi-back was sitting in a chair. Pictures of familiar people on the wall. Enver, Talat, Niyazi Djemal, Gentlemen..."

"Rifat he thought about the early days of constitutional monarchy. Hugs to here with her uncle. What had accumulated from the excitement she was going to say and kept silent for a while. Then the room was doluvermis with the other members. Then in the month of September, sky the color of yellow-painted trees from time to time bulutlanan, enthusiasm, joy, residual, flying, scattered and missing parts..." (p.144)

We received a few chapters of the novel in this perspective, we see the dominant feature of perspective. After telling that the author here sees everything from a location to move it around, sitting in Coffee gives your brain a little information about Hashim. Then it describes what you think Rifat: "Rifat he thought about the early days of constitutional monarchy. Hugs to her uncle here."

Our realm in the novel, are subject to the political upheaval in the Balkans that took place during migration events. I. after the Declaration of constitutional monarchy against the Ottoman Empire Greek, Bulgarian, and with the instigation of Armenians of Russia are rebelling. The Ottoman state left to live in this mess of a hard time.

The author of the novel the hero, Gülsüm Ali Bey, with the Ladies, after stating that minorities live with every day for many years; make sense of their rebellion against minorities. Gülsüm Mother she made the rugs, socks, coats of the same neighboring Serbian and Greek ladies weave too. Gülsüm Ana, Arts and crafts keep these as a souvenir. The soldiers pray for Ali and his family the war in the Balkans. With the instigation of Russia's minorities, the Turks are upset when they see the enemy they are. (s. 13)

Acting to subvert the power of the Sultan, enemies, receive the support of local collaborators. Those who are fighting for freedom to come to criticize the author. Don't know who you serve these people's struggles. The Ottoman Empire, the events in the novel who is the hero of the Father, Son rifaat Ali and even leads to a difference of opinion. Father Rifat, given new rights for minorities in the country, Turkish traditions, language, religion, comes under pressure against removal. The real owners of this land, the Turks have the same rights as it would be unfair to the minorities, he says. However, with the pressures of the western world, where most of the ceremony has been lost are highlighted:

"Rifat: 'well, where should I start. Used to be that door was locked? It is nice to hear from the iron arms of the Mother outside the gates is lowered. Here is felt, is the weakness of the state? Nested in all these years has been experienced. But you can't break with a kind; it is still give you Water hello to yiorgos. Ali Bey: 'peace and blessings is God the Son. You are given. Way doesn't make these sweet?

'Promise me that you'll tell me how? I found two gunshot wounds. How many people have been lost in this cause. Dad owned this land for how many years to how it was calculated. Children, women, old man, all from head to toe with this thought became a solid rock. You can't wash, but you can't learn. The death of a Bulgarians, Bulgarians such as the death of a far cry from the hundred breaks. In the Balkans, a squished fly.. why death does not rise up in our window?..

'Son, you the span between the tools and the Sultan? If with Two if it is turned on you will be kept with the Sultan and tools. Rifat remained in thought for a moment. 'If it is declared Constitutional, sirb, Greece, arnavud, Bulgarians, where do you send it? Cypriot equality.. language, religion, when you have manners you can tell. How the son to be equal with them. Changing our manners? Because we are living together. The subject must be one or the other. Of course who is going to be? You did they? My mind that he didn't.

When we live together brings the promise of equality between us. However, we see the persecution. We make our voices anyone. The big States he's blaming us. We have to wonder if these mansions were looted. Informal in a land that does not pass our verdict. What we want is equality here, dad. Let's plant peace in our land, in our village we can live without fear. Nice I ran into unmarked graves in the border villages.

Conclusion

Nice rundown, minarets, I saw abandoned houses that wiped out the sound of the adhan. Our people who migrated in the way I saw it. 'We're running away from gangs,' they said. How our provision is said to have still passed? Here are to whom it was abandoned? Hungry, tired, weary, a soldier, a gang of fed on pig farms can handle? These places are rampant Domination of foreign police, we give them ownership.

'Son, said Mr Ali. You're not wrong on the idea. Don't blame this all but the king. This is a wound that is so nice bleed. Debt is the size of the larynx. Our hands are tied from all sides. Otherwise, why bow down and tools? We have diklenece? There was a war on the territory of rumeli water, he goes down the Ottoman Empire. Both the long collapse." (s. 105, 106)

Resources

ÇOKUM Sevinç, **Our Realm**, Istanbul 978.

GÜNGÖR Erol, "**The Historical Novel",** Journal of Turkish Literature, Vol: 42, August 1975.

KAPLAN Mehmet; **Medical Tests**, Istanbul, 1991.

KAPLAN Mehmet, **Studies On Turkish Literature**, Istanbul 1992.

FETHİ Naci, "**Our Contacts Novelists and Novels**", Hürriyet gösteri, vol. 27, February, 1983.

FEYTİ Naci, **The Conquest; and Social Change**, Roma in Turkey, Istanbul, 1981.

TANPINAR Ahmet Hamdi, **Articles On Literature,** Istanbul 1992.

YALÇIN Alemdar, **The Turkish Novel In The Republican Period**, Ankara 1992.

OCAK Yaşar Ahmet, **'Geyikli Baba'** <mad.>, Turkish religious Foundation Encyclopedia of Islam, V. XIV.

YETİŞ Kazim, **"Anovel Type of Three That Are Related to the Establishment of the Ottoman State"**, Journal of Turkish Language and Literature, C: XXX, 2000-2003.

YETİŞ Kazım, "**Three Historical Novels, Two Motif",** Wise, Issue: 12th July 1994.

YETKİN Suut Kemal, **"History and The Novel", Challenge Magazine**, Issue No. 564, December.

CHAPTER 11

THE PIONEER OF MODERN CHINESE LITERATURE BA JIN AND HIS MASTERPIECE "THE TORRENTS TRILOGY: THE FAMILY"

Lale AYDIN[218*]

Introduction

Early 20th century witnessed "May Fourth", the New Culture Movement in China. At such a historical point in time, the Chinese literature went through quite a versatile transformation incorporating transformation of literary opinions, literary contents and language and even the ties between the Chinese literature and world literature. Since that time, couple of millennium old traditional literature began to lose altitude towards an eventual downfall, giving birth to a new modern Chinese literature. After that, quite a number of novelists, essayists, playwrights, poets, literary theorists and critics all of whom tended to think utterly different from one another centred, at the heart of their ongoing research studies and articles, on themes of cultural innovation, national liberalism, class struggle of the time that responded to social realism with different genres of literature.[219]

---

218 * Res. Asst., Lale Aydın, Istanbul University, Faculty of Letters, Department of Chinese Language and Literature, PhD(C), Xiamen University, Department of Modern and Contemporary Chinese Literature (lale.aydin@istanbul.edu.tr)

219 Yao Dan, Chinese Literature/ Great Tradition Since the Book of Songs, Translated by Sinan Baykent, Kaynak Publishing, Istanbul 2016, p. 217.

One of these writers is Ba Jin, one of the pioneering figures in modern Chinese literature. His original name is Li Yaotang. As an author he wrote about anti-feudalism, one of the widely read topics in modern Chinese literature. This study will provide information about effects of "May Fourth" movement upon modern Chinese literature, as well as the role and literary identity of Ba Jin, a pioneering figure in modern Chinese literature, within the context of "May Fourth" movement. Also, "The Torrents Trilogy", a masterwork by Ba Jin, will be discussed, and particularly "The family", the first serial of the trilogy, which is loaded with anti-feudalism findings and traces, will be quoted.

1. The Effects of May Fourth Movement on Modern Chinese Literature

The "May Fourth" Movement in China broke out when a group of students protested Germany that signed the Versailles Peace Treaty, which transferred China's rights on Shandong state to Japan, and also the Beijing government that surrendered to the treaty. The movement broke out on May 4, 1919 and escalated quickly to transform to an extensive social movement embracing workers and merchants lower to middle class of the society. Reflected in education, culture, art, political spheres of life in the early 20th century, the movement paved the ground for the "New Culture Movement", which, in turn, exposed concepts of democracy, science, human rights, law, freedom to the spheres of thinking, politics and culture. The movement formed a reference for the youth and the intelligentsia, whom unquestionably loved their country, had good intentions to protect it but also turned their face to the west. This was the time when the history of Chinese literature produced most yielding, rich and creative works and it also marks a time when young authors were the most productive.[220]

Along with the movement came "The Vernacular Movement" that blew down the conventional narrating style that was in use for centuries in China and replaced colloquial language with written language. Materialised with good efforts of the intelligentsia living in big cities like

[220] Gonca Ünal Chiang, May Fourth Movement and Modern Chinese Literature: Zhu Ziqing, The Pioneer of Modern Chinese Literature and His Memorable Work "Beiying", Cyprus International University, Vol: 23, Issue: 89, 2017/1, p. 37-38.

Beijing and Shanghai, the new language found a place in literature in a short time. Hu Shi was the man of knowledge that was influential on materialisation of the New Culture Movement that supported Culture Revolution.

In this regard, Hu Shi adopted a few principles. These are adopting narration with concrete contents, not to refer to examples of ancient scholars, linking narration with logical rules, not to rely on classics, adopting a clear and genuine narration rather than idioms and proverbs. As is seen they relate not to the form but to the content of a given work. Accordingly, printed book fonts prevail in handwriting, horizontal scripts are preferred to vertical scripts, punctuation marks not in use in old Chinese language are observed, Christian era prevails without showing the date, and numbers are shown in Arabic numbers in international standards. Modern dictionary and grammar works also commenced at the same period of time, Chinese meanings were produced for foreign words, and more importantly, particular attention was given to prefer works with concrete and real contents when selecting words, and when writing a script the real meaning of the words was recommended.[221]

In the light of the aforecited principles, the Chinese language was simplified after the May Fourth Movement, works of the time were produced by using the updated literary language, and the tendency increased in the course of time.

2. Biography and Literary Identity of Ba Jin

Born in Chengdu city of Sichuan State in 1904, the author used the pen name Ba Jin, and his original name is Li Yaotang . As for the story of the of 'Ba Jin' the pen name, the author decides on the name Ba Jin, a combination of syllable Ba, the last name of his friend who committed suicide, and Jin, the last syllable of Kropotkin's name in Chinese as his favourite author.

Born to a bureaucratic and wealthy family, Ba Jin closely witnessed conflicts of interest in a big and feudal family and how his elder brother was victimised in the feudal family. His early experience followed by anarchist and humane opinions drove him to harshly criticise feudalism. When he was studying in France in 1927, he wrote 'Destruction'《灭亡》 his

221 Gürhan Kırilen, Çin Dili, Gece Kitaplığı, Ankara 2016, p. 12-13.

first novella and made progress in his career as an author since then. His primary works are: The Torrents Trilogy: "The Family, Spring, Autumn", The Love Trilogy : "Fog, Rain, Ligthtning", "A Garden of Repose", "Cold Nights", "Ward No 4" etc.[222]

Ba Jin's works are divided into two, as early works and late works in modern literature process of thirty years. Early period starts with the time he wrote 'Destruction' in September 1928 and lasts until the war of resistance against Japanese aggression while the late period is accepted to have started upon the war of resistance against Japanese aggression and to have lasted until the liberation of China. In this process that covers a period of approximately twenty times as a whole, Ba Jin produced more than twenty long and medium-length novels, over seventy short stories in addition to a number of essays. He also translated from more than thirty foreign literatures. What has caught most attention amongst them has been the novels and particularly the long and medium-length ones.[223] Ba Jin's novels are subjective and lyrical and have an idiosyncratic place in modern Chinese literature. His fame is not limited to the boundaries of China but goes beyond the rest of the world and the author was awarded with the The Legion of Honour in 1983, followed by the Fukuoka Asian Culture Prize in 1990.

Ba Jin expresses his passion for writing as follows:

"My major works were all written in the twenty years from 1927 to 1946. In the long period before Liberation (1949), my life as a writer was painful. I have confessed before: When I'm burning with passion, my heart is about to explode and I don't know where to place it; I feel that I must write. I am not an artist, and writing is only part of my life, which, like my works, is full of contradictions. The conflicts between love and hate, thought and action, reason and emotion—these combine to weave a net enwrapping my whole life and all my works. My life, as well as my works, is a painful struggle. Every novel of mine carries my cry in my pursuit of light…At the same time, the picture of extreme pain and suffering is like a whip lashing me from behind. Inevitably, I could only pick up my pen and write. I wrote to my heart's content, throwing all caution to the winds."[224] It is hardly possible

---

222 Yao Dan, Chinese Literature/Great Tradition since The Book of Songs, Translated by Sinan Baykent, Kaynak Publishing, Istanbul 2016, p. 217.

223 Qian Liqun, Wen Rumin, Wu Fuhui, Zhongguo Xiandai Wenxue San Shi Nian, Peking University Press, Beijing, 2014, p. 199.

224 Ba Jin, Selected Works of Ba Jin, Translated by Sidney Shapiro and Wang Mingjie, Foreign Language Press Beijing China, 1988.

to disregard the author's passion for literature. We understand from his following remarks that he never gave up on writing despite the harsh times he had to go through during the culture revolution in particular:

"During the ten calamitous years of the cultural revolution (1966-1976), I was forced to give up writing for for a long time. But now my pen is finally back in my hand. In my heart, the fire is still burning. In my mind, is still the same old voice which continually urges me, "Keep writing, keep writing." I feel inside me emotions rising and falling like mighty waves, waiting for a free outlet. So deep is my love for my country and my people! I want to write. I will continue to write. Let that fire burn me out, fiercely. When only the ashes of my body are left behind, even then, I know my love and my hate will never disappear."[225] Ba Jin was banned from writing at the Culture Revolution, and he unfortunately lost his wife to cancer during the early years of the revolution. He wrote about the challenging times of 1978-1986 in his work, "Random Thoughts" in 5 volumes. Composed of 150 essays in total, the work discusses human weaknesses and feudalist thinking from a historical point of view. Masterfully combining his realist and humanist opinions, he attained ideological and artistic success.

As an author, a translator and social activities Ba Jin lived until 101. Having produced numerous works in his long life, Ba Jin always valued virtues of love, freedom, anti-imperialism, anti-feudalism, romance, happiness; discussed them elaborately in his works and communicated them to masses. Discussing May Fourth Movement with all details in his well-known novel 'The Family', the author died in Shanghai in 2005 at the age of 101.

2.1. Chronological Table of Ba Jin

1904

He was born on 25th November in Chengdu. His real name is Li Yaotang, his another pen name is Li Fei Gan.

1920

He passed the entrance exam of the Chengdu Foreign Language School. While he was studying under the influence of "4 May Movement" new ideology, at the same time he edited developing

225 Ibid, p.foreword iii.

magazines such as “Ban Yue”, “Ping Ming Zhi Sheng” and he joined in "Jun She" youth group.

1923

He left Chengdu and went to Shanghai and Nanjing for education in May.

1925

He gratuated from Nanjing South East Secondary School in August and returned to Shanghai for treatment.

In September, he joined an anarchism organization, Shanghai People’s Society and published “Min Zhong” magazine twice in a month. In the same period he published articles about the new poetry and social political issues. He translated some books of anarchist writers such as Kropotkin.

1927

15th January, he left Shanghai and went to France. He stayed for more than a year in France, read a lot about The French Revolution, The Russian Empire and The Narodniks. He

came into contact with some European Revolutionists and also received a letter from the Italian worker movement activist Vincetti who was tortured by the American government of that time. Started to write “Destruction”.

1928

In December, he turned back to Shangai, started to work as a literatüre editor and also started to write formally.

1929

In January, “Destruction” was published in the 20th volume/ 1-4 issues of “Xiaoshuo Yuebao” in series. In the same year of October, Kaiming Bookstore published it.

1931

In April, “The Family, with the name of “The Torrent” at that time, was published by Shanghai “Shi Bao” from 18th April to 22th May 1932 in series.

In April 1933, Kaiming Bookstore published it.

In August, "Vengeance Collection" (Short Story Collection) was published by New China Publishing.

He wrote his novel "Fog" in summer and was published in the 28. volume/ 20-23. issues of "Dongfang Zazhi" in series. It was published in 11th November, 1931 by New China Publishing.

By the end of year, he wrote "Rain" and was published in the 3.volume/ 1.-6. issues of Nanjing "Wenyi Yuekan" in series.

1932

In May, he wrote "Autumn in Spring". It was published in Shanghai "Shi Bao" from 23th May to 3th August in series. In the same year of October, it was published by New China Publishing.

In May also "Brightness Collection" (Short Story Collection) was published by New China Publishing.

In June, he wrote "Miners" and published in the 1.volume/ 1.-2. issues of "Shenbao Yuekan" in series. It was published by New China Publishing in January.

In July, he wrote again "New Life" and published in the 4.-11. issues of "Dongfang Zazhi" in series. After one year in september, it was published by New China Publishing.

1933

In December, he wrote "Lightning" and in 1934, published in the 1.volume/ 2.-3. issues of "Wenxue Jikan" in series. By the end of year, he was assigned to

Wenxue Jikan as an editor.

1934

In June, "The General" (Short Story Collection) was published by Shenghuo Publishing.

In October, he editted monthly magazines; Bian Zhilin and "Shuixing".

In November, he travelled to Japan.

1935

In August, he came back from Japan. He became editor of Shanghai Wenhua Shenghuo Publishing. On the other hand, he also edited other magazines such as; Wenhua Shenghuo Congkan, Wenxue Congkan, Wenxue Xiao Zongkan .

In November, "Gods, Ghosts and Men" (Collection of Short Story) was published by Wenhua Shenghuo Publishing.

1936

In June, he helped to publish Wenji Yuekan. Also published the first part of "Spring" novel in the 1. volume/1. issue and in the 2. volume/1. issue of Wenxue Jikan in series.

1937

In January, "The Immortality Pagoda" (Collection of Children Literature) was published by Wenhua Shenghuo Publishing.

In March, he started to edit monthly magazine Wen Cong.

In August, he edited weekly magazine "Nahan" (The name of the magazine changed as "Fenghuo" in the third issue.) and newspaper "Jiuwang Ribao".

1938

In February, he finished "Spring" and the novel was published by Shanghai Kaiming Publishing.

In March, became the director of Literary Association.

In May, he started to write the first volume of the "Fires" novel. In 1940 September, he finished it and in December it was published by Shanghai Kaiming Publishing.

1939

In October, he started to write "Autumn" novel. In 1940 May, he finished it and in July the novel was published by Shanghai Kaiming Publishing.

1940

At the beginning of July, he passed through Kunming, Chongqin, Chengdu, Guilin, Guiyang etc cities and engaged in anti-Japanese cultural propaganda activities.

1941

In 29th March, he started to write second volume of "Fires" novel. In 23th May, he finished writing and in 1942 January, the novel was published by Chongqing Kaiming Publishing.

In 4th December, he wrote "Resurrection Grass". In 1942 it was published in the 1.volume/1.issue of "Wenyi Zazhi".

1943

April-September, he wrote the third volume of "Fires" and the novel was published by Kaiming Publishing in 1945 July.

1944

In 8th May, he married with Xiao Shan in Guiyang/Huaxi.

May-July he wrote "A Garden of Repose" and was published by Wenhua Shenghuo Publishing in October.

In winter, he started to write "Cold Nights" and finished by the end of 1946. In 1946, it was published in the 2.volume/1.-6. issue of Wenyi Fuxing in series. In 1947 March it was published by Chenguang Publishing Company.

1945

May-July he wrote"Ward No 4" and in 1946 January, it was published by Liangyou Book Company.

In November, he went from Chengdu to Shanghai.

1947

He became editor of Wenhua Shenghuo Publishing and editor-in-chief of "Series of Modern Novels".

1949

He joined The Meeting of the Representatives of the Literary Federation that was the first time holded by the whole country and he was elected comittee member of Literary Federation.

1950

In July, he was elected vice president of Shanghai Literary Federation.

1957

In July, he was editor-in-chief of "Shouhuo".

He edited "Collection of Ba Jin" in 14 volumes and published in 1961.[226]

[226] Qian Liqun, Wen Rumin, Wu Fuhui, Zhongguo Xiandai Wenxue San Shi Nian, Peking University Press, Beijing, 2014, p. 209-210-211.

3. The Torrents Trilogy: "The Family"

"The Torrents Trilogy" narrates the story of a feudal family's rise and fall. It is composed of three novels, namely The Family (1931), Spring (1938) ve Autumn (1940). The trilogy fully and exactly criticises hypocritical mask of the feudal autocracy and feudal family order, revealing how the system has made a bloody massacre, what lies and sins lied beneath that mask; it claims that the feudal system is destined to come to an end, calling on the youth to rebel. 'The Family' is the most successful -as far as literature is concerned- out of the three novels.[227]

'The Family' essentially discusses tragedies of love in the Gao family, and their clash of cultures formed around the incidents in a modern history of literature. The plot of the novel is centred on the elder son Juexin and his cousin Mei, whom are in love since their childhood. Mei's mother is against her daughter getting married to Juexin, and forces her to marry off to another man. Forced to an unwilling marriage, Mei loses her wife a year after getting married and dies soon after. Although Juexin tries hard to be happy with his wife Ruijue after the loss of Mei, Ruijue dies because of excessive bleeding at delivery. Juehui is the youngest son of the family and he is in love with the maid Mingfeng. The family is also against their love and forces Mingfeng to become a concubine to a 60-year old man. Mingfeng commits suicide by jumping into a lake, Juehui leaves home. 'Spring' and 'Autumn', the sequels to the novel, narrates the fall of the Gao family, and the tragedy of the young generation.

Eldest son Juexin's characterisation within the large feudal family is a great success. Juexin has become a classical figure in the history of modern Chinese literature. As a matter of fact Juexin is the result of transformation of old and new societies. He has become a loyal representative of feudal codes of ethics and also experiences "May Fourth Movement". After his father's death, he assumes responsibility for the large feudal family as the eldest son and grandson of the family. Since he is well aware of the fact feudal family order and of feudal codes of ethics destroyed his youth and dispossessed him of his happiness in life, he secretly sympathises his brothers' rebel, whereas responsibility he has assumed as a son has clipped his wings. Though superficially, he

---

227 Yao Dan, Chinese Literature/Great Tradition since The Book of Songs, Translated by Sinan Baykent, Kaynak Publishing, Istanbul 2016, p. 217.

self-sacrificed for the sake of keeping his large family together and reeled under heavy responsibilities, and this, at the end of the day, made him an insecure and coward person. His attempts to keep the family together failed, and this drove him to unhappiness.[228]

The middle brother Juemin makes his dreams come true with the help of his brother Juehui. Although he is seemingly a calm character, he is definitely a go-getter. He is in love with Qin, the daughter to his father's sister. As his grandfather wants to marry him off to somebody else he abandons home and makes plans to marry Qin. Qin represents women that seek modernity in the new age. She is a character that fights for equality of women and men in society. How brave equality of women and men is revealed from Mei's remarks in the novels:

"Our circumstances are very different. I can't be like you. I can't keep up with the changing times. All my life I've been a plaything of Fate. I was never allowed to make up my own mind about anything. What hope have I for happiness? I certainly envy you. You have courage and strength. You never let yourself be pushed around."[229]

Mei shows determination with all her courage, despite the reactions, to be the first girl to go to school at a time when co-education is implemented, and she manages to persuade her family thanks to her will. Especially these words that he read on the New Youth Magazine supported her not to give up on hope:

"...I believe that before all else I am a human being, just as much as you are—or at least that I should try to become one... I can't be satisfied with what most people say... I must think things out for myself, and try to get clear about them..."[230]

The third brother Juehui appears as a completely different character than his elder brother. At the beginning of the novel, he succumbs to the family orders even though those orders were not always in tune with those of his own, but he does not hesitate to fight for his own freedom as the maiden he loves commits suicides because of his own family matters and calculations. In his personal fight, he criticises his elder brother, whom does not resist anything. Unlike his elder brother's meek and submissive stance, Juehui comes to the forefront with his stance against his family's traditional and feudal structure. In addition, his

---

228 İbid, p.218-219.

229 Ba Jin, Selected Works of Ba Jin, Translated by Sidney Shapiro and Wang Mingjie, Foreign Language Press Beijing China, 1988, p.112.

230 Ibid, p.26.

commitment to his case, hatred for injustice and oppression, keenness on education, and love for the maid Mingfeng are deeply discussed in the novel. Interestingly, Juehui is a naive and shy person as a character. Consequently he is just the perfect one that reflects the spirit of the May Fourth Movement youth.

Juehui would read Turgenev novels and one day he began to read aloud from Turgenev's novel, On the Eve:

"Love is a great word, a great feeling... But what kind of love are you talking about? What kind of love? Whatever kind of love you like, so long as it's love. For my part I confess that there is just aren't different sorts of love. If you fall in love—then love with all your soul." His two brothers were looking at him in surprise, but Juehui was unaware of it. *He continued to recite: "It's the thirst for love, for happiness, nothing else. We're young, we are not monsters, not fools. We'll conquer happiness for ourselves."* While Juehui was reading these lines, at the same time he was thinking: *"In this kind of society, what other kind of existence is simply a waste of youth, a waste of life!".*[231]

Conclusion

With his way of lyrical and subjective narration in his novels, Ba Jin has contributed novelty to the Chinese literature and became a leading author in the modern Chinese literature. 'The Family' is one of the masterpieces that perfectly reveal the spirit of May Fourth Movement in modern Chinese literature. Elaborately and deeply discussing anti-feudalism motifs, the novel is even more attractive as the author personally experienced the process in real life. In addition to anti-feudalism, reactions to fanatical opinions, clash of generations, equality of men and women, importance of education, modern love are discussed. Each theme has been discussed through the eyes of an individual character to convey dilemma of the time effectively. Characters in the novel do actually function as symbols for the May Fourth Movement. In this context, rebellious acts and efforts of the May Fourth youth triggered thousands of more youth to act. They are, just like Juehui, took courage steps and fought for their freedom and ideals.

---

[231] Ibid, p.83-84.

References

Yao Dan, Chinese Literature/Great Tradition Since The Book of Songs, Translated by Sinan Baykent, Kaynak Publishing, Istanbul 2016.

Gonca Ünal Chiang, May Fourth Movement and Modern Chinese Literature: Zhu Ziqing, The Pioneer of Modern Chinese Literature and His Memorable Work "Beiying", Cyprus International University, 2017.

Gürhan Kırilen, Çin Dili, Gece Kitaplığı, Ankara 2016.

Qian Liqun, Wen Rumin, Wu Fuhui, Zhongguo Xiandai Wenxue San Shi Nian, Peking University Press, Beijing, 2014.

Ba Jin, Selected Works of Ba Jin, Translated by Sidney Shapiro and Wang Mingjie, Foreign Language Press Beijing China, 1988.

PART THREE

PHILOSOPHICAL STUDIES

CHAPTER 12

CALL OF CONSCIENCE AND RISK OF ACCUSATION

Nedim YILDIZ[232*]

Abstract

Ethics is a living phenomenon now and here. It can not be spooled or postponed. It starts and ends in an unique context just for once. It can not be generalized in this aspect and it can not be extended to other people or incidents. The fact is that in addition to not touching human beings and their lives, it is not possible to find, uncover, or fabricate idealized universal ethical or ethical principles as external elements that are always alien to them, but to carry out ethical attitudes in ethical processes and actions in living situations. All this orientation may not always be appropriate for the positive or natural environment of the social environment in which it lives. This situation can also lead to the risk of guilty with ethical behavior. In this respect, the moral self has to take into account the risk of a certain accusation when it is directed to fulfill the necessity of the conscience that calls itself to the responsibility and publicity of being human. The existence of the risk causes to possibility of moral attitude and behavior.

Key Words: Ethics, Conscience, Accusation, Nietzsche, Dostoyevsky.

---

232 * Istanbul University, Philosophy Department, Associate Professor.

The moral conduct takes place in the direction of moral demand. But the moral demand is universal. The fact that the moral claim is universal also means that it is absolute and necessary. It is impossible for the moral demand to be practiced in terms of being universal.[233] In this regard, the person is faced with an impossible demand which, in a certain way, arises from himself, but again, against himself. The invalidity of the demand creates trauma to the collocutor. One goes to the philosophy, the amazement created by the helplessness of not surviving this trauma. The goal in philosophy is to make the situation that is perceived as traumatic and inexplicable to be overcome. This is also a trauma that Raskolnikov showed when he did not mean that he would not consider himself guilty of murder. The process of recognization of the situation begins with the process his confession.

As the conscience of the world human live in, one can position himself only in the processes we are experiencing, not as a representative of an out-of-time truth or necessity. According to S. Critchley, conscience is ultimately associated with the upper self in the sense of Freud, and the upper self has contingent content in connection with life accidents. Perhaps it is possible to be able to speak about sense of conscience for all people, but they can only participate in living activities, that is, activities of living, as different representations of a common sense of conscience. Here, the upper self is out-of-time and determinist-judge in form, although it is contingent in content and relative in time. Its prudence and direction is the main dynamic of moral action.[234]

Ethical experience is the experience of living. In this experience, the object and the subject in this experience are mutually and equally positioned and formed each other. In this sense, experience is not an activity that is exposed in a passive position. The subject in the activity realizes the "ethical" by his own action, thus realizing itself as the subject. [235] But this is a duality. The duality between my present-self and my self who head for 'must' is related to the unquestionable commitment to the 'must goal', which can not be achieved. "That is, without the experience of a demand to which I am prepared to bind myself, to commit myself, the whole business of morality would either not get started ..." [236] Otherwise, it is very clear that this claim can not

---

233 Simon Critchley, **Infinitely Demanding: Ethics Commitment, Politics Resistance**, Verso Press, London, 2008, p. 49.

234 **ibid.**, pp. 83-84.

235 **ibid.,** p. 14.

236 **ibid.**, p. 23.

be fulfilled.[237] The fact that the moral claim can not be realized can lead to a fragmentation in my present self trying to comply with the demand. The moral subject I choose to be is divided self, forcing him to become a subject other than the ideal situation he or she is leading. [238]

Some philosophers see Socrates as the source of these imperatives, the divide that divides and breaks up the person that often has to be, and the distinction that must be. It is possible that we should make one of the most beautiful criticisms of Socrates' understanding that the situation encountered without a certain conception of truth can not be recognized.[239] So there is a dilemma. We have to reach a definition as universal, or we have to suspend the whole moral thing. The existence of the universal will make possible the moral one? "Will the existence of the universal the existence of the moral one possible ? But it is the resultant end to which we will never be able to notice it when we are faced with courage or truth because we do not have this kind of theory."[240] Nietzsche claims Socrates is the first one who is moralizing value proposition.[241] Before, as values prevailed in the natural and living stream continue to exist in the context of certain time and space, now the values have become moralized and turned into an absolute timeliness agent outside time and space parallel to the emergence of philosophy, or conceptual thought. According to Nietzsche, Socrates had two great contributions. The first is that he has emphasized the mind and dialectic against the inner rhyme, and the second is that he has put morality forward and named it. Thus, for the first time, Socrates is the person who has made philosophical reasoning and grounding on traditional forms of behavior. In addition to this understanding, the second contribution of Socrates has argued that a rational reason for a behavior is valid for all intelligent beings. This approach is also valid for Nietzsche.[242] "Nietzsche answers that Socrates became master over himself by turning "*reason* into a tyrant"[243] Thus, "Socrates destroyed the tragic Greek world and its art

---

237 **ibid.**, p. 87.

238 **ibid.**, p. 22.

239 Alexander Nehamas, **The Art of Living *Socratic Reflections from Plato to Foucault,*** University Of California Press, 1998. pp. 147-148.

240 **ibid** p. 148.

241 **ibid.**, p. 144.

242 **ibid.,** p. 133.

243 **ibid.,** p. 138.

and introduced the seeds of what we now are: he is in a serious sense the first modern individual."[244]

The moral demand forbids one you to be how he is. It now demands from the individual to be as how s/he is not. But this is an impossible claim. So why are we going after this impossible question. Is there a moral side of the moral effort in an understanding that we accept that we are not moral and that we can never be?[245] Why does one suggests and directs a state that should be, not what it is, but what it should be.[246]

What makes human beings human, but can not realize in their lives is this demand which is a request to be human. The person tries to make the human being in his or her own efforts, and the effort to achieve this will definitely be inconclusive. But having this demand and following it will be enough for man to become human. Someone might think this: Life is not the life I think I should live, and I think that this difference will never come to pass.

Morality wants what is impossible from man. Morality is a utopia in this regard. Because, in this conception of morality, it seems to be related to what should be, not what is. This approach will mean a closure of way back to the morality of the contingent world and the struggle and concern, from the safeguard of the ideal, and from the safe haven. According to the representatives of this understanding, morality is the desire for impossible. Why can not morality become real? Those who pursues Socrates are directed to suppress what is possible, daily, sensual, earthly in favor of the 'impossible'. However, it can be said that it will be possible to realize morality as a human being, as sophists like Protagoras suggest, that if a certain ideality is pursuing a goal that can not always be reached, it is possible to live a good life in the *phronesis* of Aristotle as the living people of the world.

Will this orientation mean that we, as human beings, position ourselves as bourgeoisie in the sense that Adorno means? Adorno says: "The bourgeoisie however, is tolerant. His love of people as they are stems from his hatred of what they might be."[247] The approach that all this understanding has becomes concrete in the debate about utopias. The main argument for utopias is the two arguments used in the evaluation

---

244 **ibid.,** s. 133.

245 Crispin Sartwell, **Obscenity, Anarchy, Reality**, State University of New York Press, 1996, pp. 1-6.

246 **ibid.,** p. 13.

247 Thedor W. Adorno, **Minima Moralia: Reflections On A Damaged Life,** Translated from the German by E. F. N. Jephcott, Verso, 2005, p. 25.

of utopias. The first is that utopias must be the source of the search for alternative worlds in relation to the current situation. The second evaluation, together with having the same root as the first one, is that utopias inspire coercion regimes as fascism etc. and it is related to the fact that people play a role in the adoption of such inhuman regimes. If we remember the beginning of the discussion, we argue that the differentiation of 'must' goal and the 'fact' which is the main direction of morality can be interpreted in the same axis. Ultimately, morality is a 'must' goal, which is appeared as conscience, means a utopia.

> "This strength, though manifesting itself as individual resistance, is by no means of a merely individual nature. In the intellectual conscience possessed of it, the social moment is no less present than the moral super-ego. Such conscience grows out of a conception of the good society and us citizens. If this conception dims - and who could still trust blindly in it - the downward urge of the intellect loses its inhibitions and all the detritus dumped in the individual by barbarous culture - half-learning, slackness, heavy familiarity, coarseness - comes to light."[248]

According to Adorno, Socrates, unlike the Sophists, absolutisize the values by moralizing and positioning them out of time and space. This understanding constitutes the second front for morality. The first facade is the training of people through the system of traditional education and social sanctions according to the oscillations of time-space within the tradition-customs conception and the continual renewal and change in accordance with this custom of the fluid tradition.

> "By severing the moral principle from the social and displacing it into the realm of private conscience, goodness limits it in two senses. It dispenses with the realization of a condition worthy of men that is implicit in the principle of morality."[249]

However, the existence of the conscience calls the person out of the public self. The conscience invites one to leave their ownership of all the

---

[248] **ibid.,** p. 29.

[249] **ibid**., p. 94.

others to move away from the guaranteed area of being innocent. In this respect, conscience has also called for the one to take risks and embrace those which are uncertain. Adhering to the call includes the possibility of being described as 'criminal'. This approach can be argued from Shestov's assessments of Dostoyevsky's ability to make bad and criminal acts of Raskolnikov or other heroes based on their conscience. In this state of conscience, not only in the usual sense of 'good' but also in the unusual sense of 'evil' has become a place of residence. According to Shestov, there is a very basic dilemma in the inquiry about where truth is. One side of this dilemma is on the way of "mind and conscience" which Tolstoy loves, and the other side is Dostoyevsky's new and destructive approach which has effects on the world of literature and philosophy. The essence of this new and revolutionary orientation attributed to Dostoyevsky is the wishes that spring from the soul of man. These requests seem to have torn apart conventional wisdom and conscience conformity and dominance.[250]

Here comes the emergence of a heroic type who derives conventional states of mind and conscience from human life. Shestov argues that this situation was made by Dostoyevsky for heroic novels. Especially Dostoyevsky, who has lost his most basic belief and hope in the years of exile and conviction, in his novel which calls 'The House of the Dead', performs an 'overcoming' through the minds and consciences of the inmates there. This transgression is the 'going beyond the good and the bad', which will later show up in Nietzsche by putting his name. This transition relies on the situation in the human psyche, which constitutes the subject of examination of the psychology that emerged as a brand-new field at that time. According to Shestov, the revolution realized on this new ground by Dostoyevsky resulted in an awareness which ended the millennium reign of both mind and conscience. [251]

This opinion, which is claimed to have represented Tolstoy, appears to be an expression of a never-before-mentioned tradition. This tradition is an enlightened, naturalistic line, especially spoken by John Locke, positioned

---

250 Lev Shestov, **Dostoyevsky and Nietzsche: The Philosophy of Tragedy**. Translated by Spencer Roberts. In **Dostoyevsky, Tolstoy and Nietzsche: The Good in the Teaching of Tolstoy and Nietzsche: Philosophy and Preaching&Dostoyevsky and Nietzsche: The Philosophy of Tragedy**. Translated by Bernard Martin and Spencer Roberts. Athens: Ohio University Press, 1969, p. 24.

251 ibid., p. 25.

at the point of conscience and intelligence.[252] There is a second tradition besides this main tradition of Shestov offering the mind and conscience duality through Tolstoy. One of the main characters in Tolstoy's War and Peace novel, as a representative of this tradition, Princess Mary says: "Is Russia to go to pot, or am I to go without my tea? I tell you, let Russia go to pot, as long as I can get my tea." [253] This approach is manifested on the line created by D. Hume, who is particularly striking with his criticisms of the traditional understanding of reason.[254]

The transgression seen in Dostoyevsky's novel Crime and Punishment is an overcoming that manifests itself as going beyond good and evil, through life-giving action. Crime and Punishment Raskolnikov's essay represents legitimacy of the murder as a manifesto has a comparison between different forms of killing. This comparison is made between the killing of a person by a certain process of murder, the death of a state by death or a similar way. The conscious blood-smearing of one is seen as the main problem, and the question of how the blood-smearing can be accomplished with a conscientious comfort is on the agenda. In this respect, Raskolnikov's stance is beyond the good and bad.[255] Their standing beyond the good and bad of the heroes of Dostoyevsky manifests itself in their journey between their confidence and their suspicions in these positions. Going and going does not mean guilty in advance, but it means standing in the field of being a potential criminal. So the possibility of being guilty and conscience are located together. The understanding and realizing of the good and evil has a natureless nature which requires re-valuation for every single situation which is complicated and relative. Ivan Karamazov's question appears for the situations which one totally rejects this complication: "Why must we get to know this *devilish*

---

252 In Locke, conscience witness is used in the same way. The natural order is the original, straight. He states that he does not have to be inspired by God to find this order, that man can find this order in his mind. John Locke, **Reasonableness of Christianity**, London, 1824, pp. 13, 14, 81, 139, 151, 396, 418.

253 Shestov, **ibid.**, p. 28.

254 It is seen that D. Hume brought criticism here in two places. The first is that passion and intelligence, in particular, speak about the absolute victory of the mind, and the second is that the preference of the destruction of the whole world for a single fret damage is not a more worthless orientation. David Hume, **Treatise Of Human Nature**, Oxford 1965, p. 415-416.

255 Shestov, **ibid.**, p. 55-56.

good and evil, when it costs so much?"[256] This total rejection of the essence of the good and evil, what brings with it? Is it going beyond or transgression? The situation presented in the presence of Raskolnikov is the fallacy created by the breakup brought about by the loss of the usual morality. The main theme of the break is a committed murder. Raskolnikov's main problem is not being able to perceive how he feels guilty, even with a murder. The wobbling brought about by this lack of understanding is a sign that his understanding is lagging behind the act of living. He is amazed and can not recognize the new situation.

The most creepy situation is in the traditional sense of mind and conscience duality, mainly in the development of attitude towards the realization and support of the wickedness of the conscience in the present case, while there is an effort and attitude to favor and sustain goodness from the duality of the goodness and evil. In fact, evil is carried out with the conscientous comfort, so that it has become a mediating position to evil itself.[257] Conscience in this position threatens all current structure, dragging and facing him the danger of extinction, and dragging the individual out of secureness into the uncanny spaces that may meet catastrophes may lead to destruction of him.

Now another meaning can be given to the call of conscience. Conscience calls us to the ground of Kant's approach to base 'moral' on natural religion.[258] Conscience calls on the person to be a person other than the condition of the socio-cultural environment in which he lives. According to this understanding, there are two possibilities. I either go to myself in accordance with the voice of my conscience, or continue to act publicly, not in accordance with the call. This call is the call for the possibility of being guilty. To get out of publicness is to take the possibility of being 'to be self', on the other

---

256 **ibid.**, p. 65.

257 **ibid.,** p. 56.

258 Kant, **Within The Religion Boundaries of the Pure Reason**, has attempted to transcend one's relative life and understanding by claiming that whatever authority or court is, regardless of the authority of the human being, instrumentalization of any kind is void. The mainstay in this phase is the truth ground which is understood with the understanding of natural religion. Immanuel Kant, **The Religion Boundaries of the Pure Reason, edited by Allen Wood and George di Giovanni, Cambridge University Press, 1998.**

hand taking the risk 'to be guilty'. The possibility of being guilty begins to emerge with a tendency, regardless of whether or not they have gone beyond the public domain. The calling of conscience is frightening and uncanny in this respect. Listening to this call offering the possibility of becoming a human will mean leaving the boundaries of publicity. But conscience does not call for crime in the ordinary sense. Conscience makes a call to remind that the public situation in the present is not absolutely valid.[259]

The caller here is super ego, which Heidegger revealed in 1923. The super ego in this sense is uncanny and uncertain.[260] Adhering to the call of the unconscious does not mean to be guilty, but it brings the possibility of being guilty. Taking a blame for being a criminal is a condition taken to get the possibility of becoming a human being.

The position of conscience is related to the possibility of realizing itself as the direction of man's basic existence. It is possible to talk about this in terms of conscience as the possibility of people to realize themselves with other people, but independent of other people. Conscience is private. The existence of conscience is independent of the determinations, restrictions or approvals of social or social rules. The independence of conscience is related to its inability to be grounded in a certain chain of causality. An example of the existence of consciousness that conscience can be regarded as unfounded is expressed as 'unfounded' situation that Bauman offers as 'moral impulse'. The moral impulse in Bauman allows the person to differentiate from others in a pure manner.[261] Bauman refers to the process of taking over the whole decision-making burden from his shoulders, rather than the moral repudiation of the person, indicating that the responsibility that one carries on his/her shoulders is taken over by the belonging society or state or authority. The sole obligation of the person who delegates his responsibilities is to fulfill himself as one of the laws and regulations of the society in which he is a member. The self here, is seen as the self of 'them'. From this point of

---

259 Simon Critchley, **The Faith of The Faithless: Experiments in Political Theology**, Verso Press, London 2012, p. 185.

260 **ibid.**, p. 186.

261 Bauman wrote: "But when concepts, standards and rules enter the stage, the moral impulse makes an exit; Ethical reasoning takes its place, but ethics is made in the likeness of Law, not the moral urge." Zigmund Bauman, **Postmodern Ethics**, Blackwell, 1994, p. 61.

view, the base of the practical mind as the conscience of one is only sociality.[262]

However, all sorts of proposals of sociality are not 'forced' to be fulfilled 'unconditionally', may not be met regarding to the risk of accusation. Ultimately, whatever internal or external influence, oppression, or suggestion, it is the autonomous individual who has the ability to carry out the action as the true bearer of action or not, and to have a certain body, a willingness to do business and a discourse. Here, the position of conscience and the influence on the human being contacted is not to command what should or should not be done. Conscience calls on people to realize that they can live beyond the good and the bad. Man is invited to act responsibly, knowingly and willingly in the face of a situation he confronts in some way. In this respect, the meaning of the call of conscience is to remind that there is no other way than to bear responsibility for being human.

Bibliography

Adorno, Thedor W. **Minima Moralia: Reflections On A Damaged Life,** Translated from the German by E. F. N. Jephcott, Verso, 2005.

Asad, Talal. **Formations of the Secular: Cristianity, Islam, Modernity**, Stanford University Press, 2003.

Bauman, Zigmund. **Postmodern Ethics**, Blackwell, 1994.

Critchley, Simon. **Infinitely Demanding: Ethics Commitment, Politics Resistance**, Verso Press, London, 2008.

Critchley, Simon. **The Faith of The Faithless: Experiments in Political Theology**, Verso Press, London 2012.

Hume, David., **Treatise Of Human Nature**, Oxford 1965.

Inwood, Michael. **Heidegger: A Very Short Introduction**, Oxford University Press, 1997.

Kant, Immanuel. **The Religion Boundaries of the Pure Reason,** edited by Allen Wood and George di Giovanni, Cambridge University Press, 1998.

Locke, John. **Reasonableness of Christianity**, London, 1824.

Sartwell, Crispin. **Obscenity, Anarchy, Reality**, State University of New York Press, 1996.

262 Michael Inwood, **Heidegger: A Very Short Introduction**, Oxford University Press, 1997, p. 79.

Shestov, Lev. **Dostoyevsky and Nietzsche: The Philosophy of Tragedy**. Translated by Spencer Roberts. In **Dostoyevsky, Tolstoy and Nietzsche: The Good in the Teaching of Tolstoy and Nietzsche: Philosophy and Preaching&Dostoyevsky and Nietzsche: The Philosophy of Tragedy**. Translated by Bernard Martin and Spencer Roberts. Athens: Ohio University Press, 1969.

PART FOUR

ECONOMICS STUDIES

CHAPTER 13

OPEC' S DWINDLING INFLUENCE ON OIL PRICES

M. Büşra ENGİN ÖZTÜRK[263*], Esma SANCAR[264]**

1. Introduction

OPEC controls more than 80% of the world's proven crude oil reserves and these reserves account for more than 1.2 trillion barrels of crude oil. Moreover, member countries produce more than 33 million barrels of crude oil a day, nearly 40% of global supply. Because of this market share, OPEC's actions influence international oil prices. Some countries in OPEC like Saudi Arabia and Venezuela, which have considerable amount of oil, can affect the oil prices. The oil prices are controlled by the amount of oil. Thus, OPEC's announcements about the production policy are crucial for the world economy. After the drop in the oil prices in 2014, OPEC declared that they would not cut the supply. Two years later, OPEC announced the opposite strategy this time. Because there have been many damage for the economy of OPEC especially in Saudi Arabia. Oil prices have begun to rise again because of the OPEC's influence on oil prices. In this study we first examine the falling oil prices, it's reasons and results. Second, we discuss the OPEC's actions in this time period. And then, after the OPEC's announcements

263 * Yrd.Doç.Dr. İstanbul Üniversitesi/Sosyal Bilimler Meslek Yüksekokulu/ Dış Ticaret Bölümü, *mbusra@istanbul.edu.tr*

264 ** Öğr.Gör.İstanbul Üniversitesi /İletişim Fakültesi, *demireresma@gmail.com*

we observe the oil prices movements. By using standardized estimation method we analyze the effectiveness of OPEC's oil production on oil prices from the end of 2014 to the beginning of the 2017 and show how this affect is dwindling.

2. Falling Oil Prices in 2014

Oil prices change over time. All major oil price fluctuations are related to flow of global production levels that can be affected by the wars or revolutions in some countries. In 2014 global oil supply overtook demand and the oil price started to fall. Since mid 2014 the oil prices fell from above 100$ to an average of $50 during 2015. (Behar, Ritz, 2016: 4) June 2014-December 2014 the monthly average price of crude oil fell by 44% (Baumeister, Kilian, 2015: 2) Oil prices fell under the 28 dollars in January 2016 since 2003. (Williams, 2016). There are so many factors affecting this drop in oil prices.

2.1. The Reasons of Falling Oil Prices

i. One of the most important factor is an *increase in supply.* The level of petroleum inventories in the US and other consuming countries have been rising. (Williams, ibid). USA increased the oil production via shale oil investments. US oil and shale gas production has been expanding in recent years and with diminishing domestic fuel demand, reliance on crude imports and a lifting of its oil export bar had reduced. (Aljazeera, Business & Economy, 2015). The IEA notes US oil production increased during 2014 by 1.2 million barrels per day.

ii. *Decreasing demand* is another factor. Decreasing demand for oil is related to decreasing growth of China and other developing countries' economy. China has purposely moved from a manufacturing-oriented economy to a service-driven economy, using a less-energy intensive approach to growth. As a result, the demand for crude oil in the world's largest oil consuming country has gone down drastically. As an another reason of decreasing oil prices, Hamilton (2014) argues that around two-fifth of the decline in oil prices in the second half of 2014 are thought to result from weak global demand, particularly in the Eurozone economies with the rest attributable to increases in oil supply. (Worldbank, 2015)

iii. *Problems in OPEC*, is an important reason. Changing policies, diminishing price control and conflict in members is also a reason. Some OPEC members have recessions in recent years. OPEC's weakening price control on oil and lack of trust among members are the important problems in OPEC.

iv. *Monetary policy* is another factor. Monetary policies in the United States, Euro Area and Japan have played an important role in the general decline of commodity prices and US dollar appreciation. (Frankel, 2014) Appreciating dollar reduces demand for crude oil in importing countries because crude oil is traded in dollars. A weak US dollar has a negative impact on oil exporting countries but increase the purchasing power of oil importing countries. (Altarturi, 2016: 422)

2.2. The Results of Falling Oil Prices

Drop in oil prices affects the countries in two ways. If the country is an exporter country, like Saudi Arabia, Russia, Iraq, Venezuela then, take a disadvantage of this drop, where the oil importer country like USA, Japan take an advantage.

As a crude oil importer, USA has been being in a good position in general. The oil production jumped to 10 million barrel a day in USA in 2014, from 5 million barrel a day in 2007. (http://www.bbc.com) US output has been only dropped to about 8.5 million barrels per day compared with 9.1 million barrels per day last September. As a result, global prices have stayed low. (Buxbaum, 2016) In 2015, USA became the world's largest oil producing country beating Saudi Arabia.

Libya, Iraq, Syria combined have been able to increase their oil production since June 2014 by 18% and Saudi Arabia reduced its oil production by 0.23 %. (Baumeister, Kilian, 2015: 4). Saudi production in September 2015 was down to 10.39 million barrel per day while Iraq's output is up by 105.000 barrel per day to 4.455 million barrel per day. (Smith, 2016)

Iran is reenter the world of oil markets after years of sanctions and isolations. It has world's fourth largest crude oil reserves. Iran will see billions of dollars in lost revenue to the oil price decrease.

The Russian situation may be worse than Iran's. Russia is the one of the largest oil producing country. However, Russia loses about $2 billion in revenues for every dollar fall in the oil price, and the World Bank has warned that Russia's economy would shrink by at least 0.7% in 2016 if oil prices do not recover. (Rishabh, Chaubey: 2016: 379) It is already struggling to compete with sanctions put on them by many western countries.

Venezuela announced that the economy is unable to handle with dropping prices as a being an exporter country.

3. OPEC'S ACTIONS

The Organization of the Petroleum Exporting Countries (OPEC) is established in 1960 and an international organizational that attempts to coordinate the price of oil coming from 14 oil producing countries: Algeria, Angola, Ecuador, Gabon, Iran, Iraq, Kuwait, Libya, Nigeria, Qatar, Saudi Arabia, United Arab Emirates, Venezuela, Indonesia. (www.opec.com)

OPEC aims at promoting the interests of key oil-producing countries. The mission of OPEC is to coordinate and unify the petroleum policies of its member countries and ensure the stabilization of oil markets in order to secure an efficient, economic and regular supply of petroleum to consumers, a steady income to producers and a fair return on capital for those investing in the petroleum industry. (www.opec.com)

OPEC's actions means its announcements which have bearing on the expectations and volatility of the crude oil markets. The announcements come out in the form of "cut", "maintain", and "increase" decisions regarding changes in oil production levels. If the market prices are high, as an exporter OPEC announces an increase in production. If the market prices are low, then, OPEC announces cutting decision. Mensi,.et al, found that the maintain policy decreases the price volatility while the cutting policy increases the oil price volatility. (Mensi, et al, 2013: 4)

From rise in oil prices in 1973 and 1979, to the oil price plunge of 1986, and to the roller-coaster story from 2005 to 2008, OPEC has been labeled for exercising quasi-monopolistic control over rising oil prices, and dismissed for being incapable of applying any control over plunging oil prices. (Lin, Tamvakins: 2010: 1011). OPEC increased its production in the face of supply disruptions in other producers or rises in demand, and reduced it in the opposite case. (Anton, Golo, 2013: 1345)

When oil prices dropped significantly in the past, OPEC countries would cut their oil production to bolster the price of oil: for example, in 2008/9 with the global economy in deep recession, and oil prices plunging from $145 to $35, OPEC cut production by nearly 3 Mb/d helping to stabilize prices. Similarly, OPEC raised production sharply in 2004 when global demand suddenly surged. However in the recent episode of oil plunge, inspite of growing fiscal deficits in many OPEC nations [32], the cartel did nothing.

Since being oil exporter countries, lower prices over the past year have negatively impacted the economies of the OPEC countries. OPEC's actions vary over time depending on economic, market and geopolitical conditions and thus, announcements can be different. OPEC announcements have an impact on oil prices. (Louta, Mellios and Andriosopoulos, 2016: 262). After the drop in the oil prices, OPEC announced its strategy a few times.

Despite the falling prices, in its November 2014 meeting, OPEC decided to not to reduce supply and prices fell further to $35. Some OPEC members have been reluctant to accept this, because these members needed higher prices to compensate domestic expenditures. (Fortune Turkey, 2014) According to many analysts, this decision was for to squeeze higher cost competitors including US shale oil extracted using hydraulic fracturing out of the market. This inaction policy more probably reflected an unwillingness to repeat the mistake of cutting output between 1980-1985. Because those cuts had little effect on world over supply and damaged OPEC market share and revenue.

At the end of 2015, OPEC decided to increase its collective output to 31,5 million barrels per day. (www.aljazeera.com) Some countries like Venezuela, which has 95 percent of its income from oil, wanted OPEC to change its policy. However influential players like Saudi Arabia insisted on keeping production levels high, because they don't want to lose customers to non- OPEC producers like the United States. OPEC members didn't cut the production specifically. Even Saudi Arabia and Iraq increased their production. In 2015, OPEC had budget deficit for the first time since 1998. At the same time, OPEC's oil export revenues decreased 45,8 % compared to previous year 2014 because of the falling oil prices. (Engin Öztürk, 2016: 85)

Because of these economic problems, On September 2016, OPEC members decided to decrease production around 700.000 barrel per day from a current level of just over 33 million barrel a day. (Krauss, Read: 2016) OPEC's actions occurred against the backdrop of weakening global demand for crude and several years of steadily rising capacity from non-OPEC sources. (Behar, Ritz, 2016: 4)

By keeping production high and prices low, OPEC especially Saudi Arabia, hoped to drive down shale oil production, which in turn would best prices. Some American oil companies have had difficult time when the prices decreased. However this strategy was more harmful for Saudi Arabia and other exporter OPEC members. The oil price has been stuck for months in the $40 to $50 per barrel range. USA production excessed Arabian production and Saudi Arabia's economy weakened. (Engin Öztürk, Sancar, 2016: 325)

For Saudi Arabia the revenue losses have been much more unbearable. Iran's economy today is far less addicted to oil than Saudi Arabia.

Saudi Arabia has growing fiscal problems and thus has greater interest in higher oil price.

Saudi Arabia's strategy for dealing with this price so far has been to preserve its market share. However, during this time period Saudi Arabia has burned $150 billion of foreign exchange reserves. OPEC, who is basically controlled by Saudi Arabia, might actually stand to gain from lower oil prices.

Oil prices rose 6% to around $48 per barrel after OPEC agrees to limit crude output. (The Guardian, 2016) OPEC explained that member states agreed on to fix crude oil production around 33,24 million barrels. However Iran, Nigeria and Libya are exempted due to economic conditions. The crude oil prices begun to fall right after the meeting held at the end of October, because all of the OPEC members didn't agree on cutting policy clearly.

On November 4, the crude oil price were on course for their biggest weekly percentage declines since January of just under 10 percent as signs of tensions resurfaced between Saudi Arabia and Iran that could scupper a key supply cut pact. World Bank increased its prediction of crude oil prices from $53 to $55 due to decision of OPEC. In the future the oil prices wont be low because of the need of the growing countries. According to World Energy Outlook 2014 Report, in the 2040s oil demand will reach 111 million barrel per day. And OPEC will supply the large part of this demand. (Duran, 2016)

4. OPEC'S ACTIONS AND OIL PRICE MOVEMENTS

In historical framework, both OPEC's oil production affect the oil prices and oil prices also affect the OPEC's oil production. OPEC especially Middle East group has an impact on oil price fluctuations. (Chen, et al: 2016, 48) The costs per barrel of oil are fairly independent of OPEC, since they are driven by technological progress and characteristics of the resource stock. On the other hand, the oil price may be indirectly influenced by OPEC, since its existence leads to an imperfectly competitive market. (Zietlow, 2015: 67) The main reason of the drop in the oil prices in 2014 was US shale oil supply and thus, the oil prices affected OPEC's oil production. Since we aim to show the effect of OPEC's oil production on oil prices, we used the monthly data of oil prices and OPEC's oil production over the period between March 2014 and March 2017.

In the Table 1 below, there is the data of average OPEC's oil production (million barrel) and oil prices monthly. Since November 2014, OPEC announced that they would increase the oil production. OPEC didn't cut the production until November 2016. From November 2014 to November 2016, OPEC oil production was stable and tended to increase. Since OPEC announced on September its intention to reinstate a production cap, the price of oil has fluctuated within a range of $44-54 per barrel. (ECB, 2016) Because of the damage of this strategy to many economies, especially Saudi Arabia, OPEC changed its strategy and announced its cutting oil production policy on November 2016. Late in 2016 OPEC agreed to cut production from 33,24 million barrels per day to between 32,5 and 33 million barrels per day to increase the price of oil. Prices had fallen from around $65 per barrel in 2014 to around $30 barrel in early 2016. After the meeting held on September 2016 prices begun to rise. However prices did not increase substantially. There are two factor affecting this. One of them is oil inventories are preventing oil prices from rising quickly. When OPEC cuts production, supply is reduced, OPEC countries draw on their oil inventories to supplement the reduced production. The market price reaction to the production cut is delayed until the inventories are depleted. (Owyang, 2017:2)

Table 1: OPEC's Oil Production And Oil Prices Nov 2014-Feb 2017.

Date	Oil Prices	Opec's Oil Production
November 2014	65,94	30,05
December 2014	53,45	30,2
January 2015	47,79	30,15

February 2015	49,84	30,02
March 2015	47,72	30,79
April 2015	59,62	30,84
May 15	60,25	30,98
June 2015	59,48	31,38
July 2015	47,11	31,51
August 2015	49,2	31,54
September 2015	45,06	31,57
October 2015	46,6	31,38
November 2015	40,43	31,7
December 2015	37,13	32,18
January 2016	33,66	32,33
February 2016	32,74	32,28
March 2016	36,94	32,25
April 2016	45,98	32,44
May 2016	49,1	32,36
June 2016	48,27	32,86
July 2016	41,54	33,11
August 2016	44,68	33,24
September 2016	47,72	33,39
October 2016	46,83	33,64
November 2016	49,41	33,87
December 2016	53,75	33,08
January 2017	52,75	32,14
February 2017	54	31,96

Source: This table was created by the authors using the data from www.investing.com

In January 2015, oil prices were down at levels around $45-$55. During that time, OPEC's Secretary-General declared that the prices have reached the bottom. However, prices didn't go as OPEC expected and oil prices are still falling till today to levels not OPEC nor anyone else has expected at that time. At the time of OPEC's decision in 27th

November 2014, the global markets were probably oversupplied by 1–2 million barrel per day. (Khan, et al, 2017: 614) .

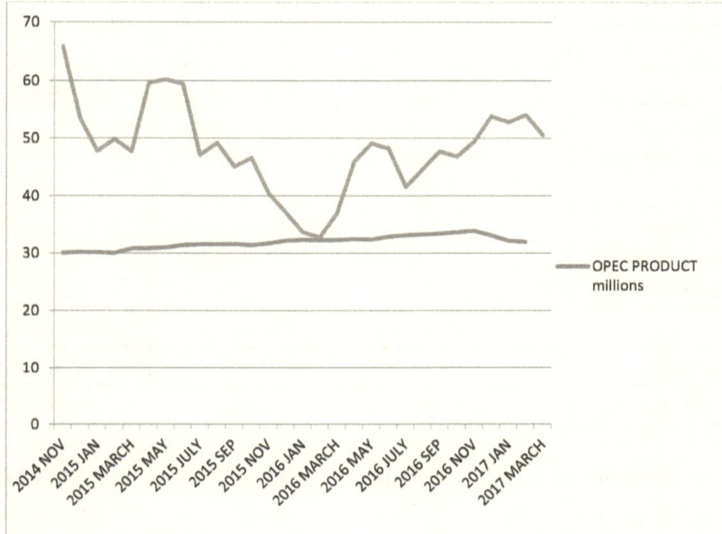

GRAPH 1: The Relation Between OPEC's Oil Product and Oil Prices
Source: This graph was created by the authors using
the data from www.investing.com

The Graph 1 above, shows the relation between oil prices and OPEC' s oil production clearly. Because of many factors, the oil prices are fluctuating over the time. Despite of this, the production of OPEC is more stabile. Below, the analysis shows the relation between OPEC's production and oil prices.

5. AN ANALYSIS OF THE OPEC'S INFLUENCE ON OIL PRICES

After November 2016, the diminishing OPEC's oil production affected oil prices. To analyze this impact we analyze the relationship between OPEC production and Oil Prices. We can analyze this relation, using alternative estimation techniques. We have used, standardized estimation method to determine the effectiveness. For 2014-2016 monthly data, first, we have estimated three model separately. Our main hypothesis are:

Estimation result can be given below:

Table 2: Standardized OLS for 2014

Standardized Least Squared Estimation (2014)			
Variables	Parameter Value	t statistic	Probability
OPEC Production (Dependent Variable)	-0.85	24.12	0.000
Oil Prices (Independent Variable)			
	Value	F-statistic	Probability
R-squared	0.912	25.47	0.000
Adjusted R-squared	0.908	24.11	0.000

As can be seen in Table 2, 3 and 4, the oil prices effects OPEC production negatively. In addition, all parameters are statistically significant at 1% significance level. All three model generally have meaningful, because F-statistics are statistically significant at 1% significance level. As we used standardized model, there is no constant parameter. In first model, the estimated parameter is -5.85, this means that, if oil prices get 1% higher, OPEC production decrease 0.85 % on average. Same results have been obtained for other models. These estimated values support our hypothesis given above.

Table 3: Standardized OLS for 2015

Standardized Least Squared Estimation (2015)			
Variables	Parameter Value	t statistic	Probability
OPEC Production (Dependent Variable)	-0.22	24.74	0.000
Oil Prices (Independent Variable)			
	Value	F-statistic	Probability
R-squared	0.924	20.14	0.000
Adjusted R-squared	0.915	19.58	0.000

Table 4: Standardized OLS for 2016

Standardized Least Squared Estimation (2016)			
Variables	Parameter Value	t statistic	Probability
OPEC Production (Dependent Variable)	-0.05	19.58	0.000
Oil Prices (Independent Variable)			
	Value	F-statistic	Probability
R-squared	0.954	24.47	0.000
Adjusted R-squared	0.933	23.33	0.000

Table 5: Standardized OLS for all periods

Standardized Least Squared Estimation (2016)			
Variables	Parameter Value	t statistic	Probability
OPEC Production (Dependent Variable)	-0.05	19.58	0.000
Oil Prices (Independent Variable)			
	Value	F-statistic	Probability
R-squared	0.954	24.47	0.000
Adjusted R-squared	0.933	23.33	0.000

Although these results support our hypothesis, we especially wish to analyze time effect of OPEC production on oil prices. For this, we have expanded our model, using time variable. We have included time and time-squared as individually independent variables and re-estimated our relation. Results can be seen below:

Table 6: Standardized OLS with time effects

Standardized Least Squared Estimation (with time effect)			
Variables	Parameter Value	t statistic	Probability
OPEC Production (Dependent Variable)	0.37	5.08	0.000
Oil Prices (Independent Variable)			

Time (t)	0.83	3.03	0.006
Time-squared (t^2)	-2.82	3.67	0.001
	Value	F-statistic	Probability
R-squared	0.992	55.41	0.000
Adjusted R-squared	0.989	49.77	0.000

For Table 6, we have taken into account these hypothesis:

Because of the time-squared parameter is negative (-2.82), is rejected and we can say that, in time, OPEC' s effect on oil prices are dwindling.

Conclusion

OPEC members have been suffering from the dramatic decline in oil prices over the past two years, which has seen crude dropping to between $40 and $50 per barrel from more than $100 in 2014. Since OPEC declared its non-cutting policy on November 2014, both government budgets and economies of oil exporting countries felt tremendous pressure. Especially Saudi Arabia's economy had affected seriously because of the strategy against USA.

Faced with these challenges, OPEC members finally agreed in a September 2016 meeting in Algeria to cut production in principle. Exact quotas were determined in late November. After this meeting OPEC oil production begun to decrease and the oil prices begun to increase. In this study, we found that there is a relation between OPEC's oil production and oil prices. We observed the monthly data from November 2014 to May 2017 and we showed the OPEC's influence on oil prices are dwindling. OPEC is still important on prices and the announcements have effect on these prices, however, this impact is dwindling.

Recently, on May 2017, OPEC and other oil producers are on course to agree an extension of supply cuts by a further nine months. According to Forbes, crude oil prices had gone up by more than 9% in November following the initial agreement to reduce output, as opposed to just 2 % jump in oil prices when OPEC announced the extension of the cut. This is not only indicates that the proposed output restrictions are not enough to have a meaningful impact on oil prices, but also hints at the fact OPEC's power to influence crude oil prices waning.

References

Aljazeera, Business & Economy (2015, December 13), Why is OPEC refusing to cut oil production?, Accessed October 4 2016, http:// www.aljazeera.com.

Altarturi, B.H.M., Sishammri, A.A, Tau Tuan M, Hussin T. (2016, March) oil price and exchange rates: a wavelet analysis for organization of oil exporting countries members, *International Journal of Energy Economics and Policy*, 6(3), 421-430.

Anton N, Galo N.(2013): "Saudi Arabia and the Oil Market." Economic ournal, 123(573):1333–1362.

Baumeister, C., Kilian L. (2015, February) Understanding the decline in the price of oil since june 2014, *CESifo Working Paper Series* No. 5755.

Baumeister, C., & Kilian, L. (2016). Forty years of oil price fluctuations: Why the price of oil may still surprise us. *The Journal of Economic Perspectives, 30*(1), 139-160.

Behar, M. A., & Ritz, R. A. (2016, Winter). An Analysis of OPEC's Strategic Actions, US Shale Growth and the 2014 Oil Price Crash, New York: International Monetary Fund.

Buxbaum, P. (2016, October 20) "What's Up With OPEC? Can Production Can Yield Sustained Higher Prices? Accessed: October 21 2016, http://www.globaltrademag.com.

Chen, Hao, Liao, Hua, Tang, Bao Jun, Wei, Yi Ming, (2016), "Impacts of OPEC's political risk on the international crude oil prices: An empirical analysis based on the SVAR models", Energy Economics, 52, pp.42-29.

Duran, Orhan (2015, Şubat 7) Düşen petrol fiyatları ve etkileri, *Türkiye Enerji Vakfı,* Accessed: July 17 2016, http://www.tenva.org

ECB Economic Bulletin, Issiue 8, "Impact of The November 2016 OPEC Agreement On the Oil Market", Accessed: 16.02.207, //www.ecb. europa.eu/

Engin Öztürk, M.B. (2016), Uluslararası Ekonomik Entegrasyonlar ve Kuruluşlar, Bursa: Ekin Yayınevi.

Engin ÖZtürk, Sancar (2016): "*Why Did OPEC Changed It's Oil Production Policy",* ICOMEP, 323-335.

Forbes (2017, June 2): OPEC's Influence On Oil Prices Wanning, Acessed June 2, www.forbes.com

Fortune Turkey (2014, November 25), Enerji Fiyatları Neden Düşüyor? Accessed: August 26 2016, http://www.fortuneturkey.com

Frankel J. (2014, December 15) "*Why Are Commodity Prices Falling?", Project Syndicate,* Accessed: September 12 2015, http:/www.project.

Khan, Muhammad Imran, Yasmeen Tabassam, Shakoor, Abdul, Khan, Niaz Bahadur, (Feb 2017), "2014 Oil Plunge: Causes And Impacts On Renewable Energy", 2014 Oil plunge: Causes And Impacts On Renewable Energy, 68 (1) pp.609–622

Krauss, C., Rad S., (2016, September 28), Energy Environment, New York Times, Accessed: September 29 2016, http://www.nytimes.com/2016/09/29

Lin, Sharon Xiaowen, Tamvakis, Michael, (2010), "OPEC Announcemnets and their Effects on Oil Prices", Energy Policy, 38 (2), pp.1010-1016.

Louta, Amine, Mellios, Constantin, Andriosopoulos, Kostas: (2016): "*Do OPEC Announcements Influence Oil Prices?,* Energy Policy, pp.262-272.

Mensi, Walid, Hammoudeh, Shawkat, Min Yoon, Seong, (2013): "How do OPEC news and structural breaks impact returns and volatility in crude oil markets? Further evidence from a long memory process

Owyang, Michael, (2017): "*Is OPEC Losing Its Ability to Influence on Oil Prices?",* Accesses, 21.03.2017, www.stlouisfed.org

Rishabh Dev, Chaubey, D.S. (2016) "World's Oil Scenario- Falling Oil Prices Winners and Losers A Study on Top Oil Producing and Consuming Countries", Imperial Journal of Interdisciplinary Research, Vol 2, issue 6, 378-383.

Smith, M. (2016, October 12), Oil Prices Under Fire From Rogue, Accessed: October 12 2016, http:// www.oilprice.com

The Guardian, (2016, September 29), Oil prices rise 6% after OPEC agrees to limit cruse output, Accessed: October 6 2016, http://www.theguardian.com

Williams, J.L., (2016, October 26), Oil Price History and Analysis, *Reuters*, Accessed: October 26 2016, http://www.wtrg.com

World Bank (2015) "Global Economic Prospects", Washington DC: World Bank

Zietlow, Kim J., "What Is Left Today? Analyzing Opec's Influence On The Crude Oil Price", Journal of Self-Governance and Management Economics, Volume 3(4), 2015, pp. 61–69,

http://www.bbc.com

http://www.investing.com

http://www.opec.org

www.ingramcontent.com/pod-product-compliance
Lightning Source LLC
Chambersburg PA
CBHW030437290526
45786CB00001B/329

* 9 7 8 1 4 9 0 7 8 8 5 0 0 *